Five-Plant Gardens

Five-Plant Gardens

52 Ways to Grow a Perennial Garden with Just Five Plants

NANCY J. ONDRA
Photography by Rob Cardillo

Storey Publishing

The mission of Storey Publishing is to serve our customers by publishing practical information that encourages personal independence in harmony with the environment.

Edited by Carleen Madigan
Art direction, book design, and diagrams by Alethea Morrison
Text production by Jennifer Jepson Smith

Photography by © Rob Cardillo
Photo styling by Nancy J. Ondra
Illustrations by Beverly Duncan

Indexed by Christine R. Lindemer,
Boston Road Communications

Pictured on the cover:
1. Japanese painted fern (*Athyrium nipponicum* var. *pictum* 'Pewter Lace')
2. Lily-of-the-valley (*Convallaria majalis*)
3. Hellebore (*Helleborus* species)
4. Creeping Jacob's ladder (*Polemonium reptans* 'Stairway to Heaven')
5. Strawberry foxglove (*Digitalis* x *mertonensis*)

Storey books are available for special premium and promotional uses and for customized editions. For further information, please call 1-800-793-9396.

Storey Publishing
210 MASS MoCA Way
North Adams, MA 01247
www.storey.com

Storey Publishing is committed to making environmentally responsible manufacturing decisions. This book was printed on paper made from sustainably harvested fiber.

Printed in China by R.R. Donnelley
10 9 8 7 6 5 4 3 2 1

Library of Congress Cataloging-in-Publication Data on file

Contents

Why Five Plants?

When the gardening bug bites, you're left thinking of beautiful flowers and lush leaves, the thrill of going shopping to find the perfect plants, and the satisfaction of making your yard look great. After you've been gardening for a few years, you develop a sense of which plants look good and grow well together, and you don't need a plant-by-the-numbers plan to get great results. But when you're new to the process, starting with a manageable-sized space, a clear shopping list, and a simple-to-follow planting plan can make the difference between inspiring success and frustrating disappointment.

Enter *Five-Plant Gardens*. These plans I've created are collections of five different perennials (sometimes in multiple quantities of each plant), carefully chosen to complement each other and grow well together. It's enough variety to give you a good mix of flowers and foliage, heights and shapes, and seasons of interest, but not so much that the collection looks like a jumbled mess. It's also a manageable number of new plants to learn about at one time, as well as a limited amount of money to spend.

The perennials in these plans aren't the very newest, cutting-edge releases; instead, they're time-tested selections that are widely available and reasonably priced, and that have been proven to perform in a variety of climates and growing conditions. If you want to tweak the plans to suit your own taste, I've suggested alternatives, too, so you don't have to guess at which other plants might work.

Whichever plan and plants you start with, it's my hope that you'll have great success with your new perennial garden, and that it's the start of an enjoyable and rewarding new obsession for you.

Happy planting!

Starting a Perennial Garden from the Ground Up

There are lots of great reasons to start any sort of flower garden: to add beauty to your yard, to enjoy months of colorful flowers, to attract birds and butterflies, to indulge your creative side, and to have a fun reason to get outside for fresh air and exercise. So, why choose to plant a *perennial* garden? Well, once you know the difference between an "annual" and a "perennial," it's easy to see the advantages.

Annual plants last through just one growing season. "True" annuals die once they complete their life cycle by flowering and producing seeds. Some true annuals include common flowers such as marigolds and zinnias. There are also plants sold as annuals that live for years in very warm climates but die when touched by frost or freezing temperatures, which are a yearly occurrence in most parts of the country. Examples here include begonias, coleus, and bedding geraniums (*Pelargonium*). Either way, most of us have to start over every year with annuals by sowing new seeds or buying new plants each spring.

Perennial plants sprout from their roots in spring, flower at some point, die back to their roots at the end of the growing season, and then repeat the cycle the following year. Many perennials can live for 3 to 5 years with hardly any attention, and some can last much longer. That means less work and worry on your part, and often less expense, too, because you don't need to deal with seeds or purchase new transplants and find time to get them planted every year.

That's not to say that annuals are bad, of course: they're just as pretty as perennials, and they give you the chance to experiment with new kinds and colors each year. But when life gets hectic, you can depend on a perennial garden to do its thing year after year with little help from you — and that's a big plus in anyone's book!

Exploring Your Options

So, you know you want a perennial garden; now, where's it going to go? Instead of grabbing a shovel and randomly digging up part of your lawn, consider playing off an existing feature in your yard. How about planting a small bed of perennials by your front door, or perhaps a border along the main path to your home, to add curb appeal and a welcoming touch? A border of perennials also makes a great alternative to boring shrubs in the strip of ground along the front of the house, or along the wall of a garage or shed. Consider surrounding your deck or patio with a planting of lush leaves and bountiful blooms. A garden could also be a good solution for a problem area, such as a hard-to-mow slope or a soggy spot in the yard.

Another option is to first think about what *kind* of garden you want, and then try to find the perfect spot for it. Maybe you'd like a garden filled with flowers in your favorite color, or one that's at its best during your favorite season. If you enjoy watching wild critters in your yard, a garden filled with perennials that attract seed- and bug-eating birds, hummingbirds, or butterflies can be a real delight.

This book includes 52 plans for simple perennial gardens in a variety of shapes and themes, about half for sites that are sunny to partly shady (with about 5 hours or more of direct sun a day) and half for those in partial to full shade (less than 5 hours of direct sun a day). Flip through the plans that suit your site, and you'll find dozens of ideas for inspiration.

Be a Smart Shopper

Each plan in this book includes a shopping list that tells you which perennials to buy and how many of each to get. The suggested quantities are based on plants growing in 2-quart pots (about 5 inches wide and deep) or 1-gallon pots (these are usually 6 to 7 inches wide and deep). Perennials of these sizes are usually reasonably priced and large enough to look nice the first year, though they may not fill the area completely until the second or third year.

To double check the plant quantities before you buy, try arranging the pots according to your chosen plan while you're still at the garden center. You might decide that you need a few more or a few less pots, depending on how large the actual plants are and how much you can afford to spend.

If you really want an "instant garden" effect, feel free to buy more of each plant and set them close together at planting time so they'll fill the area within a few weeks after planting. Keep in mind, however, that the garden might look overcrowded and messy in two or three months, and you'll probably have to take out some of the extra plants by the end of the first growing season. (You could use those extras to start a new garden, so that's not necessarily a bad thing.)

If you're working with a very limited budget, buy as many of the perennials as you can, then add some inexpensive annuals as fillers until you can afford the rest of the perennials. Or, wait for end-of-the-season sales and start your new garden in fall instead of spring.

Don't worry if you can't find the exact perennials specified for each plan; that's why each of the five plants in the shopping list comes with suggestions of other perennials that could work as replacements.

Smaller Is Smarter

THERE'S AN OLD SAYING to the effect of "Admire large gardens but plant small ones," and that's excellent advice. When you're excited by the idea of a new garden, it's easy to get carried away with grand plans and dig up way too much space. That translates into a big expense in buying enough perennials to fill the garden, and a lot of time spent on planting and caring for the garden, especially the first year.

Starting small makes your garden project way more manageable cost- and time-wise, and the success you'll enjoy with a reasonably sized starter garden will give you a more realistic idea of how much more garden you can handle. The plans in this book are large enough to make a good show of color for months but small enough to dig and plant over the course of a weekend and maintain with a few hours a year. As time and money (and available space) allow, you can easily expand an existing small garden or add a new perennial planting in another part of your yard.

Let's Get Growing

You've got a plan; you've got the plants. Now it's time to dig in and get this garden started! If you're completely new to gardening, the prospect may seem a little daunting, but really, it isn't very complicated. And if you've had any sort of flower garden before, the basics of planting and caring for perennials will be easy for you.

Starting with the soil. When you're ready to start your garden, use stakes and string to mark the outline of the shape and size you've chosen. Use a sharp shovel or spade to cut around the outline. To remove existing grass and weeds, slip the blade of the tool into the soil as close to horizontal as you can to cut off the grass roots just below the soil surface. Use the chunks of sod you remove to patch holes in other parts of your lawn or to fill in low spots, or pile them in an out-of-the-way spot to decompose.

Once the grass is gone, spread a 1-inch-thick layer of chopped leaves, compost, or dehydrated manure over the area, and use a shovel or spading fork to loosen the top 8 inches or so of soil. Lift one shovelful or forkful at a time, turn the chunk of soil onto its side or flip it over completely as you drop it, and then use the blade of the tool to chop the chunk into smaller pieces. Pick out larger rocks; it's fine to leave small ones (those about 2 inches across or smaller). Once you've dug up the whole area, go over it once more to break up any remaining soil chunks, and then use a rake to level the surface. Avoid stepping on the loose soil; you don't want to pack it down again.

Planting your perennials. You can plant pretty much any time the ground isn't frozen or muddy-wet, though spring is generally prime time for planting, especially for perennials that bloom in summer and fall. Early to mid fall, when temperatures are mild and rainfall is fairly reliable, is another ideal planting time, particularly for perennials that bloom in spring to early summer.

To make sure the rootballs (the mass of roots and potting soil) of your perennials are thoroughly moist, lower each plant — pot and all — into a bucket of water and hold it down so the water covers the surface of the potting soil. Once bubbles stop rising to the top of the water (anywhere from 1 to 10 minutes, depending on how dry the soil is), remove the pot from the water and set it down somewhere to drain for a few minutes.

Getting in the Zone

IN THE SHOPPING LIST for each plan in this book, you'll notice a USDA Hardiness Zone rating for each of the five recommended perennials. This rating relates to the USDA Plant Hardiness Zone Map, which you can find on page 176. This map divides North America into 11 numbered zones based on each area's average minimum winter temperature. Once you know which zone you live in, you can use the zone rating to figure out if a particular perennial is likely to survive the winters in your area. If a perennial recommended in the shopping list isn't rated for your hardiness zone (if it's rated for USDA Hardiness Zones 5 to 8, for instance, and you live in Zone 4), then consider the suggested alternates instead.

Set the watered pots out on the prepared soil according to the plan. Once you're happy with how they're arranged, plant them one at a time. Dig a hole that's about as deep as the rootball and a few inches wider, and remove the plant from its pot. If the pot is thin, you may only need to squeeze the sides with your fingers or hands. If that doesn't help to loosen the pot from the roots, lay the plant on its side and gently tap or roll the pot with your foot to help release the rootball. You should be able to slip off the pot by cradling the base of the plant and the top of the rootball with one hand and sliding off the pot with your other hand. If that doesn't work, don't tug on the leaves to get the plant out; instead, carefully slit the sides of the pot with a knife to get it off.

With your fingers, tickle all sides of the rootball to loosen any circling roots and knock off any loose growing medium. Set the rootball in the planting hole, and add or remove soil under the rootball so that the plant's crown (the point where the top joins the roots) is about even with the soil surface. Push the soil back around the roots to fill the hole, crumbling any remaining lumps with your hands and using moderate pressure to get good contact between the soil and the rootball. Unless you're expecting a steady rain right after you finish planting, water your new garden as soon as you get all of the plants in the ground.

Watering wisely. Water a newly planted perennial garden regularly (about once or twice a week, unless you get a soaking rain) through the rest of that growing season. After the first year, the garden should be fine for at least 2 weeks after a soaking rain, unless the weather is exceptionally hot or windy.

Instead of watering on a set schedule, let the plants or soil tell you when your garden needs water. If the plants wilt a bit in the afternoon but perk up in the evening, they can probably wait a day or so for water. If they're still wilted the next morning, though, water them as soon as possible. An even more reliable approach is to dig down 3 to 4 inches in one spot with a trowel. If the soil is dry down that far, it's a good idea to water as soon as possible. If only the top 1 to 2 inches are dry, replace the soil and check again in another spot in 2 or 3 days if no rain is due.

When you do water, the key is to water deeply: enough to soak the top 4 to 5 inches of soil. That sounds like a lot, but in small areas like these starter gardens, that'll probably take less than an hour. If you're using a sprinkler instead of watering by hand with a hose, check every 10 minutes or so to make sure that the water is soaking into the soil. If water is puddling on the soil surface or running off, turn off the sprinkler until the water soaks in, then turn it on again until the area has gotten a good soaking.

Managing mulches. Covering the soil between your perennials with some kind of mulch will go a long way in reducing watering chores. Mulches also help to insulate the soil from rapid temperature changes, which can interfere with root growth. They discourage weed seeds that are already in the soil from sprouting, and they make it easier to pull out any weeds that do poke through. Organic mulches — those derived from plants — such as chopped leaves, grass clippings, pine straw (needles), or shredded bark, have the extra benefit of adding organic matter to the soil as they decompose, building the fertility of your garden's soil over time.

Two inches is about the right thickness for an effective mulch layer. Mulch new gardens soon after planting. Organic mulches break down over time, so you'll probably need to add more each spring to keep the layer at the ideal thickness. Do your spring garden cleanup chores first; then spread the mulch. It's all right if the mulch touches the leaves and stems a little, but avoid piling it right against the leaves and stems.

Grooming your garden. A bit of attention every now and then through the season helps to keep your perennial garden looking great. Grooming is mostly a matter of removing the dead flowers (a process called deadheading), either individually or all at once. This makes the plants look tidier, prevents them from producing seed (which can lead to unwanted seedlings), and may encourage them to produce new flowers later in the season. Some perennials, though, produce seed heads that are very interesting, especially in fall and winter, so sometimes you may decide to skip summer deadheading. You'll find specific tips for what to cut and what to leave in place in the care calendar for each starter garden plan. Also, take a few minutes every few weeks to pull or dig out any weeds that pop up between your perennials.

After a few years, you may notice that some of your perennials are starting to crowd out their companions, or that they are gradually producing fewer flowers than they used to. In either case, it's a good idea to dig up those plants and divide them (ideally in early to mid spring, or in early fall). Use an old knife or a sharp spade or trowel to cut the clump into three or four pieces, making sure that each piece has some roots and some buds or top growth. Replant one of the pieces where the original clump was growing. Use the leftovers to start new gardens, or share them with friends.

At the end of the growing season, when frosts or freezes have nipped your plants and turned them brown, you have a choice to make: cut down the dead tops in mid to late fall or leave them in place for the winter. Both options have advantages and disadvantages. Fall cleanup gives the garden a very tidy look for winter, and spring cleanup will take practically no time at all. If you leave the dead tops on through the winter, though, they help to protect the buds and roots from excessive cold and damaging freeze-and-thaw cycles. Dried stems and seed heads give you something to look at through the winter, and they provide a source of winter shelter and food for birds, too. The care calendar for each starter garden plan gives you some suggestions about how to handle fall cleanup for that particular garden, but really, the choice is yours. Perennials tend to be pretty sturdy plants, so chances are good that yours will be fine either way!

Growing Beyond the Five-Plant Garden

Ready to expand your perennial plantings? Repeat your favorite plan, using the same plants each time or mixing in some of the alternate suggestions for variety, or combine two or more plans into one larger garden. Here are some ways to build bigger beds and borders out of the simple starter-plan shapes.

SQUARE OR SMALL RECTANGLE: Plant on one side of a bench, arbor, or set of steps, then repeat the plan on the other side of the feature. Repeat the squares or rectangles side to side to create longer borders, or leave space between each part for a path. To fill even more space, add additional sets of beds and paths to create a grid pattern.

LARGE RECTANGLE: Repeat the plan end to end to create a longer border along a driveway, house wall, fence, or property line.

LONG, NARROW RECTANGLE: Repeat the plan end to end to create an even longer edging border for a sidewalk or walkway. Set two rectangles side by side with space in between for a path, or join their ends at a right angle to fit the planting into an inside corner or wrap it around an outside corner.

TWO SHORT RECTANGLES: Start with a single set to flank a gate, arch, bench, or walkway. Repeat each of the rectangles end to end to create a longer narrow border, or set them side by side to make a longer and wider border.

HALF-CIRCLE: Flip the plan along the flat side to create a mirror image of the original. Set the two parts right next to each other to make a complete circle, or leave 2 to 3 feet between the two halves to create a walk-through planting.

TRIANGLE: Flip the plan along one of the shorter sides, or along the longer side. Set the mirror image right next to the original plan, or leave some space between the two parts for a path.

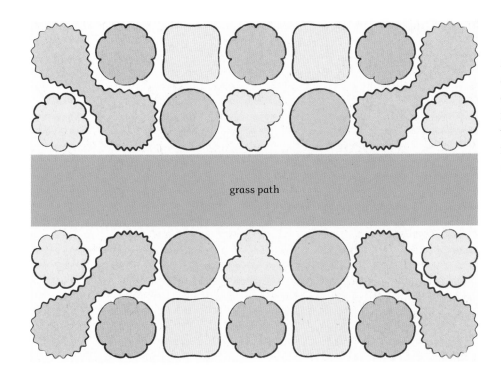

grass path

A DOUBLE BORDER: Flank a path with a long rectangle or a half circle and its mirror image for an elegant walk-through garden. This layout is ideal for a long, narrow space, such as a side yard.

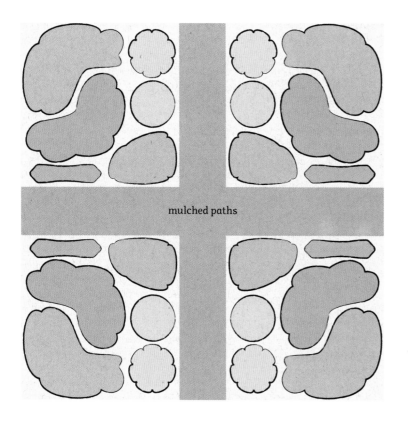

mulched paths

A GRID GARDEN: Multiple squares or small rectangles set in a grid pattern create a charming formal-garden effect. The paths make it easy to reach all parts of each bed, so maintenance is a breeze.

A U-SHAPED GARDEN: Use a half-circle, short rectangle, or triangle for the base of the U, with two short or long rectangles as the sides. The inside creates a perfect nook for a garden bench.

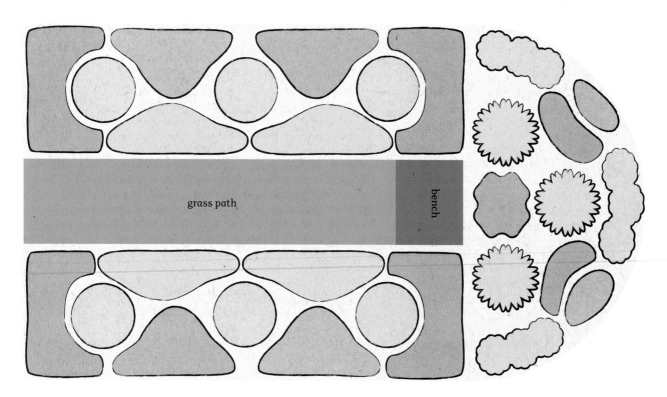

grass path

bench

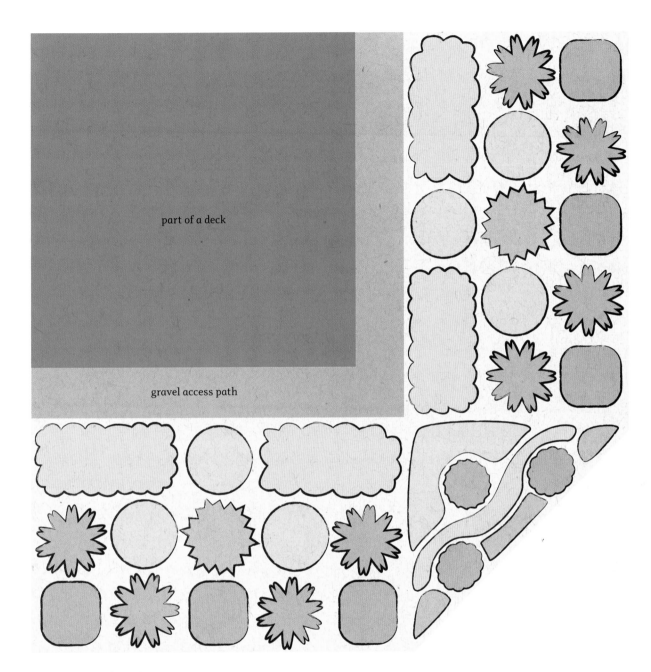

part of a deck

gravel access path

A WRAP-AROUND BORDER: Dress up the corner of a deck, patio, or paved area with short or long rectangles along the sides, with a triangle or square plan tucked into the area where they meet.

Five-Plant Gardens

for Full Sun to Partial Shade

Bright White Garden

Brilliant white blooms create a bright, eye-catching accent for any part of your yard. There are loads of white-flowered perennials to choose from: pure whites, creamy whites, blue-tinged whites, greenish whites, and pinkish whites. Greens, of course, are always part of a white garden, and deep green leaves make an especially good backdrop for crisp white blossoms. Companions with silvery, gray, or white-variegated leaves complement the white-garden theme and add color even when the flowers aren't around.

● ◐ Full sun to partial shade

◆ ◇ Average to dry soil

➤ 'White Swan' purple coneflower (*Echinacea purpurea*)

◀ 'David' phlox (*Phlox paniculata*)

❯ 'Snow Fairy' bluebeard (*Caryopteris divaricata*)

◀ Perennial candytuft (*Iberis sempervirens*)

▲ 'Big Ears' lamb's ears (*Stachys byzantina*)

The Garden Plan

Shopping List

❶ 'DAVID' PHLOX
Phlox paniculata | 3 plants
Zones 4–9
Alternates: Another 3- to 4-foot-tall perennial with white flowers, such as white gaura (*Gaura lindheimeri*) [3 plants] or 'Snowbank' false aster (*Boltonia asteroides*) [3 plants]

❷ 'WHITE SWAN' PURPLE CONEFLOWER
Echinacea purpurea | 3 plants
Zones 3–8
Alternates: 'Virgin' or another white-flowered purple coneflower or other 2- to 4-foot-tall perennial with white flowers, such as 'Miss Manners' obedient plant (*Physostegia virginiana*) [6 plants] or white blazing star (*Liatris spicata* 'Alba') [3 plants]

❸ 'SNOW FAIRY' BLUEBEARD
Caryopteris divaricata | 2 plants
Zones 5–9
Alternates: Another 2- to 3-foot-tall perennial with green-and-white leaves, such as variegated Japanese iris (*Iris ensata* 'Variegata') [6 plants] or 'Overdam' feather reed grass (*Calamagrostis × acutiflora*) [2 plants]

❹ PERENNIAL CANDYTUFT
Iberis sempervirens | 6 plants
Zones 3–9
Alternates: Another 6- to 12-inch-tall perennial with white flowers, such as wall rock cress (*Arabis caucasica*) [6 plants] or 'Greystone' dianthus (*Dianthus*) [6 plants]

❺ 'BIG EARS' LAMB'S EARS
Stachys byzantina | 3 plants
Zones 4–8
Alternates: Another 6- to 12-inch-tall perennial with silvery leaves, such as 'Berggarten' sage (*Salvia officinalis*) [3 plants] or 'Silver Brocade' beach wormwood (*Artemisia stelleriana*) [3 plants]

Planting Plan

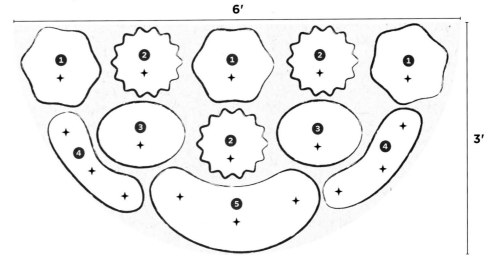

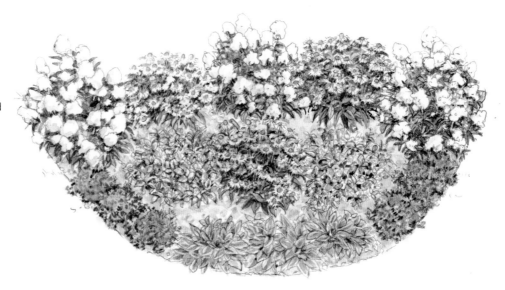

Season by Season

Spring: Leaves are the main keys to the white theme in spring, starting with the silver-furred new leaves of 'Big Ears' lamb's ears and the bright green new foliage of perennial candytuft, joined later by the white-and-green new shoots of 'Snow Fairy' bluebeard. Blooms come along in mid spring, when the perennial candytuft is covered with white flowers. In mild-winter areas, 'White Swan' coneflower may start flowering by late spring.

To get your white garden off to a great start for the season, cut down any remaining top growth on the phlox, coneflower, bluebeard, and lamb's ears and clip out any winter-damaged parts on the candytuft in early spring. Early to mid spring is also a fine time to divide the phlox, coneflower, and lamb's ears if they were starting to outgrow their spaces last year and you didn't divide them in fall. When you're done with these spring tasks, apply a fresh layer of organic mulch over the soil.

Summer: Perennial candytuft is usually finished blooming by early summer. In southern gardens, the white, daisy-form flowers of 'White Swan' coneflower start in early summer, if not earlier; in the North, 'White Swan' may not start until midsummer. 'David' phlox, with its large clusters of fragrant, bright white blossoms, is generally at its best in mid to late summer. Throughout the summer, the gray-green mature leaves of the lamb's ears and the bushy, green-and-white clumps of the bluebeard add loads of foliage interest.

Remove the dead flowers regularly to keep your white garden looking fresh. On the phlox, clip the finished flower clusters off the top of the stems; on the candytuft, snip off individual dead bloom clusters or wait until they're all done to shear them off just above the leaves. Clip off the finished coneflower blooms just above a bud lower down on the stem. 'Big Ears' lamb's ears occasionally sends up fuzzy spikes with tiny pinkish flowers, but they're not especially showy, so it's best to clip off the flowering stems at the base when they appear. Shearing off all of the top growth to about 2 inches above the ground in mid to late summer encourages lamb's ears to produce a flush of fresh leaves for fall. Water the garden during extended dry spells.

Fall and Winter: 'David' phlox and 'White Swan' coneflowers often continue flowering into early fall, and perennial candytuft may send up a few flowers then, too. 'Snow Fairy' bluebeard usually starts flowering in early fall, with blue flowers over its white-variegated leaves, and continues until frost. The leaves of 'Big Ears' lamb's ears and perennial candytuft continue to look good through fall, and through most or all of the winter as well.

Divide the phlox, coneflower, and lamb's ears in early fall if they're crowding out their companions. Keep clipping off the dead flowers through fall. Cut down the top growth of the phlox and coneflower in mid to late fall, if desired, or leave all cleanup until spring.

Digging Deeper

THIS HALF-CIRCLE DESIGN is well suited for use as a border against a wall, fence, hedge, or other vertical surface. Or, you could flip the plan along the flat side and separate the two parts with a walk-through path or with a short path that leads to a bench. Make the two sides identical, or mix in some of the suggested alternate plants for variety.

White gardens are very pretty in the daytime, but when they really shine is the low-light times at dawn and dusk. The pale petals reflect the slightest bit of light, popping out of the gloom when richer colors fade into the background. That makes white gardens great for sites where you'll enjoy them early — along the path you walk to your car when you leave for work in the morning, for instance — or around a deck or patio where you like to sit on summer evenings.

"Deadheading" — a term gardeners use for the process of removing dead flowers from plants — isn't a serious chore for most gardens. Usually, clipping or pinching off the faded blooms once or twice a week is fine for keeping a garden looking tidy and preventing the plants from producing unwanted seeds. White flowers, though, turn brown and look ugly very quickly as they decline, so you may want to think twice about putting an all-white garden in a high-visibility spot (near your front door, for example), unless you're willing to spending a few minutes deadheading it daily to keep the perennials looking pristine.

Stunning in Silver

● Full sun

◆ ◇ Average to dry soil

Perennials with silvery leaves, stems, and flower heads are naturally well adapted to hot and bright conditions, so they're perfectly suited for sunny, dry sites. They're beautiful in their own right and even more elegant with accents of other colors, such as the cool blue choices in this plan. For a brighter effect, try white flowers instead; for high-impact contrast, replace some of the silvers with near-black leaves.

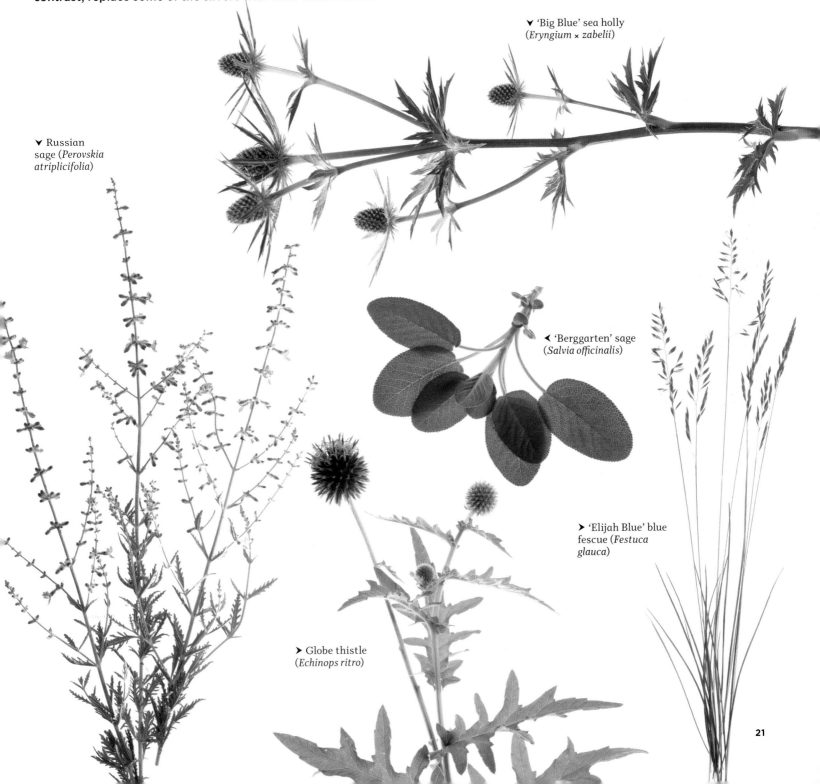

⌄ 'Big Blue' sea holly
(*Eryngium × zabelii*)

⌄ Russian
sage (*Perovskia
atriplicifolia*)

◄ 'Berggarten' sage
(*Salvia officinalis*)

➤ 'Elijah Blue' blue
fescue (*Festuca
glauca*)

➤ Globe thistle
(*Echinops ritro*)

21

The Garden Plan

Shopping List

❶ RUSSIAN SAGE
Perovskia atriplicifolia | 2 plants
Zones 5–9
Alternates: Another 3- to 5-foot-tall perennial
with blue flowers and/or silvery leaves, such as
'Powis Castle' wormwood (*Artemisia*) [2 plants]
or blue mist shrub (*Caryopteris × clandonensis*)
[2 plants]

❷ GLOBE THISTLE
Echinops ritro | 1 plant
Zones 3–9
Alternates: Another 3- to 4-foot-tall
perennial with blue flowers and/or gray-blue
leaves, such as 'Heavy Metal' switch grass
(*Panicum virgatum*) [1 plant] or blue oat grass
(*Helictotrichon sempervirens*) [1 plant]

❸ 'BIG BLUE' SEA HOLLY
Eryngium × zabelii | 6 plants
Zones 5–9
Alternates: 'Blaukappe' or other sea holly
or another 1- to 3-foot-tall perennial with
blue flowers and/or gray-blue leaves, such as
rosemary (*Rosmarinus officinalis*) [6 plants] or
'Blue Ice' bluestar (*Amsonia*) [4 plants]

❹ 'BERGGARTEN' SAGE
Salvia officinalis | 3 plants
Zones 5–8
Alternates: Another 6- to 18-inch-tall
perennial with blue flowers and/or silvery
leaves, such as English lavender (*Lavandula
angustifolia*) [3 plants] or 'Silver Brocade' beach
wormwood (*Artemisia stelleriana*) [3 plants]

❺ 'ELIJAH BLUE' BLUE FESCUE
Festuca glauca | 5 plants
Zones 4–9
Alternates: 'Siskiyou' or other blue fescue
[5 plants] or another 6- to 12-inch-tall perennial
with silvery or gray-blue leaves, such as
'Firewitch' or 'Greystone' dianthus (*Dianthus*)
[3 plants] or wall rock cress (*Arabis caucasica*)
[3 plants]

Planting Plan

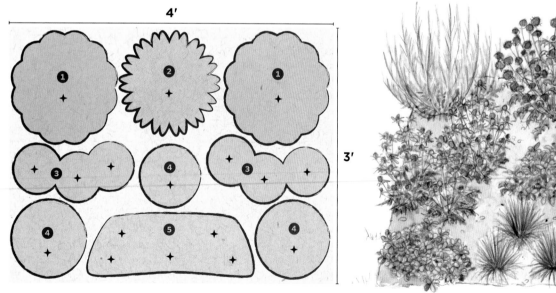

Season by Season

Spring: 'Elijah Blue' blue fescue jumps into growth as soon as the weather gets a bit milder, with very slender, blue-gray leaves in dense, spiky clumps. The other perennials start sending up new growth in mid to late spring: lacy gray Russian sage; spiny, gray-green globe thistle; toothed green 'Big Blue' sea holly; and oval, silvery 'Berggarten' sage. By late spring, the sea holly sends up large, cone-shaped flower buds, each surrounded by a ring of spiky leaflike "bracts." Russian sage may also start producing its airy, branching, silvery blue flower clusters in late spring in mild-winter areas.

In early spring, trim the blue fescue clumps back to about 4 inches, and cut the dead tops of the globe thistle and sea holly. Wait until you see new growth sprouting before you trim the Russian sage back to about 6 inches tall and the 'Berggarten' sage back by about half. Add more mulch, if needed, to cover the soil.

Summer: In southern gardens, Russian sage continues to bloom through early summer; elsewhere, it's at its best in mid to late summer. Globe thistle's spherical, silvery gray buds appear in early summer, opening to silvery blue flowers in mid to late summer. The silvery buds and upper stems of 'Big Blue' sea holly also develop a rich blue color in mid to late summer. 'Berggarten' sage generally doesn't flower, but its silver-gray leaves look great all through the summer. 'Elijah Blue' blue fescue, too, is mostly a foliage accent, though it also produces blue-green flower heads and tan seed heads in midsummer.

If the Russian sage was flowering in early summer, cut it back by one-half to two-thirds in midsummer to prevent self-sowing, encourage bushy new growth, and possibly get more flowers later in the season. Clip off the dead flower heads of the globe thistle above a lower bud or close to the base of the plant, or let them dry in place for late-season interest. It's normal for the lower leaves of globe thistle to turn crispy and fall off at some point during the summer; remove the browned leaves, if you wish. Clip off the stalks of the blue fescue just at the leaf tips before they turn tan and drop their seeds, or even earlier if you don't find the flowers attractive. Water the garden during extended dry spells.

Fall and Winter: Russian sage, globe thistle, and 'Big Blue' sea holly often continue flowering into early fall, at least, and their dried stems and seed heads add lots of winter interest. 'Berggarten' sage hangs on to its leaves well into winter. 'Elijah Blue' blue fescue can hold its color all through the winter in mild areas.

Divide the blue fescue clumps every 3 or 4 years in early fall. Otherwise, leave the garden alone until spring cleanup.

Digging Deeper

A SMALL, RECTANGULAR PLAN like this one looks great on its own if you only have room for a small garden. Where space allows, you can easily expand this starter garden by repeating the plan end to end as many times as you wish to create a longer border. For more variety in the extended planting, replace some of the perennials with their suggested alternates. A silver border looks stunning along a driveway or sidewalk (silvery plants tend to be particularly tolerant of hot, dry sites, such as those right next to paved surfaces), or as a foundation planting along a dark house wall.

When you're shopping for plants to put in a silver garden, don't forget to check out the herbs for sale as well as the perennials. Several herbs have silvery or gray leaves, with the added benefit of being delightfully aromatic and even, in some cases, richly flavorful. Culinary sage (*Salvia officinalis*), for instance, typically has gray-green leaves, and some of its cultivars, such as wide-leaved 'Berggarten', are distinctly silvery. Lots of lavenders (*Lavandula*), too, fall in the gray-to-silver category.

Using gravel instead of chopped leaves, shredded bark, or other organic materials as a mulch generally isn't a good idea in perennial gardens, because you'll need to dig up and divide most perennials every few years. If you're growing silver-leaved plants in a humid climate, or in soil that's on the moist side, though, a bit of gravel mulch may be helpful in keeping the leaves and stems dry and preventing rot. Instead of covering all of the soil, spread gravel in a ring that extends out 6 to 12 inches from the base of each plant. Also, use gravel that is pea-sized or smaller; that way, you can easily dig it into the soil when you need to divide or replace the plants.

Think Pink

A pink planting is one of the easiest themes to try, because there are so many wonderful pink-blooming perennials to choose from. Pale pinks may bleach out and appear near white in strong sun, so if you want flowers that stay distinctly pink in full sun, look for rich rosy pinks. They'll look as good with the soft yellows, baby blues, and crisp whites of spring as they do with the rich purples and golds of summer and fall.

◖◑ Full sun to partial shade

◆ Average soil

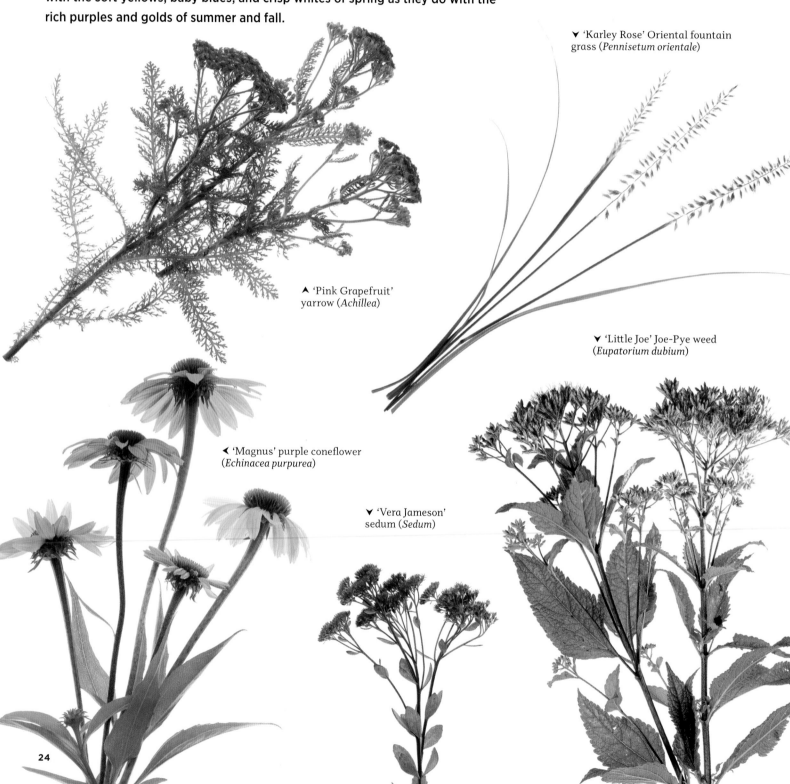

❯ 'Karley Rose' Oriental fountain grass (*Pennisetum orientale*)

▲ 'Pink Grapefruit' yarrow (*Achillea*)

❯ 'Little Joe' Joe-Pye weed (*Eupatorium dubium*)

◀ 'Magnus' purple coneflower (*Echinacea purpurea*)

❯ 'Vera Jameson' sedum (*Sedum*)

The Garden Plan

Shopping List

❶ 'LITTLE JOE' JOE-PYE WEED
Eupatorium dubium | 1 plant
Zones 4–9
Alternates: Another 4- to 5-foot-tall perennial with pink flowers, such as 'Marshall's Delight' bee balm (*Monarda*) [1 plant], 'Shortwood' phlox (*Phlox paniculata*) [1 plant], or 'Robina' Orienpet lily (*Lilium*) [3 bulbs]

❷ 'KARLEY ROSE' ORIENTAL FOUNTAIN GRASS
Pennisetum orientale | 2 plants
Zones 5–9
Alternates: Another 3- to 4-foot tall perennial with pinkish flowers, such as 'Cedar Waxwing' daylily (*Hemerocallis*) [2 plants] or a blazing star (*Liatris spicata* or *L. pycnostachya*) [6 plants]

❸ 'MAGNUS' PURPLE CONEFLOWER
Echinacea purpurea | 3 plants
Zones 3–8
Alternates: Another 2- to 4-foot-tall perennial with pink flowers, such as 'Oertel's Rose' yarrow (*Achillea*) [3 plants] or hummingbird mint (*Agastache cana*) [3 plants]

❹ 'PINK GRAPEFRUIT' YARROW
Achillea | 5 plants
Zones 4–8
Alternates: Another 18- to 24-inch-tall perennial with pinkish flowers, such as 'Crimson Butterflies' gaura (*Gaura lindheimeri*) [5 plants] or 'Pilgrim' oregano (*Origanum laevigatum*) [5 plants]

❺ 'VERA JAMESON' SEDUM
Sedum | 2 plants
Zones 4–8
Alternates: Another 6- to 12-inch-tall perennial with purplish leaves and white or pinkish flowers, such as 'Encore', 'Midnight Rose', or 'Plum Pudding' heuchera (*Heuchera*) [2 plants] or red-leaved thrift (*Armeria maritima* 'Rubrifolia') [6 plants]

Planting Plan

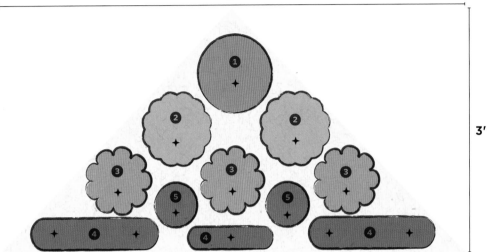

Season by Season

Spring: In southern gardens, the 'Magnus' purple coneflower may begin flowering in mid to late spring. There's also some interesting color from the leaves of 'Vera Jameson' sedum, which are a purple-tinged blue-green in spring, along with the feathery, bright green foliage of the 'Pink Grapefruit' yarrow.

In early spring, cut down the remaining top growth on all of the perennials. This is also a good time to divide any of the perennials that were starting to outgrow their space last year. Then, spread a fresh layer of organic mulch over the soil.

Summer: 'Pink Grapefruit' yarrow usually begins blooming in early summer, with deep pink flowers that age to soft pink, and keeps going through the summer. 'Magnus' purple coneflower typically peaks in early to midsummer in southern gardens and in mid to late summer elsewhere. The other three perennials are also at their best in mid to late summer: the domed clusters of 'Little Joe' Joe-Pye weed, the fluffy pink-turning-tan spikes of 'Karley Rose' Oriental fountain grass, and the clustered pink flowers of 'Vera Jameson' sedum.

Through the summer, trim off dead purple coneflower and yarrow blooms just above a bud lower down on the stem if you want to extend the bloom season. The other perennials don't need any attention in summer; just water the whole garden during summer dry spells.

Fall and Winter: 'Little Joe' Joe-Pye weed may continue to bloom into early fall. Eventually, its flower heads age to deep rosy pink, and then turn into fluffy seed heads that last well into winter. 'Karley Rose' Oriental fountain grass, too, keeps producing new pink flowering spikes that age to tan; by mid to late fall, the whole plant turns brown. 'Magnus' purple coneflowers and 'Pink Grapefruit' yarrow keep producing a few flowers until freezing weather, and the seed heads stick around into winter. The flowers of 'Vera Jameson' sedum age to deep red as the seed heads form. The leaves drop after frost, but the seed heads and stems dry in place to provide winter interest.

In early fall, divide the yarrow if it is crowding its companions. Cut down the top growth of the Oriental fountain grass in late fall. You could cut down the Joe-Pye weed, purple coneflower, and sedum then, too, or leave them in place to enjoy their winter structure.

Digging Deeper

BY ITSELF, THIS TRIANGULAR GARDEN fits easily into a corner. Flip it to create a mirror image, and you have two triangles that would work great to mark the beginning of a path or walkway, or to flank a doorway or set of steps.

Want to add some zip to your pink plantings? Include some more dark-leaved perennials, such as 'Obsidian' or other deep purple heucheras (*Heuchera*) or black mondo grass (*Ophiopogon planiscapus* 'Nigrescens'). Or, soften the rosy pink blooms with silver or gray leaves, such as lamb's ears (*Stachys byzantina*) or wormwoods (*Artemisia*).

Despite their common name, Joe-Pye weeds (*Eupatorium*) aren't really weeds; they're hardy perennials that make a great addition to sunny gardens. Their individual flowers are tiny, but they bloom in large clusters held at the top of tall stems. Some Joe-Pyes can reach 6 to 8 feet tall in moist soil, which can be rather too big for an average-sized yard, but they also come in smaller forms, such as 4- to 5-foot tall 'Little Joe' or 3- to 4-foot-tall 'Phantom'. Or, plant a common cultivar such as 'Gateway' and cut it back by about half its height in early summer or by a third in midsummer.

Red All Over

● ◑ Full sun to partial shade

◇ ◆ Average to moist soil

Red flowers never fail to catch the eye, so they're an excellent choice for jazzing up any sunny garden. The fact that many red-flowered perennials are also favorites with hummingbirds is an added bonus. Bright blooms aren't your only option for filling a red bed or border, though. Companions with red in their leaves contribute color all season long. Silvery and purple-leaved perennials also make perfect partners for red flowers.

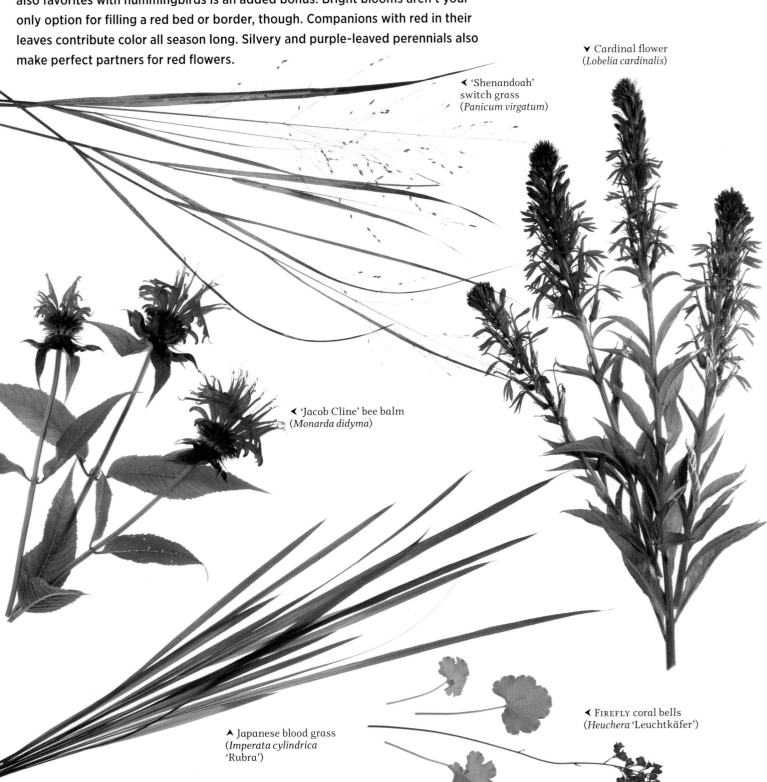

❯ Cardinal flower
(*Lobelia cardinalis*)

◀ 'Shenandoah' switch grass
(*Panicum virgatum*)

◀ 'Jacob Cline' bee balm
(*Monarda didyma*)

◀ FIREFLY coral bells
(*Heuchera* 'Leuchtkäfer')

▲ Japanese blood grass
(*Imperata cylindrica*
'Rubra')

27

The Garden Plan

Shopping List

❶ 'JACOB CLINE' BEE BALM
Monarda didyma | **3 plants**
Zones 3–9
Alternates: Another 2- to 4-foot-tall perennial
with red flowers, such as 'Red Jewel' or 'Ruby
Tuesday' Helen's flower (*Helenium*) [3 plants]
or 'Paprika' yarrow (*Achillea*) [3 plants]

❷ 'SHENANDOAH' SWITCH GRASS
Panicum virgatum | **2 plants**
Zones 4–9
Alternates: Another 3- to 4-foot-tall switch
grass selection with red-tinged leaves,
such as 'Cheyenne Sky', 'Huron Solstice', or
'Rotstrahlbusch' [2 plants], or a red-flowered
daylily (*Hemerocallis*), such as 'Chicago Apache'
[2 plants]

❸ JAPANESE BLOOD GRASS
Imperata cylindrica 'Rubra' | **10 plants**
Zones 5–9
Alternates: Another 1- to 2-foot-tall perennial
with red flowers, such as 'Arizona Red Shades'
blanket flower (*Gaillardia × grandiflora*)
[4 plants] or a red-flowered chrysanthemum
(*Chrysanthemum*), such as 'Ruby Mound'
[4 plants]

❹ FɪREFLY CORAL BELLS
Heuchera 'Leuchtkäfer' | **5 plants**
Zones 3–8
Alternates: Another coral bells or heuchera
with red flowers and/or purple leaves, such as
'Obsidian' [5 plants], or another 1- to 2-foot-tall
perennial with reddish flowers and purplish or
red-tinged leaves, such as 'Lynda Windsor' or
'Red Cauli' sedum (*Sedum*) [5 plants]

❺ CARDINAL FLOWER
Lobelia cardinalis | **6 plants**
Zones 3–9
Alternates: 'Fan Scarlet' or other red-flowered
lobelia, or another 1- to 2-foot-tall perennial
with red flowers, such as wild columbine
(*Aquilegia canadensis*) [6 plants] or 'Heart
Attack' sweet William (*Dianthus barbatus*)
[6 plants]

Planting Plan

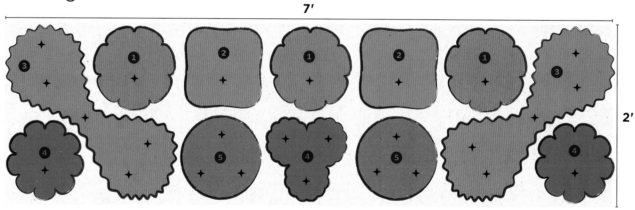

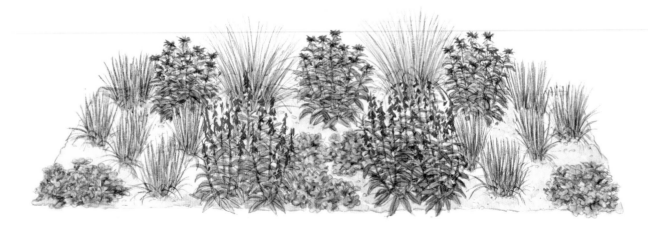

Season by Season

Spring: Early color in this garden comes from the emerging leaves: the greens of the 'Jacob Cline' bee balm, 'Shenandoah' switch grass, FIREFLY coral bells, and cardinal flower, and — by late spring — the red-tipped green blades of Japanese blood grass.

To get your red garden off to a good start for the growing season, cut down any winter-damaged or dead stems and leaves in early to mid spring. It's also a good time to divide any of these perennials: for bee balm and heuchera, every 2 to 3 years; for grasses and cardinal flower, whenever they start crowding out their companions. Finish up by applying a fresh layer of organic mulch over the bare soil (except around the base of the cardinal flower clumps if you want them to produce seedlings).

Summer: FIREFLY coral bells sends up its loose spikes of brilliant red bells in early summer (possibly even earlier in southern gardens) and continues through midsummer. The Japanese blood grass holds its red leaf tips through the summer, and the 'Shenandoah' switch grass develops red tips too, usually in early to midsummer. The switch grass also bears airy reddish flower plumes in mid to late summer, around the same time that the 'Jacob Cline' bee balm produces its shaggy-looking flower clusters and the cardinal flower sends up its brilliant red spikes.

Snip off the heads of the bee balm as soon as the blooms drop to encourage the plants to produce more flowers, or leave them on for later interest. On the cardinal flower, cut off the finished part of the flower spike above the leafy part of the stem; often, the remaining stem will produce a flush of shorter bloom spikes later in the season. And on the coral bells, clip off the finished flower spikes close to the base of the stalk. Water the garden during summer dry spells.

Fall and Winter: Cardinal flower may continue to produce some flowers into early fall, but the grasses are the real color highlight in fall, when their leaves turn bright red (in the case of blood grass) to burgundy red (on the 'Shenandoah' switch grass). 'Jacob Cline' bee balm has interesting seed heads in fall, if you didn't remove the spent summer flowers, and they can last on the dried stems well into winter. The coral bells leaves may develop some purplish or silvery marbling as cool weather arrives, and the leaves generally look good through the winter.

Cut the bee balm, grasses, and cardinal flower stems to the ground in mid to late fall, or leave them in place for winter interest.

Digging Deeper

YOU HAVE LOTS OF PLANTING OPTIONS with a long, narrow border like this one: set it against a wall, fence, or hedge; use it as a foundation planting around your house or garden shed; or enjoy it along the edge of a path, sidewalk, or driveway. If you want to fill a longer space, repeat the plan end to end as many times as needed. Consider mixing in some of the suggested alternate plants to give the extended border more variety.

Want to enjoy your red bed even sooner in spring? Tuck in some tulips! These sun-loving spring favorites come in a range of heights, from 6-inch-tall *Tulipa linifolia* and 10-inch 'Red Riding Hood' to the classic 'Kingsblood', at 24 inches. Or start the season with a softer palette of pinks, such as 15-inch 'Toronto' bouquet tulips or 20-inch 'Barcelona'. They'll look super with the green, silvery, and red-tipped leaves of the emerging perennials.

Add even more intensity to your red-themed garden by mixing in plants with deep purple to near-black leaves. Many heucheras (*Heuchera*), for instance, come in that color range; 'Obsidian' is one outstanding practically black selection that you could use in place of the green-leaved FIREFLY coral bells in the front row. In the back row, replace the 'Shenandoah' switch grass (*Panicum virgatum*) with purple fountain grass (*Pennisetum setaceum* 'Rubrum') or 'Purple Majesty' millet (*P. glaucum*). These dark-leaved grasses are generally annuals, not perennials, but it's worth replacing them each spring if you enjoy the effect.

Vision in Blue

Blue flowers never fail to please, so when you plan an entire garden around them, you have a plan for success. From intense cobalt blue to palest sky blue, from icy silver blues to sumptuous purple-blues — your options for beautiful blue blooms are seemingly endless. Even some leaves get into the act, in cool powdery blues that keep the color theme going when the flowers take a break.

●● ◐ Full sun to partial shade

◆ Average soil

▼ 'Heavy Metal' switch grass (*Panicum virgatum*)

◀ Blue Fortune' hyssop (*Agastache*)

➤ Rozanne geranium (*Geranium* 'Gerwat')

➤ Arkansas bluestar (*Amsonia hubrichtii*)

➤ 'Caradonna' ornamental sage (*Salvia*)

30

The Garden Plan

Shopping List

❶ ARKANSAS BLUESTAR
Amsonia hubrichtii | **2 plants**
Zones 4–9
Alternates: Another 2- to 3-foot-tall and -wide perennial with blue or purple-blue flowers, such as 'October Skies' aromatic aster (*Aster oblongifolius*) [2 plants] or blue false indigo (*Baptisia australis*) [2 plants]

❷ 'BLUE FORTUNE' HYSSOP
Agastache | **2 plants**
Zones 5–9
Alternates: Another 3- to 5-foot-tall perennial or shrub with spiky blue or purple-blue flowers, such as Russian sage (*Perovskia atriplicifolia*) [2 plants] or ADONIS BLUE ('Adokeep') or 'Blue Chip' butterfly bush (*Buddleia*) [2 plants]

❸ 'HEAVY METAL' SWITCH GRASS
Panicum virgatum | **3 plants**
Zones 4–9
Alternates: A 3- to 4-foot-tall, blue- or purple-blue flowered perennial, such as a Siberian iris (*Iris sibirica*) [2 plants], globe thistle (*Echinops ritro*), or a blue mist shrub (*Caryopteris × clandonensis*)

❹ 'CARADONNA' ORNAMENTAL SAGE
Salvia | **5 plants**
Zones 4–8
Alternates: Another blue-flowered perennial sage, such as 'May Night', or another 18- to 30-inch-tall perennial with blue or purple-blue flowers, such as 'Sapphire Blue' sea holly (*Eryngium*) [5 plants], blue lobelia (*Lobelia siphilitica*) [5 plants], or 'Grosso' or 'Provence' lavender (*Lavandula × intermedia*) [5 plants]

❺ ROZANNE GERANIUM
Geranium 'Gerwat' | **5 plants**
Zones 5–8
Alternates: Another 6- to 18-inch-tall perennial with blue or purple-blue flowers, such as catmint (*Nepeta × faassenii*) [5 plants] or leadwort (*Ceratostigma plumbaginoides*) [9 plants]

Planting Plan

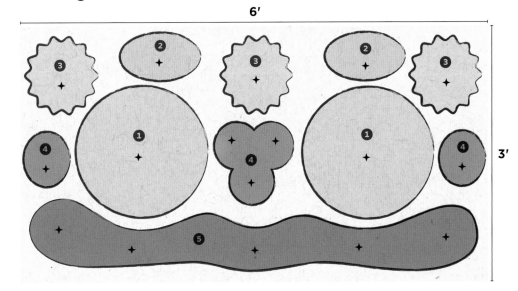

Season by Season

Spring: Leafy growth starts sprouting in early to mid spring on most of these perennials, though the gray-blue new shoots of 'Heavy Metal' switch grass usually rise a bit later, in mid to late spring. By late spring, the clustered, pale blue flowers of Arkansas bluestar are in full bloom, and the deep purple-blue spikes of 'Caradonna' ornamental sage may be opening, too.

To get your blue garden off to a great start for the growing season, cut down all the remaining dead stems and leaves in early spring. This is also a good time to divide the hyssop, switch grass, ornamental sage, and geranium if they were starting to crowd out their companions by last fall. Finish up by applying a fresh layer of organic mulch around the plants.

Summer: Arkansas bluestar finishes flowering in early summer, but the 'Caradonna' ornamental sage is in full glory well into summer. The purple-blue spikes of 'Blue Fortune' hyssop and bowl-shaped blooms of ROZANNE geranium join in now, too, and contribute color for much, if not all, of the summer. You also get the gray-blue leaves of the 'Heavy Metal' switch grass all summer. ('Heavy Metal' flowers, as well, with loose, reddish green plumes in mid to late summer, which are pretty even though they don't add much to the blue theme.)

Once the Arkansas bluestar is done flowering, cut it back by one-third to one-half of its height to remove the developing seedpods and encourage lower, bushier regrowth. Trim the ornamental sage back by about one-third in mid to late summer and the hyssop back by about one-quarter in late summer to promote rebloom later in the season. If the geranium stops flowering or looks straggly by late summer, snip off all of its trailing stems close to the center of the plant, where new growth will quickly sprout if it hasn't already. Water the garden during summer dry spells.

Fall and Winter: The blues keep coming into fall, with more flowers from the 'Blue Fortune' hyssop, 'Caradonna' ornamental sage, and ROZANNE geranium from early fall to frost. Cooler weather brings out some other colors, too: the leaves of Arkansas bluestar usually turn bright yellow, as do the leaf blades of 'Heavy Metal' switch grass, and the foliage of ROZANNE geranium often turns showy shades of orange and red.

In mid to late fall, cut down the freeze-killed tops of the Arkansas bluestar, switch grass, and geranium and clip off the finished flower stems of the ornamental sage back to the ground-level leaves, if you wish, or leave all of the tops in place for winter interest. (Even if you cut down the other perennials, it's a good idea to leave the hyssop stems alone until spring cleanup, to improve the odds of the plants surviving the winter.)

Digging Deeper

THIS BLUE GARDEN would show off beautifully against a light-colored background, such as a white or pale gray house wall or fence. Try it as a foundation planting along the front of your home, as a multiseason border next to a deck or patio, or as an edging along a driveway or sidewalk. If you need to fill a longer space, repeat the plan end to end, mixing in some of the suggested alternate plants to add some variety.

Blue flowers tend to fade into the background, so keep them for areas where you'll see them at close range: by your front door, for instance, or around your favorite summer sitting area. Complement their soft colors by pairing them with gray and blue leaves, or give them a bit of zip by combining them with white and yellow flowers or white-striped, yellow-striped, or bright silver foliage.

As you can guess from their common name, bluestars (*Amsonia*) are obvious choices for blue gardens. The starry flowers are light blue to near white on Arkansas bluestar (*A. hubrichtii*) and eastern bluestar (*A. tabernaemontana*), both of which have an upright to vase-shaped form at their late-spring bloom time and a bushy, mounded shape from midsummer on. The hybrid 'Blue Ice' is a richer blue in flower and forms lower-growing clumps. After their bloom display, bluestars offer rich green leaves for summer interest and often turn showy shades of yellow in fall. These dependable, long-lived perennials also tend to be deer resistant — a big plus where these animal pests are a problem.

Touch of Gold

Yellow flowers are a great choice for sunny gardens, because their bright petals show up well even in strong light, adding lots of cheerful color whether you enjoy them up close to your house or plant them farther out in your yard. Besides blooms, yellows can come from yellow-striped or -spotted leaves, as well as from the yellow centers of many daisy-form flowers.

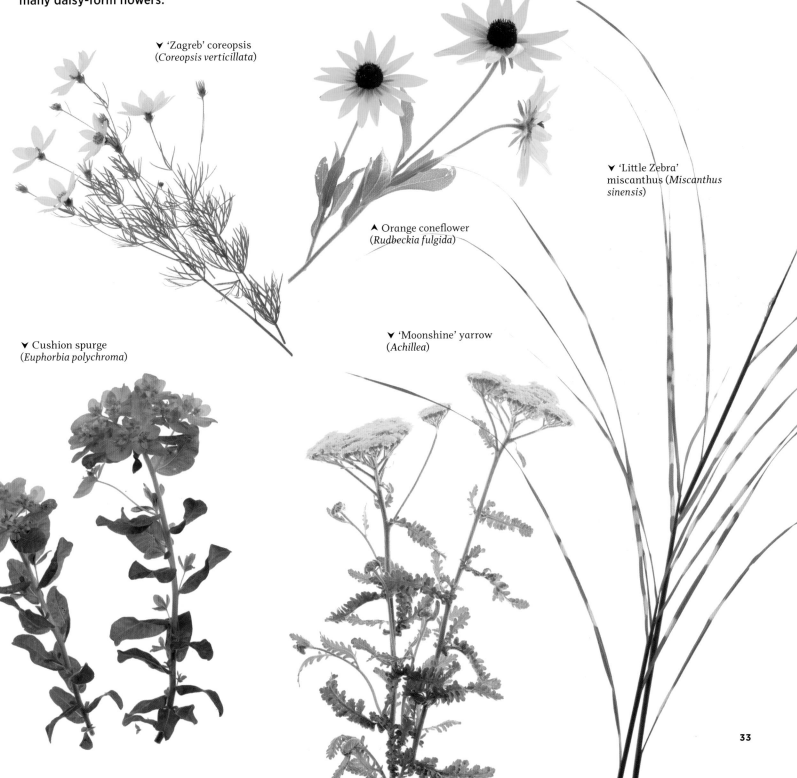

⌄ 'Zagreb' coreopsis
(*Coreopsis verticillata*)

⌄ 'Little Zebra' miscanthus (*Miscanthus sinensis*)

⌃ Orange coneflower
(*Rudbeckia fulgida*)

⌄ Cushion spurge
(*Euphorbia polychroma*)

⌄ 'Moonshine' yarrow
(*Achillea*)

33

The Garden Plan

Shopping List

❶ 'LITTLE ZEBRA' MISCANTHUS
Miscanthus sinensis | 1 plant
Zones 5–9
Alternates: A 3- to 5-foot-tall, yellow-flowered perennial, such as 'Hyperion' or another yellow daylily (*Hemerocallis*) [1 plant] or 'Fireworks' goldenrod (*Solidago rugosa*) [1 plant]

❷ 'ZAGREB' COREOPSIS
Coreopsis verticillata | 3 plants
Zones 4–9
Alternates: 'Early Sunrise' coreopsis, or another 1- to 2-foot-tall perennial with yellow flowers, such as a golden marguerite (*Anthemis*) [3 plants]

❸ 'MOONSHINE' YARROW
Achillea | 3 plants
Zones 3–8
Alternates: Another 2- to 3-foot-tall, yellow-flowered yarrow, such as 'Schwellenberg', or another perennial with those traits, such as 'Summer Solstice' sundrops (*Oenothera fruticosa*) [3 plants] or 'Golden Alexander' yellow loosestrife (*Lysimachia punctata*) [3 plants]

❹ CUSHION SPURGE
Euphorbia polychroma | 3 plants
Zones 4–9
Alternates: Another 12- to 18-inch-tall perennial with yellow flowers, such as basket-of-gold (*Aurinia saxatilis*) [3 plants] or lady's mantle (*Alchemilla mollis*) [3 plants]

❺ ORANGE CONEFLOWER
Rudbeckia fulgida | 3 plants
Zones 3–9
Alternates: Another 18- to 24-inch-tall perennial with yellow flowers, such as 'Mesa Yellow' blanket flower (*Gaillardia × grandiflora*) [3 plants] or Broadway Lights ('Leumayel') or 'Banana Cream' Shasta daisy (*Leucanthemum*) [3 plants]

Planting Plan

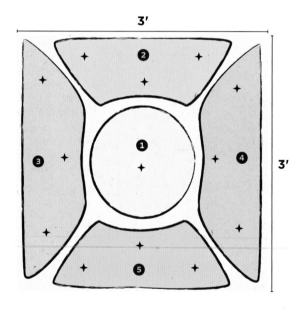

Season by Season

Spring: The yellow theme here is evident early on, when the cushion spurge jumps into growth with yellow shoot tips, with peak color as the shoots expand in mid to late spring. The other perennials are generally just leaves at this time of year, with the ferny gray foliage of 'Moonshine' yarrow and broad, fuzzy leaves of orange coneflower popping up in early to mid spring and the yellow-banded blades of 'Little Zebra' miscanthus and feathery, bright green shoots of 'Zagreb' coreopsis appearing a bit later, in mid to late spring.

In early to mid spring, cut down any remaining dead stems and leaves, and divide the miscanthus, coneflowers, coreopsis, or yarrows if they were starting to outgrow their space last year. When you're done with spring cleanup, apply a fresh layer of organic mulch over the soil.

Summer: Cushion spurge is usually done flowering by early summer, gradually developing reddish seed heads. Bright yellow 'Zagreb' coreopsis and 'Moonshine' yarrow generally come into full glory in early summer and continue through much or all of the season, joined by orange coneflower in mid- to late summer. The yellow banding on the leaves of 'Little Zebra' miscanthus contributes to the color theme all summer long. This ornamental grass also produces reddish brown, whisklike flower plumes in late summer.

It's a good idea to shear the mounds of cushion spurge by about half their height in early summer to prevent self-sowing and get bushier regrowth. (Wear gloves while working around the plants to protect your skin from the irritating milky sap.) On the coreopsis, clip off individual blooms as they die, or shear the clumps by about a third when flowering slows down in mid

to late summer. Cut off the finished yarrow and orange coneflower flower heads just above a lower bud on the stem, if there is one, or close to the base of the stem. Water the garden during extended summer dry spells.

Fall and Winter: The flower plumes of 'Little Zebra' miscanthus age to golden brown in fall. The leaves eventually turn yellow, too, and then dry to brown and remain all winter. 'Zagreb' coreopsis, 'Moonshine' yarrow, and orange coneflower may keep producing new flowers until frost; then their dried seed heads remain for winter interest. The cushion spurge leaves turn shades of orange, red, or purple in fall: not yellow, usually, but still very showy.

If the coreopsis, yarrows, or coneflowers are crowding their companions, divide them in early fall. Otherwise, it's fine to leave the garden as is until spring cleanup.

Digging Deeper

A SMALL SQUARE PLAN like this one is a super place to try out a new color theme. Tuck it into a corner, or use a pair of squares to flank a doorway, gate, arbor, or set of steps. To extend it into a longer border, repeat the square as many times as needed, with the squares right next to each other. Or make a larger square by putting four squares together, leaving about 2 feet between them to create paths through the area. Repeat the plan exactly the same each time for a formal look, mix in some of the suggested alternate plants for a bit of variety, combine two or more colors — two yellow and two blue squares, for instance — or go wild with four different-colored squares.

Even a "one-color" garden is never really just one color. Even if you choose just one shade of yellow for the flowers, their leaves can contribute many shades of green. Dark greens and bright greens make an especially nice setting for yellow blossoms. For a bit more variety in a yellow theme, include some orange and orange-yellows, too. Touches of white, purple, or blue in flowers or leaves add even more zip.

Bold and Beautiful

Rousing reds, intense oranges, vivid yellows, and brilliant purples are super for sunny sites, because their rich hues hold up well even in strong sunlight. They're a cheery choice for any part of the yard, welcoming visitors to your front yard, dressing up a dull side yard, or brightening up the back yard with months of lively color.

◐ ◑ Full sun to partial shade

◆ Average soil

❯ 'Prairie Sunset' false sunflower (*Heliopsis helianthoides*)

❯ 'Jacob Cline' bee balm (*Monarda didyma*)

❯ Nicky phlox (*Phlox paniculata* 'Dusterlohe')

❯ Firefly coral bells (*Heuchera* 'Leuchtkäfer')

▲ Mardi Gras Helen's flower (*Helenium* 'Helbro')

The Garden Plan

Shopping List

❶ 'PRAIRIE SUNSET' FALSE SUNFLOWER
Heliopsis helianthoides | 1 plant
Zones 4–8
Alternates: Another 4- to 6-foot-tall perennial with bright yellow, golden, or orangey flowers, such as 'Lemon Queen' perennial sunflower (*Helianthus*), 'Fireworks' goldenrod (*Solidago rugosa*) [1 plant], or 'Wayside Flame' torch lily (*Kniphofia*) [1 plant]

❷ 'JACOB CLINE' BEE BALM
Monarda didyma | 2 plants
Zones 3-9
Alternates: Another 3- to 5-foot-tall perennial with red flowers, such as 'Firetail' or 'Taurus' mountain fleeceflower (*Persicaria amplexicaulis*) [2 plants], scarlet rose mallow (*Hibiscus coccineus*) [2 plants], or cardinal flower (*Lobelia cardinalis*) [6 plants]

❸ MARDI GRAS HELEN'S FLOWER
Helenium 'Helbro' | 2 plants
Zones 4–8
Alternates: Another orangey Helen's flower, such as 'Coppelia', or another 2- to 3-foot-tall perennial with orange or golden flowers, such as orange coneflower (*Rudbeckia fulgida*) [2 plants] or blackberry lily (*Belamcanda chinensis*) [2 plants]

❹ NICKY PHLOX
Phlox paniculata 'Dusterlohe' | 1 plant
Zones 4–9
Alternates: Another purple or magenta phlox, such as 'Wendy House', or another 2- to 4-foot-tall perennial with purple or magenta flowers, such as 'Purple Profusion' spiderwort (*Tradescantia*) [1 plant] or 'Iron Butterfly' ironweed (*Vernonia lettermannii*) [1 plant]

❺ FIREFLY CORAL BELLS
Heuchera 'Leuchtkäfer' | 5 plants
Zones 3–8
Alternates: Another red-flowered coral bells, such as 'Splendens', or another 6- to 18-inch-tall perennial with red or orange flowers or foliage, such as Japanese blood grass (*Imperata cylindrica* 'Rubra') [5 plants] or 'Peach Flambe' heuchera (*Heuchera*) [5 plants]

Planting Plan

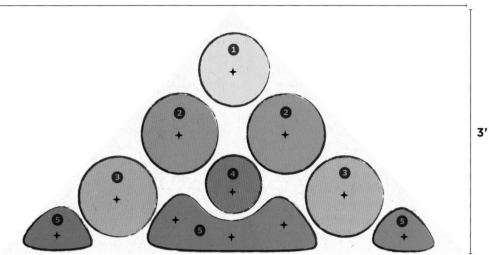

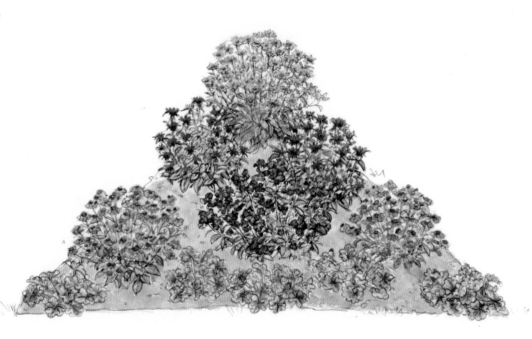

Season by Season

Spring: Early interest in this garden comes mostly from the bright green shoots of the emerging perennials. By late spring, though, the FIREFLY coral bells may be in bloom, with tiny but abundant red bells held above the leaves on upright stems.

Get this garden ready for the new season in early to mid spring. Cut down any remaining dead stems on all of the perennials, and pinch or snip off any winter-damaged leaves on the coral bells. Every 3 years, divide all of the plants to keep them vigorous and free-flowering. Spread a fresh layer of organic mulch around the plants. If the 'Prairie Sunset' false sunflower, 'Jacob Cline' bee balm, or MARDI GRAS Helen's flower sprawled last year, or if you'd like to delay their blooms until a bit later in the summer, cut the clumps back by about half in late spring.

Summer: FIREFLY coral bells is in full bloom in early summer, if not before, and continues through midsummer, at least. 'Prairie Sunset' false sunflower, with deep purple stems that bear golden yellow, orange-centered daisies, and MARDI GRAS Helen's flower, with yellow-streaked, orange-red blooms, start in early summer (or midsummer, if you cut them back in spring) and keep going through much or all of the summer. 'Jacob Cline' bee balm, with shaggy-looking clusters of brilliant red blooms, and NICKY phlox, with fragrant, deep magenta-purple flowers, are generally at their best a bit later, in mid to late summer.

Summer care is mostly a matter of keeping the dead flowers clipped off to prevent unwanted seedlings and to encourage the plants to produce more blooms. Water the garden during summer dry spells.

Fall and Winter: 'Prairie Sunset' false sunflower and NICKY phlox often produce some new flowers through early fall. Later on, the false sunflower seed heads provide welcome winter food for birds, and the FIREFLY coral bells leaves stay green (sometimes with silvery or purplish marbling) for much of the winter.

Leave the dead tops of the plants in place for winter, or cut everything (except the coral bells) to the ground in late fall.

Digging Deeper

A TRIANGLE MIGHT SEEM LIKE AN ODD CHOICE for a garden shape, but it's actually quite versatile. A single triangle fits neatly into a corner, and a pair of triangles looks great flanking a bench or arbor, marking the entrance to a path, or edging a set of steps.

Flowers aren't the only source of color in the garden: you can look to the leaves, too. Perennials with brightly colored foliage, such as golden oregano (*Origanum vulgare* 'Aureum'), bright yellow SUNSHINE BLUE bluebeard (*Caryopteris incana* 'Jason'), and rich red Japanese blood grass (*Imperata cylindrica* 'Rubra'), add interest all through the growing season. Deep purple to near-black leaves, such as 'Obsidian' heuchera (*Heuchera*) and 'Chameleon' spurge (*Euphorbia dulcis*), are super for providing contrast to bright blooms.

Garden phlox (*Phlox paniculata*) blooms in many eye-catching colors, including hot pinks, bright reds, vibrant magenta, and even orange. Their exact hues may vary through the season, darkening in cool temperatures and cloudy conditions and bleaching out a bit in very hot, sunny weather. If you see a clump producing blooms of a very different color, though, it's likely that one or more seedlings have popped up right at the base of the original clump. You can fix that problem by digging up the clump and dividing it to remove the unwanted part. To prevent this from happening in the first place, clip off the flower heads as soon as all of the blossoms drop so they don't have a chance to produce seeds.

Perennials in Pastel

Combining pastel-flowered perennials is a foolproof way to create a gorgeous-looking color-themed garden. No need to worry if you have no design experience, because it's pretty much impossible for baby blues, lavender-purples, soft yellows, and pastel pinks and peaches to look bad together. Soft colors like these can bleach out in strong light, though, so you may want to put your pastel planting in a site with a bit of shade from midday to midafternoon.

Full sun to partial shade

Average soil

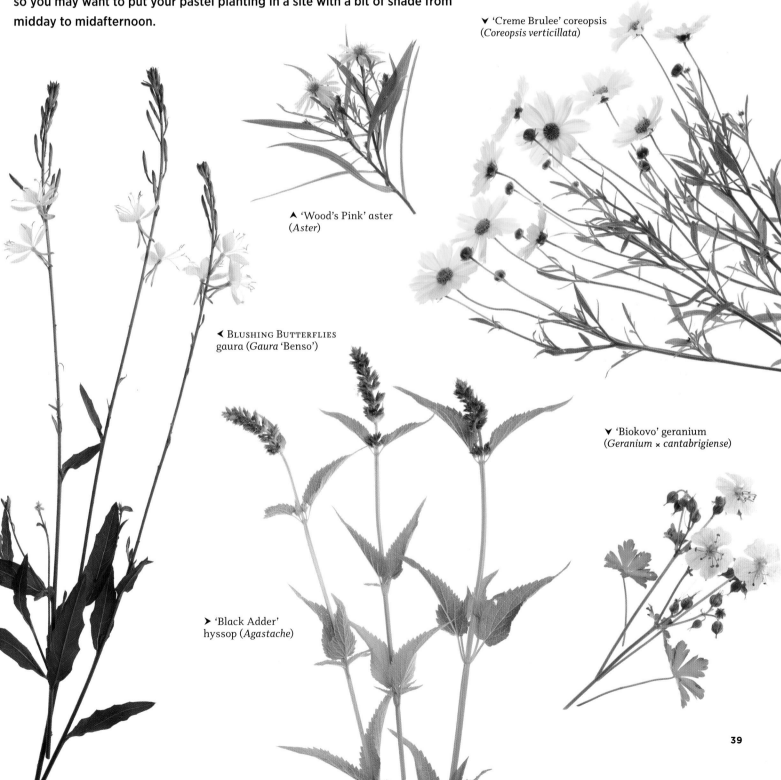

▼ 'Creme Brulee' coreopsis
(*Coreopsis verticillata*)

▲ 'Wood's Pink' aster
(*Aster*)

◄ Blushing Butterflies
gaura (*Gaura* 'Benso')

▼ 'Biokovo' geranium
(*Geranium × cantabrigiense*)

➤ 'Black Adder'
hyssop (*Agastache*)

The Garden Plan

Shopping List

1 BLUSHING BUTTERFLIES GAURA
Gaura 'Benso' | 3 plants
Zones 5–9
Alternates: Another 1- to 2-foot-tall, upright perennial with pink or peach-colored flowers, such as 'Pink Mist' pincushion flower (*Scabiosa*) [3 plants], 'Pink Grapefruit' yarrow (*Achillea*) [3 plants], or sunset hyssop (*Agastache rupestris*) [3 plants]

2 'BLACK ADDER' HYSSOP
Agastache | 2 plants
Zones 6–9
Alternates: 'Golden Jubilee' hyssop, or another 2- to 3-foot-tall, upright perennial with blue or purple-blue flowers, such as 'Provence' lavender (*Lavandula × intermedia*) [2 plants] or 'Sapphire Blue' sea holly (*Eryngium*) [2 plants]

3 'BIOKOVO' GERANIUM
Geranium × cantabrigiense | 4 plants
Zones 4–8
Alternates: Another 1- to 2-foot-tall, mounded perennial with pink or peach-colored flowers or foliage, such as 'Bath's Pink' dianthus (*Dianthus*) [4 plants] or 'Caramel' heuchera (*Heuchera*) [4 plants]

4 'CREME BRULEE' COREOPSIS
Coreopsis verticillata | 3 plants
Zones 4–9
Alternates: 'Moonbeam' or 'Moonlight' coreopsis, or another 1- to 2-foot-tall perennial with yellow flowers, such as lady's mantle (*Alchemilla mollis*) [3 plants] or 'Happy Returns' daylily (*Hemerocallis*) [3 plants]

5 'WOOD'S PINK' ASTER
Aster | 2 plants
Zones 4–8
Alternates: 'Wood's Blue' aster or another 1- to 2-foot-tall, mounded perennial with pink, blue, or purple-blue flowers, such as 'Blue Ice' bluestar (*Amsonia*) [2 plants] or 'Blue Wonder' or 'Kit Kat' catmint (*Nepeta × faassenii*) [2 plants]

Planting Plan

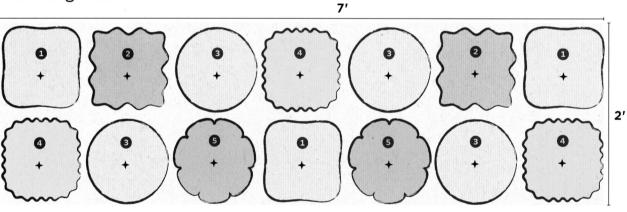

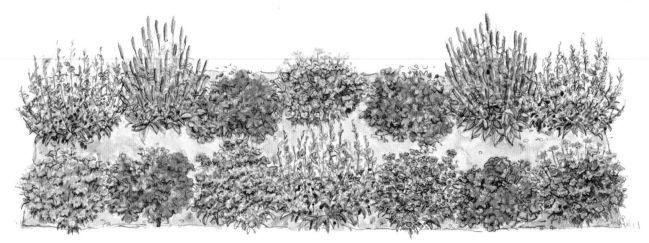

Season by Season

Spring: 'Biokovo' geranium jumps into growth early in the spring, and it may be in bloom by mid spring, with an abundance of pink-and-white flowers. The other perennials are usually just starting to leaf out at that point, in varying shades of green.

Since the geranium begins growing so quickly, give it a bit of attention very early in spring. If there are only a few winter-damaged leaves, clip them off; otherwise, simply shear off all of the leaves close to ground level, being careful not to damage any emerging new shoots. This is also a good time to divide the clumps if they are starting to outgrow their space. Early to mid spring is a fine time to cut down any remaining top growth on the hyssop, coreopsis, and aster, and to divide the clumps (every 3 years or so for the coreopsis and aster; only if the plant is crowding out its companions for the hyssop). Wait until the gaura starts growing before trimming off the dead parts, just above the vigorous new shoots. In mid to late spring, spread a fresh layer of organic mulch over the soil.

Summer: Despite its late start, BLUSHING BUTTERFLIES gaura is generally in bloom by early summer, with white flowers that age to pink. They're lovely with the butter yellow, daisy-form flowers of 'Creme Brulee', which appear around the same time. Both of these may keep blooming all through the summer, or they may take a break in mid or late summer. 'Black Adder' hyssop, too, starts flowering in early summer, and its blue-purple spikes continue for months. 'Biokovo' geranium overlaps with its companions in early summer, sometimes with a few additional blooms later in the season. 'Wood's Pink' aster finally comes along in late summer, with lots of pink daisies.

Clip off the flower stems on the geranium once the flowers finish. If the gaura or coreopsis clumps stop blooming in mid to late summer, cut them back halfway to encourage more flowers to form later in the season. It's also a good idea to give the hyssop a light trim (by about a quarter of its height) in late summer, for the same reason. Water the garden during dry spells.

Fall and Winter: This pastel planting continues to look lovely in autumn. 'Wood's Pink' aster flowers into early fall, and the gaura, hyssop, and coreopsis can keep going until frost. 'Biokovo' geranium might produce a few flowers now, too, but its main contribution is its leaves, which may turn shades of yellow, orange, and red as colder weather arrives. The geranium and gaura may hold on to their leaves for the winter, too.

No need to do any fall or winter cleanup here. Leaving the top growth in place provides some winter interest from the seed heads and provides some winter protection for the plants, too.

Digging Deeper

A LONG, NARROW BORDER like this one is great as an edging for a pathway, sidewalk, or driveway, or as a foundation planting around your home, garage, or garden shed. Repeat the plan end to end as many times as needed to fill a longer space, mixing in some of the suggested alternate plants to add more variety. These pastels would show off especially well if you set the garden against a 4- to 6-foot-tall evergreen hedge.

Rich green leaves make a great backdrop for light-colored blooms, but other leaf colors also have their own charms in a garden like this. Bright yellow or sparkling silver leaves add zip, for instance, while gray or powder blue foliage complements equally soft flower colors.

There's plenty of room in this plan for you to tuck in spring-blooming bulbs for early season color, and there are many pastel options that will complement the pale pink 'Biokovo' geranium. For early to mid spring, consider light blues, such as 'Blue Pearl' crocus (*Crocus*), 'Sky Jacket' Dutch hyacinth (*Hyacinthus orientalis*), or 'Valerie Finnis' grape hyacinth (*Muscari*). And for mid to late spring, include soft-colored tulips (*Tulipa*), such as creamy 'Ivory Floradale', frilly pink 'Angelique', or peachy pink 'Apricot Beauty'.

Welcome Spring

A garden filled with early blooming flowers is a wonderful way to mark the end of a long, dreary winter and celebrate the return of spring. Crocuses, daffodils, tulips, and other spring bulbs are an obvious choice, but there are also many early flowering perennials, with the added advantage that they stick around for the rest of the growing season instead of disappearing back underground soon after bloom.

◐ ◑ Full sun to partial shade

◆ Average soil

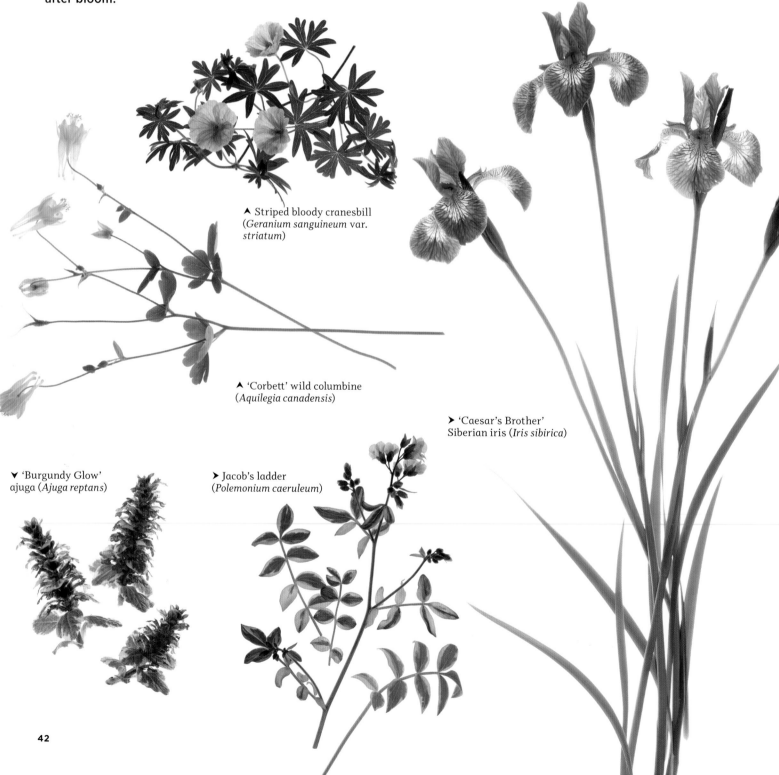

▲ Striped bloody cranesbill (*Geranium sanguineum* var. *striatum*)

▲ 'Corbett' wild columbine (*Aquilegia canadensis*)

➤ 'Caesar's Brother' Siberian iris (*Iris sibirica*)

▼ 'Burgundy Glow' ajuga (*Ajuga reptans*)

➤ Jacob's ladder (*Polemonium caeruleum*)

The Garden Plan

Shopping List

❶ JACOB'S LADDER
Polemonium caeruleum | **3 plants**
Zones 4–8
Alternates: Another 3- to 5-foot-tall, spring-blooming perennial, such as Italian alkanet (*Anchusa azurea*) [3 plants] or 'Telham Beauty' peach-leaved bellflower (*Campanula persicifolia*) [3 plants]

❷ 'CAESAR'S BROTHER' SIBERIAN IRIS
Iris sibirica | **1 plant**
Zones 3–8
Alternates: 'Moon Silk' or 'Sparkling Rose' Siberian iris, or another 24- to 30-inch-tall, spring-blooming perennial with blue, yellow, or rosy pink flowers, such as yellow foxglove (*Digitalis grandiflora*) [1 plant], strawberry foxglove (*D.* × *mertonensis*) [1 plant], or 'Swan Pink and Yellow' columbine (*Aquilegia*) [1 plant]

❸ 'CORBETT' WILD COLUMBINE
Aquilegia canadensis | **4 plants**
Zones 3–9
Alternates: Regular wild columbine (*A. canadensis*) or another 6- to 18-inch-tall, spring-blooming perennial with yellow, yellow-and-blue, or yellow-and-pink flowers, such as leopard's bane (*Doronicum orientale*) [4 plants] or 'Etain' viola (*Viola*) [4 plants]

❹ STRIPED BLOODY CRANESBILL
Geranium sanguineum var. *striatum* | **3 plants**
Zones 4–8
Alternates: Another 6- to 18-inch-tall, spring-blooming perennial with pink or white flowers, such as 'Max Frei' soapwort (*Saponaria* × *lempergii*) [3 plants] or 'Bath's Pink' dianthus (*Dianthus*) [3 plants]

❺ 'BURGUNDY GLOW' AJUGA
Ajuga reptans | **4 plants**
Zones 3–9
Alternates: 'Dixie Chip' ajuga, or another 4- to 12-inch-tall, spring-blooming perennial with blue or white flowers, such as 'Georgia Blue' (*Veronica peduncularis*) [4 plants] or perennial candytuft (*Iberis sempervirens*) [4 plants]

Planting Plan

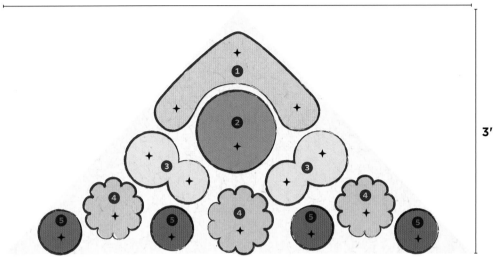

Season by Season

Spring: As soon as winter loosens its grip, you'll see your garden jump into new growth, with peak bloom by late spring. Jacob's ladder starts with clumps of lacy, bright green leaves, and then sends up upright stems topped with clusters of grape-scented blue flowers. 'Caesar's Brother' Siberian iris forms dense, grass-like clumps of medium green leaves accented with elegant purple-blue blooms. The multi-parted, light green clumps of 'Corbett' wild columbine form ferny clumps topped with dangling, light yellow blossoms. Striped bloody cranesbill grows in dense mounds of deeply cut, rich green leaves practically smothered in pale pink flowers. And then there's 'Burgundy Glow' ajuga, with short spikes of purple-blue flowers over rosettes of green and white leaves that are heavily blushed with pink.

Because growth starts so early in this garden, make it your top priority when planning your spring gardening chores. Clip off any dead stems, as well as any remaining green leaves that were damaged over the winter. Spread a fresh layer of organic mulch around the plants, and your garden is all ready for a spectacular spring display.

Summer: Jacob's ladder, 'Caesar's Brother' Siberian iris, 'Corbett' wild columbine, striped bloody cranesbill, and 'Burgundy Glow' ajuga may continue flowering into early summer. Even though new blooms stop forming, the spring foliage remains to add summer interest. The only main difference is that the leaves of the ajuga tend to lose their pinkish blush in warm weather.

Cut off the finished flower stems of the Jacob's ladder, iris, and ajuga at their base to tidy the plants. Do the same on the wild columbine, but consider leaving one or two of the stems in place to form and drop seed. (Wild columbine plants tend to fade out after a few years, but letting the plants produce some seed will allow for a few self-sown replacements.) Shear the striped bloody cranesbill clumps back by one-third to one-half to remove the developing seed heads and encourage new leafy growth. If the Jacob's ladder or wild columbine leaves turn brown during hot spells, cut off all of the foliage to promote a flush of fresh green leaves. Water the garden during summer dry spells.

Fall and Winter: Jacob's ladder holds its bright green leaves through the fall and often through much or all of the winter. 'Caesar's Brother' iris leaves eventually turn yellow and then brown as they dry. 'Corbett' wild columbine leaves stay green through the fall but die back for the winter. Striped bloody cranesbill leaves often take on shades of red and burgundy for fall, then brown in winter. 'Burgundy Glow' ajuga blushes pink again in cold weather and may hold its leaves all through the winter in mild areas.

Early fall is a good time to divide the iris, cranesbill, or ajuga clumps if they are starting to outgrow their places. Other than that, there's nothing much to do in this garden until spring.

Digging Deeper

SPRING-FLOWERING PERENNIALS generally don't rebloom later in the growing season, but their leaves can add a lot of interest to your yard, especially if you choose types with colorful foliage. Don't want to do without *any* flowers in summer? Tuck in some lily (*Lilium*) bulbs in spring or fall to enjoy large, showy midseason blooms in a wide range of bright and pastel colors. Plant the bulbs between the perennial clumps, and the lily stems will shoot up through their now-just-leafy companions for an extra show of flower power in mid or late summer.

Common ajuga (*Ajuga reptans*), also known as bugle or bugleweed, produces an abundance of short spikes of purple-blue, pink, or white flowers that are a lovely sight in spring, plus dense carpets of rich green, bronzy, or multicolored leaves that look great for the rest of the growing season. It also spreads quite quickly, a trait that makes it popular with gardeners who need to fill a lot of space without spending a lot of money. This creeping nature can make it a maintenance problem, too, though. Once it fills its allotted space, it *keeps* spreading in all directions, sometimes crowding out less vigorous companions and readily creeping into surrounding lawn areas as well. Variegated 'Burgundy Glow' tends to be a less rampant spreader than some kinds, but you may still need to pull out or transplant the excess parts once or twice a year. Using some kind of edging strip, such as a row of bricks or paving blocks, can help to slow its spread into adjacent turfgrass.

Summer Spectacular

Whether you plan to host lots of parties and picnics or simply like relaxing outdoors on summer evenings and weekends, a perennial garden planned specifically for summer color makes your yard a prettier place to be. This is the peak season for many perennials, with flowers in all kinds of colors, so the hardest part may be deciding on just a few to try. This starter garden includes a cheery variety of yellows, pinks, and blue to give you a taste of the possibilities.

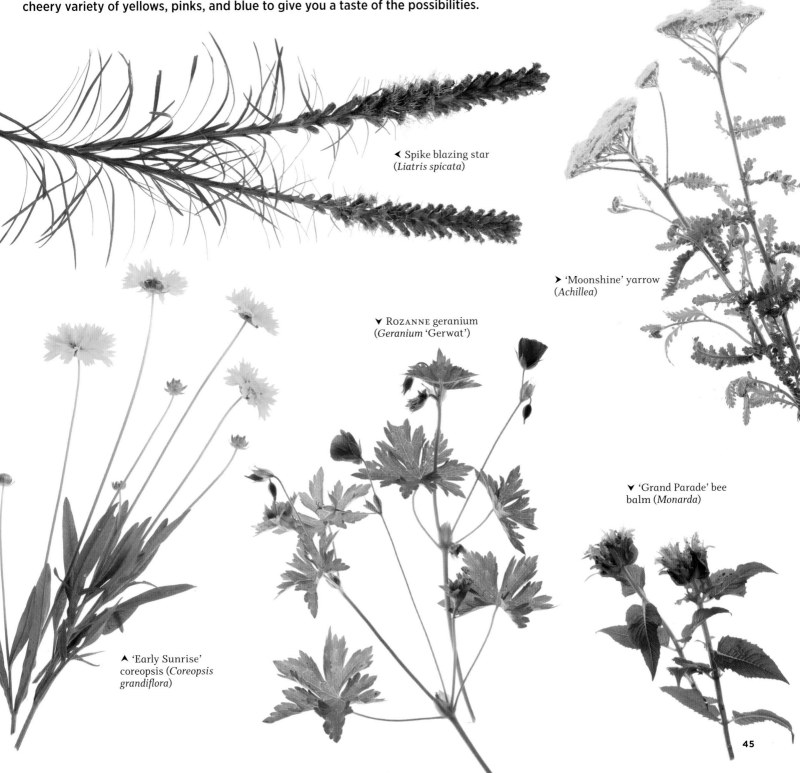

◄ Spike blazing star (*Liatris spicata*)

► 'Moonshine' yarrow (*Achillea*)

▼ Rozanne geranium (*Geranium* 'Gerwat')

▼ 'Grand Parade' bee balm (*Monarda*)

▲ 'Early Sunrise' coreopsis (*Coreopsis grandiflora*)

45

The Garden Plan

Shopping List

① SPIKE BLAZING STAR
Liatris spicata | **4 plants**
Zones 4–9
Alternates: Another 2- to 3-foot-tall, summer-flowering perennial with purplish or orange flowers, such as 'Caradonna' ornamental sage (*Salvia*) [1 plant] or 'Apricot Sunrise' hyssop (*Agastache*) [1 plant]

② 'GRAND PARADE' BEE BALM
Monarda | **2 plants**
Zones 3–8
Alternates: Another dwarf, pink bee balm, such as 'Pink Lace' or 'Pink Supreme' , or another 12- to 18-inch-tall, summer-blooming perennial with pink flowers, such as 'Kim's Knee High' purple coneflower (*Echinacea purpurea*) [2 plants]

③ Rozanne GERANIUM
Geranium 'Gerwat' | **2 plants**
Zones 5–8
Alternates: Another 12- to 18-inch-tall, summer-blooming perennial with blue or purple-blue flowers, such as 'Blue Wonder' or 'Kit Cat' catmint (*Nepeta* × *faassenii*) [2 plants] or English lavender (*Lavandula angustifolia*) [2 plants]

④ 'MOONSHINE' YARROW
Achillea | **6 plants**
Zones 3–8
Alternates: 'Schwellenberg' yarrow, or another 12- to 18-inch-tall, summer-blooming perennial with yellow flowers, such as 'Mesa Yellow' blanket flower (*Gaillardia* × *grandiflora*) [2 plants] or 'Happy Returns' daylily (*Hemerocallis*) [2 plants]

⑤ 'EARLY SUNRISE' COREOPSIS
Coreopsis grandiflora | **2 plants**
Zones 4–9
Alternates: 'Moonbeam', 'Moonlight', or 'Sienna Sunset' coreopsis, or another 12- to 18-inch-tall, summer-blooming perennial with yellow or peach-colored flowers, such as 'Oranges and Lemons' blanket flower (*Gaillardia* × *grandiflora*) [2 plants]

Planting Plan

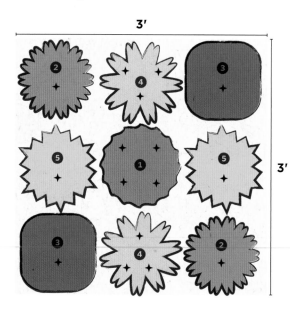

Season by Season

Spring: Lovely leaves are the main source of interest here during the spring. Bright green spike blazing star and 'Early Sunrise' coreopsis, deep green 'Grand Parade' bee balm, and silver-gray 'Moonshine' yarrow generally pop up in early to mid spring. ROZANNE geranium can be slow to sprout but is usually up and growing by mid to late spring.

In early to mid spring, cut down any remaining dead stems and divide any of the perennials that were starting to outgrow their space by last fall. Then, spread a fresh layer of organic mulch over the soil.

Summer: The fuzzy-looking, purplish pink spikes of spike blazing star are in peak bloom in early to midsummer in southern gardens and mid to late summer in northern areas. 'Early Sunrise' coreopsis is covered with bright yellow blooms in early to midsummer, while the shaggy pink bloom clusters

of 'Grand Parade' bee balm are most abundant in mid to late summer. And all through the summer months, you'll enjoy the purple-blue blooms of ROZANNE geranium and clear yellow clusters of 'Moonshine' yarrow.

Keeping the faded flowers clipped off will help to keep the garden looking great through the summer. On the blazing star, cut the finished spikes back by one-third to one-half for possible rebloom, or leave the spikes in place to form seeds for later-season interest. Snip off the bee balm flower heads just above the uppermost leaves on the stem, or leave them, too, for their seed heads. If the geranium stops blooming, snip off all of the trailing stems at the base, where new growth will emerge at the center of the plant. On the yarrow, cut off the faded flower heads just above a bud lower down on the stem (if there is one) or close to the base of the plant. And on the coreopsis, snip off the faded flowers individually through the

summer or cut the entire plant back by one-third to one-half when flowering slows in mid to late summer. Don't forget to water the garden during dry spells, too.

Fall and Winter: Spike blazing star and 'Moonshine' yarrow might produce a few flowers in fall, and ROZANNE geranium and 'Early Sunrise' coreopsis are quite likely to produce blooms until freezing weather. The foliage of ROZANNE geranium also turns showy shades of orange and red in autumn. The blazing star, bee balm, yarrow, and coreopsis have attractive seed heads, too.

If any of these perennials are crowding out their companions, dig up and divide them in early fall. Otherwise, leave garden cleanup until spring so you can enjoy the interesting seed heads. (These seed heads also provide welcome winter food for birds.)

Digging Deeper

A SMALL, SQUARE BED like this one is easy enough to dig and plant over the course of a day or two, and it fits neatly into all sorts of spots: in a corner, for instance, or around a mailbox post, or next to a doorway or set of steps. As time and money allow, you can easily expand it by repeating the plan as many times as you wish, setting the squares right next to each other or leaving some space between them for paths.

Even though this garden is planned for summer splendor, it doesn't have to be *only* a summer garden. There's plenty of space between the clumps to tuck in small bulbs for spring color as well, so you can get weeks or even months more beauty from this garden for just a few dollars and a few minutes of planting time. Early risers such as snowdrops (*Galanthus*), crocuses (*Crocus*), and grape hyacinths (*Muscari*) jump into growth as soon as the weather gets milder, adding bright spots of spring color. As the bulbs' leaves turn yellow and then brown, the emerging foliage of the perennials covers them up and quickly fills in to get ready for the summer spectacle.

Blazing stars (*Liatris*) are always a welcome addition to sunny summer gardens. Their distinctive spiky blooms make a great contrast to the abundance of summer daisies, and they're magnets for a variety of butterflies. If you can bear to cut them, they're terrific for flower arrangements, too. One warning, though: when their leaves sprout in spring, they look very much like tufts of lawn grass, so be sure to mark their spot with a label so you don't accidentally pull them out.

Autumn Abundance

This perennial planting is packed with an abundance of beautiful autumn blooms, but it's not *just* a fall garden. These late bloomers also have sturdy stems and long-lasting seed heads that remain attractive through the winter months; they provide beauty *and* a bonus of shelter and food for winter birds. Add some spring and summer bulbs, such as Dutch crocus, hyacinths, and lilies, and you can easily turn this fall garden into a multipurpose, multiseason planting!

◐ Full sun to partial shade

◆ Average soil

◄ 'October Skies' aromatic aster (*Aster oblongifolius*)

◄ 'Autumn Fire' sedum (*Sedum*)

➤ 'Fireworks' goldenrod (*Solidago rugosa*)

◄ 'Shenandoah' switch grass (*Panicum virgatum*)

◄ 'Little Joe' Joe-Pye weed (*Eupatorium dubium*)

The Garden Plan

Shopping List

❶ 'SHENANDOAH' SWITCH GRASS
Panicum virgatum | **3 plants**
Zones 4–9
Alternates: 'Heavy Metal' or 'Huron Solstice' switch grass, or another 4- to 5-foot-tall ornamental grass, such as 'Karl Foerster' feather reed grass (*Calamagrostis × acutiflora*) [3 plants] or flame grass (*Miscanthus* 'Purpurascens') [3 plants]

❷ 'LITTLE JOE' JOE-PYE WEED
Eupatorium dubium | **2 plants**
Zones 4–9
Alternates: 'Gateway' Joe-Pye weed, or another 4- to 5-foot-tall, late-summer- to fall-blooming perennial with pink or purple flowers, such as 'Harrington's Pink' or 'September Ruby' New England aster (*Aster novae-angliae*) [2 plants] or 'Plum Crazy' hardy hibiscus (*Hibiscus*) [2 plants]

❸ 'FIREWORKS' GOLDENROD
Solidago rugosa | **3 plants**
Zones 4–9
Alternates: Another 30- to 40-inch-tall perennial or shrub with yellow flowers or foliage in fall, such as Arkansas bluestar (*Amsonia hubrichtii*) [3 plants] or Sᴜɴꜱʜɪɴᴇ Bʟᴜᴇ bluebeard (*Caryopteris incana* 'Jason') [3 plants]

❹ 'OCTOBER SKIES' AROMATIC ASTER
Aster oblongifolius | **3 plants**
Zones 5–8
Alternates: Another 18- to 30-inch-tall, fall-blooming perennial, such as 'Little Spire' Russian sage (*Perovskia*) [3 plants] or 'Sheffield Pink' mum (*Chrysanthemum*) [3 plants]

❺ 'AUTUMN FIRE' SEDUM
Sedum | **6 plants**
Zones 3–9
Alternates: 'Autumn Joy' sedum, or another 12- to 18-inch-tall perennial with flowers, attractive seed heads, or colorful foliage in fall, such as 'Herrenhausen' or 'Rosenkuppel' ornamental oregano (*Origanum*) [6 plants], 'Piglet' fountain grass (*Pennisetum alopecuroides*) [6 plants], or prairie dropseed (*Sporobolus heterolepis*) [6 plants]

Planting Plan

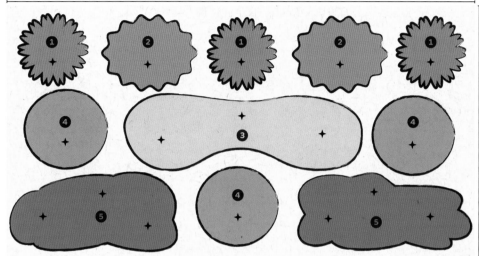

Season by Season

Spring: There are no flowers in this garden through the spring months, unless you've added some early blooming bulbs, but the flush of fresh leafy growth in various shades of green offers textural interest in mid to late spring.

Late-blooming perennials are generally slow to sprout; in fact, the 'Little Joe' Joe-Pye weed may not make an appearance until late spring. But it's still a good idea to tackle the cleanup chores — cutting down and removing all of the remaining dead stems and seed heads — in early to mid spring, so you won't damage the new growth whenever it appears. This is also the ideal time to divide any or all of the perennials, every 3 or 4 years or whenever you notice that they were getting crowded by the end of the previous growing season. When the other chores are done, spread a fresh layer of organic mulch over the soil.

Summer: The arrival of settled warm weather encourages these perennials to jump into vigorous growth. The green blades of 'Shenandoah' switch grass develop red tips by midsummer, and the clumps are topped with airy, reddish brown flower plumes in late summer. The upright stems of 'Little Joe' Joe-Pye weed are topped with rosy pink bloom clusters by about the same time, or even a few weeks earlier in southern gardens. The other perennials are usually just leafy through summer, but they're still attractive. 'Fireworks' goldenrod forms upright clumps of deep green leaves; 'October Skies' aromatic aster grows in dense mounds of tiny, medium green leaves; and the light green, leafy stems of 'Autumn Fire' are topped with tightly packed buds by late summer.

You may want to cut the sedum stems back by half in early summer to reduce the chance of them sprawling in late summer. Otherwise, the only summer maintenance is watering the garden during extended dry spells.

Fall and Winter: By early fall, the loose flower heads of 'Shenandoah' switch grass turn into tan seed heads and the leaves turn burgundy red. The clumps later age to tan-brown and last all winter. 'Little Joe' Joe-Pye weed generally finishes up flowering by early fall, but its sturdy stems and fluffy seed heads dry in place to provide interest through much of the winter. 'Fireworks' goldenrod explodes into sprays of bright yellow blooms and 'October Skies' aromatic aster is smothered in hundreds of small purple-blue daisies in early fall; both eventually drop their leaves when freezing weather returns, but their dried stems and seed heads linger for months. 'Autumn Fire' is topped with dense clusters of rosy pink blooms by early fall, aging to deep red as the seed heads form. The leaves turn yellow in mid fall and then drop, leaving the stems and seed heads to complement the dried forms of their companions.

If you wish, you could cut down all of the perennials by late fall, but it's a pity to miss out on the winter beauty of the dried plant forms, especially when they're lined with frost, dusted in snow, or encased in ice.

Digging Deeper

THIS BORDER IS DESIGNED to be seen mainly from one side, with the tallest plants at the back tapering down to the shortest at the front, so it would look best placed against a vertical backdrop, such as a wall, fence, or hedge. It would work very well as a foundation planting, too. Or, use it to enclose a ground-level deck or patio, where the tall plants will provide some shelter from wind and create screening to give you a sense of privacy.

Bright flowers and intriguing seed heads aren't the only fall features that perennials have to offer. Like many deciduous shrubs and trees, some perennials have leaves that turn showy colors before they drop in autumn. A few sun lovers that are well known for their fall foliage include Arkansas bluestar (*Amsonia hubrichtii*) and balloon flower (*Platycodon grandiflorus*), which turn yellow to orange-yellow, and Japanese blood grass (*Imperata cylindrica* 'Rubra'), which turns brilliant red.

Don't avoid adding goldenrods (*Solidago*) to your garden because you are afraid of them causing hay fever. Goldenrods' bright yellow blooms take the blame that rightly belongs to ragweeds (*Ambrosia*), which bloom around the same time but are hardly noticeable because they have tiny greenish flowers. Ragweeds have very light pollen, which is easily carried by wind and inhaled to aggravate fall allergies, while goldenrods produce relatively heavy, sticky pollen that's carried by insects.

Winter Wonderful

◐○ Full sun to partial shade

◇ Average soil

When folks talk about a "winter garden," they generally don't mean a garden that's actively growing and flowering during the winter months. Instead, they mean a garden that grows during the normal growing season and then continues to look attractive after frost, thanks to features such as evergreen leaves, showy seed heads, bright berries, or striking dried stems. So, if you're tired of looking at bare garden beds in your yard for several months a year, a perennial planting designed specifically for winter interest could be just the thing for you!

▶ 'Coronation Gold' yarrow (*Achillea*)

▲ Spike blazing star (*Liatris spicata*)

◀ 'Ruby Tuesday' Helen's flower (*Helenium*)

◀ 'Karl Foerster' feather reed grass (*Calamagrostis* × *acutiflora*)

▶ 'Southern Comfort' heuchera (*Heuchera*)

51

The Garden Plan

Shopping List

❶ 'KARL FOERSTER' FEATHER REED GRASS
Calamagrostis × acutiflora | **3 plants**
Zones 4–8
Alternates: Another 4- to 5-foot-tall perennial with persistent winter stems, such as Russian sage (*Perovskia atriplicifolia*) [3 plants] or 'Heavy Metal' or 'Shenandoah' switch grass (*Panicum virgatum*) [3 plants]

❷ 'CORONATION GOLD' YARROW
Achillea | **6 plants**
Zones 3–8
Alternates: Another 2 to 3-foot-tall, yellow- or orange-flowered perennial with long-lasting seed heads, such as orange coneflower (*Rudbeckia fulgida*) [6 plants] or 'Summer Sun' false sunflower (*Heliopsis helianthoides*) [6 plants]

❸ 'RUBY TUESDAY' HELEN'S FLOWER
Helenium | **3 plants**
Zones 4–8
Alternates: Another 18- to 24-inch-tall perennial with red or rosy pink flowers, such as 'Fireball' bee balm (*Monarda*) [3 plants] or 'Autumn Fire' or 'Autumn Joy' sedum (*Sedum*) [3 plants]

❹ SPIKE BLAZING STAR
Liatris spicata | **5 plants**
Zones 4–9
Alternates: Another blazing star, such as prairie blazing star (*L. pycnostachya*), or another 3- to 4-foot-tall perennial with long-lasting seed heads, such as purple coneflower (*Echinacea purpurea*) [5 plants], a turtlehead (*Chelone*) [5 plants], or 'Bluebird' smooth aster (*Aster laevis*) [5 plants]

❺ 'SOUTHERN COMFORT' HEUCHERA
Heuchera | **6 plants**
Zones 4–9
Alternates: Another heuchera, or another 6- to 18-inch-tall perennial with evergreen foliage, such as perennial candytuft (*Iberis sempervirens*) [6 plants] or a variegated blue lilyturf (*Liriope muscari* 'Silvery Sunproof' or 'Variegata') [6 plants]

Planting Plan

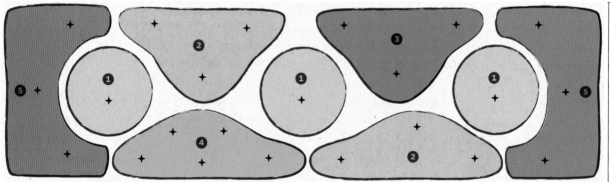

Season by Season

Spring: This garden jumps into the growing season with the bright green new shoots of 'Karl Foerster' feather reed grass, 'Ruby Tuesday' Helen's flower, and spike blazing star, the ferny gray-green leaves of 'Coronation Gold' yarrow, and the rich orange foliage of 'Southern Comfort' heuchera.

Give your winter garden a fresh start via a thorough cleanup in early spring. Cut down any remaining dead top growth on the feather reed grass, yarrow, Helen's flower, and spike blazing star, and divide any of these that were starting to outgrow their places last year. Trim off any winter-damaged leaves on the heuchera, and figure on dividing it every 3 years or so to keep it vigorous. Spread a fresh layer of organic mulch over the soil, and your work is done for the season.

Summer: Early summer brings on the blooms, with the pinkish plumes of 'Karl Foerster' feather reed grass and the golden yellow, clustered blooms of 'Coronation Gold' yarrow, and both of these remain through the summer. In southern gardens, spike blazing star typically produces its fuzzy-looking spikes of pinkish purple flowers in early to midsummer; in northern areas, it flowers in mid to late summer. Mid to late summer is also the usual bloom time of 'Ruby Tuesday' Helen's flower, with its small but abundant daisy-form, deep red flowers. 'Southern Comfort' heuchera sends up loose spikes of tiny white bells in mid to late summer, but they don't add much interest; its key attraction is its leaves, which are peachy yellow to light orange through the summer.

While you'd normally keep dead flowers clipped off, you'll want to leave them in this garden so they can dry in place and remain for winter interest. The one exception is the heuchera flowers: clip off the bloom stems close to their base after flowering, or even before the blossoms open if you don't like how they look.

Fall and Winter: The 'Karl Foerster' feather reed grass plumes turn tan by early fall, and the dried flower stalks remain through the winter. The 'Coronation Gold' yarrow, 'Ruby Tuesday' Helen's flower, and spike blazing star might still be sending up a few near flowers in early fall, and some of them might keep some leaves at the base, but they're mostly stems and seed heads that remain through fall and into winter. 'Southern Comfort' heuchera generally holds its orangey foliage through the winter.

There's not much late-season maintenance to do here: just keep the flower stalks of the heuchera clipped off through the fall; then, enjoy your winter garden.

Digging Deeper

THIS LONG, NARROW BED is designed to look good from both sides, making it ideal for edging a path, sidewalk, or driveway. The 'Karl Foerster' feather reed grass (*Calamagrostis × acutiflora*) in the center adds height without creating a solid barrier, so the bed would also make a great screen planting around a ground-level deck or patio, giving it a sense of privacy from summer through winter without the expense of a permanent enclosure.

One good reason to keep dead flowers clipped off is to stop your perennials from producing seeds, which may then drop to the ground, sprout, and produce new plants (a process known as "self-sowing"). Finding a few self-sown seedlings can be fun, but when a perennial starts producing dozens or even hundreds of seedlings every year, that can be a big problem. There are two ways to prevent over-abundant self-sowing but still be able to enjoy seed heads in your winter garden. One is to apply a new 1- to 2-inch-thick layer of organic mulch over the soil in your garden every year as soon as you finish the spring cleanup. (The mulch will prevent many of the seeds that dropped through the winter from sprouting.) The other option is to look for perennials that are "sterile" (that don't produce seeds capable of sprouting), such as 'Karl Foerster' feather reed grass (*Calamagrostis × acutiflora*), 'Coronation Gold' yarrow (*Achillea*), 'Blue Fortune' hyssop (*Agastache*), and 'Walker's Low' catmint (*Nepeta*).

Want to add a touch of color to your winter garden? Dress up the seed heads of your perennials with a quick spritz of spray paint!

A Nonstop Garden

○ ◑ Full sun to partial shade

◆ ◇ Average to dry soil

When nice spring weather puts you in the mood to plant a new garden, it's tempting to head to the garden center and pick out whichever perennials look pretty at the moment. Impulse buying like this can be fun, and your new garden will be filled with flowers right away, but there's a good chance that it won't look very pretty for the rest of the year, once the early bloomers are done. To get the longest possible season of interest, look beyond instant color to choose perennials with flowers that bloom for months instead of weeks, as well as those perennials that have attractive leaves for interesting color and texture from spring to frost, or even all year round.

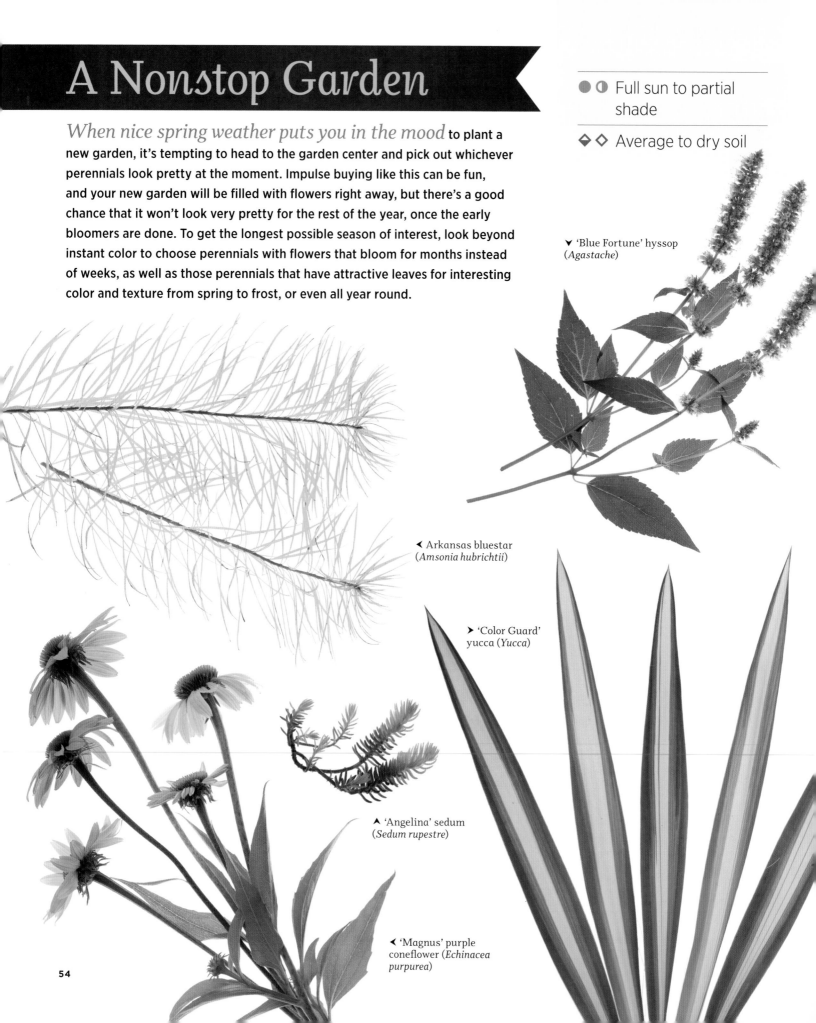

▼ 'Blue Fortune' hyssop (*Agastache*)

◄ Arkansas bluestar (*Amsonia hubrichtii*)

➤ 'Color Guard' yucca (*Yucca*)

▲ 'Angelina' sedum (*Sedum rupestre*)

◄ 'Magnus' purple coneflower (*Echinacea purpurea*)

54

The Garden Plan

Shopping List

❶ 'BLUE FORTUNE' HYSSOP
Agastache | 3 plants
Zones 5-9
Alternates: Another 4- to 5-foot-tall perennial with an extended bloom period, interesting seed heads, and/or colorful foliage, such as 'Bluebird' smooth aster (*Aster laevis*) [3 plants], Culver's root (*Veronicastrum virginicum*) [3 plants], or 'Prairie Sunset' false sunflower (*Heliopsis helianthoides*) [3 plants]

❷ 'COLOR GUARD' YUCCA
Yucca | 3 plants
Zones 5-9
Alternates: 'Golden Sword' yucca, or another spiky-looking, 2- to 4-foot-tall perennial with long-lasting seed heads or evergreen leaves, such as 'Cassian' or 'Hameln' fountain grass (*Pennisetum alopecuroides*) [3 plants] or blue oat grass (*Helictotrichon sempervirens*) [3 plants]

❸ ARKANSAS BLUESTAR
Amsonia hubrichtii | 1 plant
Zones 4-9
Alternates: Another mound-forming, 2- to 3-foot-tall perennial or shrub with colorful fall leaves, such as SUNSHINE BLUE bluebeard (*Caryopteris incana* 'Jason') [1 plant] or 'Brookside' geranium (*Geranium*) [1 plant]

❹ 'MAGNUS' PURPLE CONEFLOWER
Echinacea purpurea | 6 plants
Zones 3-8
Alternates: Another 2- to 4-foot-tall purple coneflower or other perennial with an extended flowering period, such as Gloriosa daisy (*Rudbeckia hirta*) [6 plants], orange coneflower (*Rudbeckia fulgida*) [6 plants], or red valerian (*Centranthus ruber*) [6 plants]

❺ 'ANGELINA' SEDUM
Sedum rupestre | 6 plants
Zones 3-8
Alternates: 'Fuldaglow' or 'Voodoo' sedum, or another 6- to 12-inch-tall perennial with colorful foliage, such as 'Aztec Gold' speedwell (*Veronica prostrata*) [6 plants] or 'Big Ears' lamb's ears (*Stachys byzantina*) [6 plants]

Planting Plan

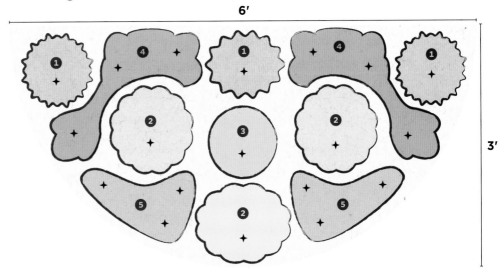

Season by Season

Spring: This garden celebrates the return of spring with the brilliant yellow leaves of 'Angelina' sedum, as well as the spiky, yellow-striped green foliage of 'Color Guard' yucca. Flowers join in by late spring: the clustered, pale blue stars of Arkansas bluestar and, in southern gardens, the large, pink daisy-form blooms of 'Magnus' purple coneflower.

A little attention in early to mid spring gets this garden off to a good start for the year. Cut down any remaining dead top growth, and trim out any winter-damaged parts on the yucca. Divide and replant the yucca, purple coneflower, and sedum if they are outgrowing their spaces. Then apply a fresh layer of organic mulch over the soil.

Summer: Bluestar finishes flowering in early summer, but the other perennials are just getting started. Purple coneflower usually peaks in early to midsummer in southern gardens and in mid to late summer elsewhere. 'Blue Fortune' hyssop starts opening its dense spikes of light purple-blue flowers in early summer and keeps blooming for several months. 'Color Guard' yucca clumps usually take a few years to reach flowering size, and then produce tall, thick stalks topped with large, creamy white bells in early to midsummer. 'Angelina' sedum also blooms in summer, but its yellow flowers aren't very noticeable against the yellow foliage.

A little regular attention keeps your multiseason garden going strong all through the summer. After the first year or two, cut the bluestar back by about half as soon as the flowers drop to encourage dense, bushy regrowth and prevent self-sowing. Cut finished yucca stalks off at the base, or, if there are more rosettes coming along, cut out that whole rosette at ground level to make room for the others, because it won't bloom again. Clip off dead purple coneflower blooms above a bud lower on the stem, or leave them in place to form dark, domed seed heads for fall and winter interest. Trim off the dead flower clusters of the 'Angelina' sedum just above the leaves, if desired, to tidy the plants. 'Blue Fortune' hyssop usually keeps flowering freely without attention, but a light trim (by about a quarter) in late summer can encourage fresh flowering later on.

Fall and Winter: 'Blue Fortune' hyssop typically keeps producing some flower spikes well into fall, especially if you gave it a light trim in late summer. Its spikes eventually dry in place and stick around through the winter. 'Magnus' purple coneflower, too, produces some fresh flowers in fall, and its dried seed heads remain attractive well into winter. Arkansas bluestar leaves typically turn bright yellow in mid fall, dry to tan-brown, and eventually drop in winter. The yucca and sedum leaves continue to look attractive through fall and all winter, too: the yucca typically takes on a pinkish blush, while 'Angelina' sedum may turn from bright yellow to orange-yellow in cold weather.

If the yucca, bluestar, or sedum are crowding out their companions, divide them in early fall. Otherwise, hold off on cutting back until spring so you can enjoy the colorful foliage and dried stems and seed heads through the winter.

Digging Deeper

WITH THE TALL PLANTS TOWARD THE BACK and shorter plants at front, this half-circle plan is ideal for a site against a vertical surface, such as a wall, fence, or hedge. Or flip the plan along its flat side, setting the two parts next to each other to create a circular bed, or leave 24 to 30 inches between the two parts to create a walkway through the planting or a short path leading to a bench or arbor.

Several features that make for great multiseason gardens — including many long-blooming flowers and those with interesting seed heads — attract the attention of wildlife as well as people. Butterflies love to feed on the tiny but densely clustered, nectar-rich flowers of many daisy-form perennial flowers, as well as those with spiky blooms. And when seeds form on those blossoms, you're likely to find a variety of songbirds picking them off the plants or up from the ground around them. Add a birdbath — perhaps with a few rocks added to provide small landing platforms for butterflies and insects — and your multiseason garden will do double duty as a wildlife-attracting planting.

Beat the Heat

◐ ◑ Full sun to partial shade

◇ ◇ Average to dry soil

Blazing sun and sandy soil is a tough combination for many plants to cope with, but with some careful choices, you can have a perennial garden that's loaded with beautiful blooms. A planting of heat-tolerant perennials also works well next to paved areas, such as along a driveway or in that tough-to-maintain strip of ground between a sidewalk and a street.

◄ 'Homestead Purple' verbena (*Verbena*)

◄ Hardy ice plant (*Delosperma cooperi*)

➤ 'Moonshine' yarrow (*Achillea*)

▼ 'Silver Brocade' beach wormwood (*Artemisia stelleriana*)

◄ Red valerian (*Centranthus ruber*)

The Garden Plan

Shopping List

❶ RED VALERIAN
Centranthus ruber | 1 plant
Zones 5–8
Alternates: Another 2- to 3-foot-tall perennial that can tolerate hot and dry conditions, such as hummingbird mint (*Agastache cana*) [1 plant], 'Grosso' or 'Provence' lavender (*Lavandula × intermedia*) [1 plant], sea holly (*Eryngium*) [1 plant], or yucca (*Yucca*) [1 plant]

❷ 'HOMESTEAD PURPLE' VERBENA
Verbena | 2 plants
Zones 6–9
Alternates: Another 4- to 12-inch-tall, purple-, blue-, or magenta-flowered perennial that can tolerate hot and dry conditions, such as winecups (*Callirhoe involucrata*) [2 plants] or 'Marcus' ornamental sage (*Salvia*) [6 plants]

❸ HARDY ICE PLANT
Delosperma cooperi | 6 plants
Zones 5–8
Alternates: Another 4- to 12-inch-tall perennial that can tolerate hot and dry conditions, such as 'Fuldaglow', 'Voodoo', or another creeping sedum (*Sedum*) [6 plants], or a green-leaved or variegated thyme (*Thymus*) [6 plants]

❹ 'MOONSHINE' YARROW
Achillea | 6 plants
Zones 3–8
Alternates: Another 12- to 18-inch-tall, yellow- to peach-flowered perennial that can tolerate hot and dry conditions, such as lavender cotton (*Santolina chamaecyparissus*) [6 plants] or 'Arizona Apricot' blanket flower (*Gaillardia × grandiflora*) [2 plants]

❺ 'SILVER BROCADE' BEACH WORMWOOD
Artemisia stelleriana | 2 plants
Zones 3–8
Alternates: Another 4- to 12-inch-tall, silver- or gray-leaved perennial that can tolerate hot and dry conditions, such as 'Cape Blanco' or 'Blue Carpet' sedum (*Sedum*) [6 plants] or 'Frosty Fire' dianthus (*Dianthus*) [6 plants]

Planting Plan

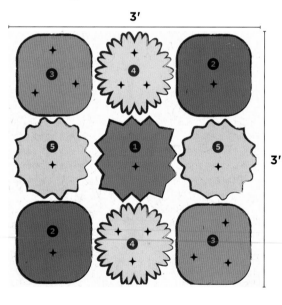

Season by Season

Spring: The growing season starts with lovely leaves: the light greens of red valerian and hardy ice plant, the bright green of 'Homestead Purple' verbena, and the grays and silvers of 'Moonshine' yarrow and 'Silver brocade' beach wormwood. Flowers join the show by late spring: rosy pink red valerian, vibrant purple 'Homestead Purple' verbena, and fuchsia-purple hardy ice plant.

Take care of cleanup chores in early to mid spring: trim off any remaining dead top growth, and divide any of the perennials that are outgrowing their space. Cut established plants of red valerian back to about 4 inches to get bushier summer growth. Finish up by applying a fresh layer of organic mulch to cover the soil.

Summer: Red valerian continues flowering through early summer, at least, and the verbena and hardy ice plant keep flowering through the summer. 'Moonshine' yarrow joins in with clustered, clear yellow blooms through the summer. 'Silver Brocade' beach wormwood flowers, too, but the blooms are tiny and greenish yellow, so they aren't very noticeable. Its lacy, silvery leaves add plenty of summer interest, though.

Clipping off the dead flowers or flower clusters every few days encourages your summer perennials to keep blooming freely through the summer months. Cut the beach wormwood back by one-third to one-half in early to midsummer to remove the upward-facing flowering shoot tips. This garden should need watering only during extended dry spells.

Fall and Winter: 'Homestead Purple' verbena and hardy ice plant usually keep flowering freely from early fall to frost, and red valerian and 'Moonshine' yarrow may produce a few flowers from early fall to frost. 'Silver Brocade' beach wormwood is silvery into winter. The hardy ice plant's leaves often blush with pink when cool weather returns, and it tends to be evergreen in mild-winter areas.

Divide the hardy ice plant, yarrow, or beach wormwood clumps in early fall if they are crowding their companions. Leave any cutting back or cleanup until spring.

Digging Deeper

A SIMPLE SQUARE GARDEN like this fits easily into any corner site. To edge a driveway or sidewalk, or to outline a pool or patio area, repeat the squares side to side as many times as needed, mixing in some of the suggested alternate plants to add variety. Or, repeat the squares with 2- to 3-foot-wide paths in between to create a pretty, easy-care patchwork planting to replace unneeded lawn space in a side or backyard.

If you're wondering whether a perennial can tolerate heat and drought, look to the leaves. Silvery or gray leaves, such as those of wormwoods (*Artemisia*), lavenders (*Lavandula*), and some thymes (*Thymus*) and sages (*Salvia*), are often a sign that a plant can deal well with hot sun and dry soil. Narrow leaves, such as those of dianthus (*Dianthus*) or ornamental grasses, and succulent leaves, such as those of sedums (*Sedum*), are also good clues to drought tolerance.

You'll often see gravel used as a mulch for gardens in hot, dry climates. Like all mulches, it has advantages as well as disadvantages. Gravel lasts for many years, unlike organic mulches, which can disappear in just a few weeks or months in sun-baked sites. Also, gravel won't blow away in strong winds. On the other hand, light-colored rocks can reflect a lot of sunlight, possibly scorching even sun-toughened leaves. Plus, they make it very difficult to maintain perennials that need to be dug up and divided every few years. If you're not sure which mulch you want to use, consider trying a couple of different kinds in small areas for a season or two and see which work best in your particular conditions.

Wet and Wild

Soggy spots in your yard can be a real maintenance headache. Weeds or lawn grass may grow so thickly there that they're tough to mow, or they may be so wet that they're nothing but puddles or bare, muddy areas. Instead of fighting with these troublesome sites, turn them into lush, colorful gardens filled with perennials that appreciate a steady supply of moisture.

◖◗ Full sun to partial shade

◆ Moist soil

◀ 'Lady Baltimore' hardy hibiscus (*Hibiscus moscheutos*)

◀ Golden creeping Jenny (*Lysimachia nummularia* 'Aurea')

▾ Dwarf goat's beard (*Aruncus aethusifolius*)

▾ 'Britt-Marie Crawford' ligularia (*Ligularia dentata*)

➤ Bowles' golden sedge (*Carex elata* 'Aurea')

The Garden Plan

Shopping List

❶ 'LADY BALTIMORE' HARDY HIBISCUS

Hibiscus moscheutos | **3 plants**
Zones 5–9
Alternates: Another pink-flowered hardy hibiscus or other 4- to 5-foot-tall perennial that can tolerate moist to wet soil, such as 'Little Joe' Joe-Pye weed (*Eupatorium dubium*) [3 plants] or swamp milkweed (*Asclepias incarnata*) [3 plants]

❷ 'BRITT-MARIE CRAWFORD' LIGULARIA

Ligularia dentata | **1 plant**
Zones 4–8
Alternates: 'Othello' ligularia, or another 3- to 4-foot-tall perennial that can tolerate moist to wet soil, such as a feather-leaved Rodger's flower (*Rodgersia*) [1 plant] or a Japanese or Siberian iris (*Iris ensata* or *I. sibirica*) [1 plant]

❸ BOWLES' GOLDEN SEDGE

Carex elata 'Aurea' | **2 plants**
Zones 5–8
Alternates: Another 18- to 36-inch-tall perennial that can tolerate moist to wet soil, such as a spiderwort (*Tradescantia*) [2 plants] or blue lobelia (*Lobelia siphilitica*) [2 plants]

❹ DWARF GOAT'S BEARD

Aruncus aethusifolius | **6 plants**
Zones 4–8
Alternates: Another 6- to 18-inch-tall perennial that can tolerate moist to wet soil, such as marsh marigold (*Caltha palustris*) [2 plants] or a pink or white Japanese primrose (*Primula japonica*) [2 plants]

❺ GOLDEN CREEPING JENNY

Lysimachia nummularia 'Aurea' | **3 plants**
Zones 3–8
Alternates: Another 3- to 12-inch-tall perennial that can tolerate moist to wet soil, such as dwarf golden sweet flag (*Acorus gramineus* 'Minimus Aureus') [5 plants] or dwarf Chinese astilbe (*Astilbe chinensis* var. *pumila*) [3 plants]

Planting Plan

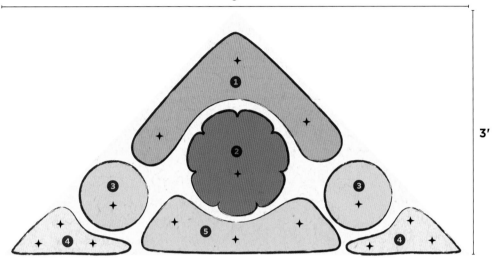

Season by Season

Spring: Wet soil tends to be slow to warm up in spring, so new sprouts may be a little slow to appear, but soon enough, you'll be enjoying the near-black shoots of 'Britt-Marie Crawford' ligularia contrasting with the bright yellow new leaves of Bowles' golden sedge and golden creeping Jenny. Dwarf goat's beard adds another element of color and texture with its ferny, bright green leaves and plumy white, late-spring flowers.

Early to mid spring is a good time to get this garden ready for the growing season. Cut down any remaining top growth, and divide any of the plants that were starting to crowd their companions by last fall.

Summer: 'Lady Baltimore' hardy hibiscus may not even sprout until early summer, but once it's up, it grows quickly and may be producing its large, red-centered pink flowers as early as midsummer, continuing through late summer. The ligularia also flowers in mid to late summer, with clusters of bright orange-yellow daisies. Dwarf goat's beard usually blooms into early summer, and then its plumes turn golden brown as the seeds form through the summer. Bowles' golden sedge and golden creeping Jenny flower too, but you probably won't even notice their blooms (brown on the sedge and yellow on the golden creeping Jenny).

Apply an organic mulch to cover any soil that's still visible in early summer. If you wish to keep the hibiscus shorter than its usual 4 to 5 feet, cut it back to half its height in midsummer. Once it starts blooming, clip off the finished flowers to tidy the plants and encourage more flowers to form. Clip off the seed heads on the dwarf goat's beard, too, if you don't find them attractive.

Fall and Winter: 'Lady Baltimore' hardy hibiscus often continues flowering until frost. The deep purple-black leaves of 'Britt-Marie Crawford' ligularia remain attractive through much of the fall, as do the yellow leaves of the sedge and the golden creeping Jenny, and the fluffy seed heads of the ligularia are interesting, too. Dwarf goat's beard starts the fall with still-green leaves and then turns rich shades of red and orange as the weather cools.

Cut down the dead tops of the plants in mid to late fall, or leave them in place until spring cleanup. If you do cut the hibiscus down in fall, trim it back to about 6 inches above the ground; the stubs will mark the location of the clumps while you're waiting for them to appear in spring.

Digging Deeper

FIT THIS TRIANGULAR PLAN into a soggy corner of your yard, or use the plan and its mirror image to flank the entrance to a path. (Adding a strip of gravel a couple of inches thick and 2 to 4 feet wide through a wet area gives you mud-free access to other parts of your yard and looks great, too.)

Spring is a fine time to start most gardens, but when you're working with a soggy spot, the soil may simply be too wet to dig early in the season. Waiting until sometime during the summer, when the site has had a chance to warm up and dry out a bit, often makes the digging and planting process much easier. If you end up planting during a dry spell, remember to water your new garden once or twice a week until regular rains return.

Keep in mind that the perennials in this garden need evenly moist soil to look their best through the whole growing season. If the site dries out in summer, they'll often wilt dramatically, bloom poorly, develop crispy brown leaf edges, and generally look awful. Weekly watering is a reasonable option if you're just trying to keep the garden alive through an unusually long dry spell. If you know that the site usually dries out at some point during every summer, though, consider the Amazing Rain Garden on opposite page instead, because those plants can adapt to both dry and wet conditions.

Amazing Rain Garden

◐ ◑ Full sun to partial shade

◆ ◆ Average to moist soil

When soil is covered up by buildings, paving, and other hard surfaces, it can't absorb rainfall as it normally would. That water has to go somewhere, though, and often, that means it flows into sewer systems that are already overtaxed by heavy rainfall. Installing a rain barrel to collect water from your roof is one great way to reduce stormwater runoff and save on your watering bills too. Planting a "rain garden" is another great way to do your part for the environment, and you'll end up with a gorgeous perennial planting to enjoy as well.

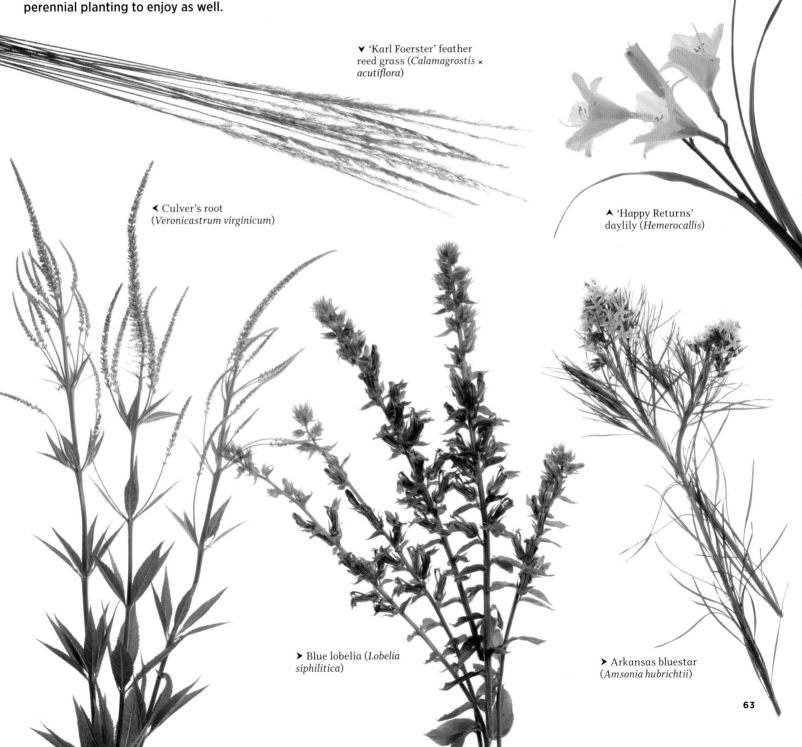

▼ 'Karl Foerster' feather reed grass (*Calamagrostis* × *acutiflora*)

◄ Culver's root (*Veronicastrum virginicum*)

▲ 'Happy Returns' daylily (*Hemerocallis*)

➤ Blue lobelia (*Lobelia siphilitica*)

➤ Arkansas bluestar (*Amsonia hubrichtii*)

The Garden Plan

Shopping List

❶ CULVER'S ROOT
Veronicastrum virginicum | **5 plants**
Zones 3–8
Alternates: Another 4- to 6-foot-tall perennial
that can tolerate occasional flooding, such
as swamp milkweed (*Asclepias incarnata*)
[3 plants] or New York ironweed (*Vernonia
noveboracensis*) [3 plants]

**❷ 'KARL FOERSTER' FEATHER
REED GRASS**
Calamagrostis × acutiflora | **4 plants**
Zones 4–8
Alternates: Another 3- to 5-foot-tall perennial
that can tolerate occasional flooding, such
as 'Rotstrahlbusch' switch grass (*Panicum
virgatum*) [4 plants] or 'Little Joe' Joe-Pye
weed (*Eupatorium dubium*) [4 plants]

❸ ARKANSAS BLUESTAR
Amsonia hubrichtii | **1 plant**
Zones 4–9
Alternates: Another 2- to 4-foot-tall perennial
that can tolerate occasional flooding, such
as a Siberian iris (*Iris sibirica*) [1 plant] or a
turtlehead (*Chelone*) [1 plant]

❹ BLUE LOBELIA
Lobelia siphilitica | **10 plants**
Zones 3–8
Alternates: Another 2- to 3-foot-tall perennial
that can tolerate occasional flooding, such as
Mardi Gras Helen's flower (*Helenium* 'Helbro')
[8 plants] or orange coneflower (*Rudbeckia
fulgida*) [8 plants]

❺ 'HAPPY RETURNS' DAYLILY
Hemerocallis | **4 plants**
Zones 3–9
Alternates: Another 1- to 2-foot-tall perennial
that can tolerate occasional flooding, such as
'Miss Manners' obedient plant (*Physostegia
virginiana*) [4 plants] or a dwarf bee balm
(*Monarda*) [4 plants]

Planting Plan

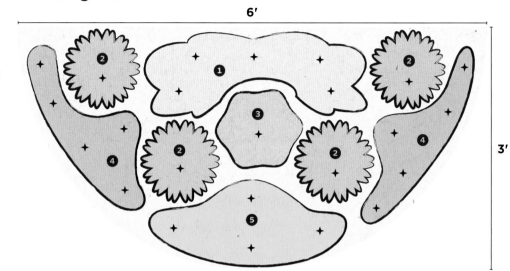

6'

3'

Season by Season

Spring: The perennials in this plan tend to jump into growth in early to mid spring. The tightly whorled, green shoots of Culver's root may be tinged with red, making an interesting contrast to the bright green blades of the grass and the daylily, the feathery foliage of the Arkansas bluestar, and the dense rosettes of blue lobelia. By late spring, the upright stems of the Arkansas bluestar are topped with clusters of pale blue, starry blooms.

Tackle cleanup chores here as soon as possible in spring. Cut down the remaining dead stems and leaves, and divide any of the perennials that were outgrowing their space by last fall. Then, spread a fresh layer of organic mulch over the soil.

Summer: Arkansas bluestar usually finishes flowering by early summer, about the time that 'Happy Returns' daylily starts its early to midsummer bloom period, with trumpet-shaped yellow blossoms. 'Karl Foerster' feather reed grass sends up its pinkish flower plumes in early summer, too; they remain for the rest of the summer, gradually turning tan. Culver's root joins in with spiky white blooms in mid to late summer, and the blue spikes of blue lobelia come along in late summer.

As soon as the flowers fade on the Arkansas bluestar, trim established clumps back by about half to prevent self-sowing and encourage bushier new growth. On the blue lobelia, cut off the finished flower spikes just above the leafy part of the stem. And on the daylily, clip off the bloom stalks at the base when the flowers are finished. Water the garden during extended dry spells.

Fall and Winter: Fresh flowers can keep coming in fall from the blue lobelia and the 'Happy Returns' daylily. Arkansas bluestar contributes cheery color, too, as the leaves turn bright shades of yellow by mid fall. The dried heads of Culver's root and 'Karl Foerster' feather reed grass remain attractive through the autumn, and well into winter, too.

There's very little maintenance to do now: wait until late fall to cut down the dead stems, or leave them in place for winter interest.

Digging Deeper

IT'S SMART TO PLANT YOUR RAIN GARDEN near a downspout from a roof gutter, but be sure to keep it at least 10 feet away from your home, because you don't want to encourage water to collect right near the foundation. Also, avoid putting it in a site that is normally slow to dry out after a storm. The point of a rain garden is to hold excess water for a very short period, not long enough to create a breeding ground for mosquitoes. So choose a well-drained site, and dig out the area to a depth of 4 to 8 inches to create a broad, shallow catch basin. If you have the room, you could easily flip this plan along the straight site to create a larger, circular bed.

The perennials in a rain garden need to be tough enough to tolerate occasional flooding as well as drier spells between rains. They'll still need weekly watering during their first growing season if rain is lacking, but after that, they should be fine without supplemental irrigation.

When you mulch your rain garden — which will help to keep weeds down and hold some moisture in the soil during dry weather — avoid using very lightweight materials, such as small wood chips or cocoa hulls. These light mulches tend to float and can easily end up out of place, or even out of the garden entirely, during heavy storms. Shredded bark mulch tends to create a more solid mat that's less likely to shift around in wet conditions.

Coping with Slopes

Slopes offer both interesting challenges and exciting opportunities when it comes to gardening. They're typically drier than nearby flat areas, because rainwater tends to run off before it has a chance to soak into the soil, especially on steep slopes. When water runs quickly down a slope, it's also likely to pick up loose soil as it flows, carving channels into the ground and dumping eroded topsoil onto the lawn or paved area at the bottom. But on the plus side, slopes give you a chance to experiment with beautiful perennials that thrive in dry, sunny sites. Slopes also display plants exceptionally well, allowing stems and leaves to trail gracefully and showing off nodding or short-stemmed blooms beautifully.

◗◑ Full sun to partial shade

◆◇ Average to dry soil

▲ 'Angelina' sedum (*Sedum rupestre*)

◀ 'Walker's Low' catmint (*Nepeta*)

▶ Mexican feather grass (*Stipa tenuissima*)

◀ 'Oranges and Lemons' blanket flower (*Gaillardia* × *grandiflora*)

◀ 'Big Ears' lamb's ears (*Stachys byzantina*)

Shopping List

❶ MEXICAN FEATHER GRASS
Stipa tenuissima | 4 plants
Zones 6–9
Alternates: Another 1- to 2-foot-tall
ornamental grass that can tolerate dry soil, such
as prairie dropseed (*Sporobolus heterolepis*)
[4 plants] or 'Piglet' fountain grass (*Pennisetum
alopecuroides*) [4 plants]

❷ 'ORANGES AND LEMONS'
BLANKET FLOWER
Gaillardia × grandiflora | 2 plants
Zones 5–9
Alternates: Another blanket flower or other
1- to 2-foot-tall, orange- or yellow-flowered,
mounded or spreading perennial that can
tolerate dry soil, such as 'Sienna Sunset'
or another coreopsis (*Coreopsis*) [2 plants]
or 'Tuscan Sun' false sunflower (*Heliopsis
helianthoides*) [2 plants]

❸ 'BIG EARS' LAMB'S EARS
Stachys byzantina | 2 plants
Zones 4–8
Alternates: Another 1- to 2-foot-tall, silver-
or blue-leaved, mounded or spreading
perennial that can tolerate dry soil, such as
'Firewitch' dianthus (*Dianthus*) [2 plants] or
October daphne (*Sedum sieboldii*) [2 plants]

❹ 'WALKER'S LOW' CATMINT
Nepeta | 2 plants
Zones 4–8
Alternates: Another 1- to 2-foot-tall catmint
or other mounded or spreading, blue-, purple-,
or pink-flowered perennial that can tolerate dry
soil, such as a lavender (*Lavandula*) [2 plants]
or an ornamental oregano (*Origanum*) [2 plants]

❺ 'ANGELINA' SEDUM
Sedum rupestre | 2 plants
Zones 3–8
Alternates: Another creeping sedum or
other 4- to 12-inch-tall, mounded or spreading
perennial that can tolerate dry soil, such as
moss phlox (*Phlox subulata*) [2 plants] or 'Snow
Flurry' heath aster (*Aster ericoides*) [2 plants]

Planting Plan

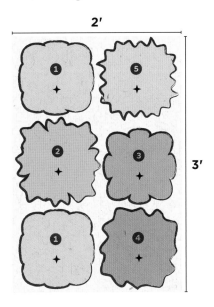
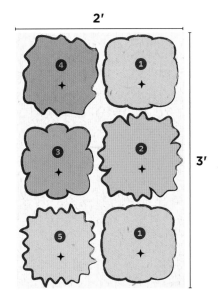

Season by Season

Spring: There's lots of early color and texture in this garden, starting with the foliage of 'Angelina' sedum. Mexican feather grass joins in early, too, quickly forming fountain-shaped clumps of hairlike, bright green leaves and bearing wispy greenish flowers by late spring. The hairy foliage of 'Oranges and Lemons' blanket flower isn't especially showy now, but the fuzzy, bright silver leaves of 'Big Ears' lamb's ears are quite attractive, as are the dense, gray-green mounds of 'Walker's Low' catmint. The catmint is also in bloom by late spring, with loose spikes of purple-blue flowers over the small, aromatic leaves.

In early to mid spring, cut the Mexican feather grass back to about 4 inches above the ground, and cut the blanket flower, lamb's ears, and catmint back to 2 to 3 inches above the ground. The sedum generally doesn't need pruning, unless you want to trim off any winter-damaged bits. This is also a fine time to divide any of the perennials that were starting to outgrow their space last year. Finish up by spreading a fresh layer of organic mulch around the plants.

Summer: Through the summer, the greenish flowers of Mexican feather grass gradually ripen to golden brown and then tan. 'Oranges and Lemons' blanket flower begins blooming in early to midsummer and continues for months, with soft orange-and-yellow, daisy-form flowers. 'Big Ears' lamb's ears occasionally sends up fuzzy stalks with small pinkish flowers, but they're not very showy; the gray-green leaves are its main summer feature. 'Walker's Low' catmint is in peak bloom in early summer, with a few new flowers possible in midsummer. 'Angelina' sedum produces yellow flowers in summer, but they're hardly noticeable against the bright yellow foliage.

Clip off the dead flowers of the blanket flowers individually through the summer or shear the whole clump back to about 6 inches in late summer. If the lamb's ears produce any flowering stems, cut them off at the base. In humid summers, the lamb's ears leaves may look tattered or start to rot; if that happens, shear the whole plant back to about 2 inches to remove all the leaves so fresh foliage can emerge. Cut back the catmint clumps by one-half to two-thirds in midsummer to get bushy new growth and promote rebloom later in the season. Clip off the dead flowers of the sedum to tidy the plants and prevent self-sowing, if desired.

Fall and Winter: Mexican feather grass's foliage continues to look good through fall, gradually turning blonde-tan as it dries and staying in place for the winter. 'Oranges and Lemons' blanket flower keeps flowering through fall, and even into early winter in mild areas. 'Walker's Low' catmint, too, often reblooms through fall, and its foliage remains into early winter, or even longer. The leaves of 'Big Ears' lamb's ears stick around for most or all of the winter. 'Angelina' sedum holds its leaves all through the winter, typically taking on a rich orangey color.

It's best to leave the plant tops in place for the winter to protect the soil from erosion from winter rains, so there are no late-season tasks to take care of.

Digging Deeper

THIS PAIR OF MINI-BORDERS is designed to edge a short flight of steps. To flank a higher set of steps, repeat each border end to end as many times as needed. To extend the planting across a slope rather than up it, set the two parts side by side and repeat them as needed to cover the area.

A perennial garden is a pretty solution for a relatively short, gentle slope, and it's certainly more interesting than straggly, hard-to-mow lawn grass. If there's more than about 3 feet from the bottom to the top of the slope, though, consider installing a low wall (6 to 12 inches tall) across the site. Breaking up one steep slope into two shorter, gentler slopes slows down water runoff and prevents erosion, providing better growing conditions for the perennials. A well-built wall also serves as an access path, giving you a place to walk or sit when you're planting, weeding, or doing other maintenance.

When you're choosing plants for sloping sites, stick with those that are about 1 foot tall or shorter, because taller stems are more likely to sprawl and look messy. Perennials that form low, spreading mounds or ground-hugging carpets do the best job in preventing soil erosion, especially once they're settled in and mingling to form a solid carpet, with no mulch or bare soil visible.

A Great Foundation

The space right around your home's foundation is a great place to experiment with a planting of perennials. Use them to replace the boring shrubs that are already there, or — if there's space — plant the flowers in front of the shrubs. This collection of perennials supplies year-round interest from a variety of features, including showy flowers, attractive leaves, fall color, and even intriguing seed heads and evergreen foliage for winter.

◐ ◑ Full sun to partial shade

◆ ◇ Average to dry soil

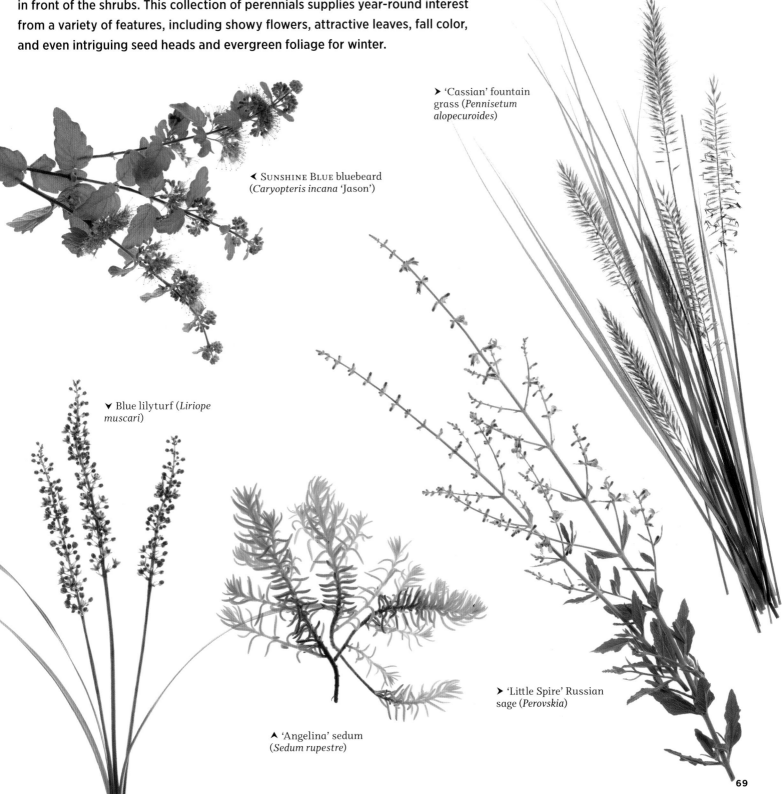

‹ SUNSHINE BLUE bluebeard (*Caryopteris incana* 'Jason')

› 'Cassian' fountain grass (*Pennisetum alopecuroides*)

⌄ Blue lilyturf (*Liriope muscari*)

⌃ 'Angelina' sedum (*Sedum rupestre*)

› 'Little Spire' Russian sage (*Perovskia*)

The Garden Plan

Shopping List

1 'LITTLE SPIRE' RUSSIAN SAGE
Perovskia | 2 plants
Zones 5–9
Alternates: Another 2- to 4-foot-tall perennial with showy blooms and/or attractive foliage, such as 'Six Hills Giant' catmint (*Nepeta*) [2 plants] or 'Blue Fortune' hyssop (*Agastache*) [2 plants]

2 Sunshine Blue BLUEBEARD
Caryopteris incana 'Jason' | 1 plant
Zones 5–9
Alternates: Another 3- to 4-foot-tall perennial with showy blooms and attractive foliage, such as 'Worcester Gold' blue mist shrub (*C. × clandonensis*) [1 plant] or 'Carolina Moonlight' or other false indigo (*Baptisia*) [1 plant]

3 'CASSIAN' FOUNTAIN GRASS
Pennisetum alopecuroides | 3 plants
Zones 5–9
Alternates: 'Hameln' fountain grass or another 2- to 3-foot-tall perennial with showy blooms and/or attractive foliage, such as Arkansas bluestar (*Amsonia hubrichtii*) [3 plants] or 'Magnus' purple coneflower (*Echinacea purpurea*) [5 plants]

4 'ANGELINA' SEDUM
Sedum rupestre | 7 plants
Zones 3–8
Alternates: Another creeping or upright sedum or other 4- to 9-inch-tall perennial with showy blooms and attractive foliage, such as 'Aztec Gold' speedwell (*Veronica prostrata*) [7 plants] or 'Firewitch' dianthus (*Dianthus*) [7 plants]

5 BLUE LILYTURF
Liriope muscari | 6 plants
Zones 5–9
Alternates: Another 6- to 12-inch-tall perennial with showy blooms and/or attractive foliage, such as perennial candytuft (*Iberis sempervirens*) [6 plants] or 'Caramel', 'Obsidian', or other heuchera (*Heuchera*) [6 plants]

Planting Plan

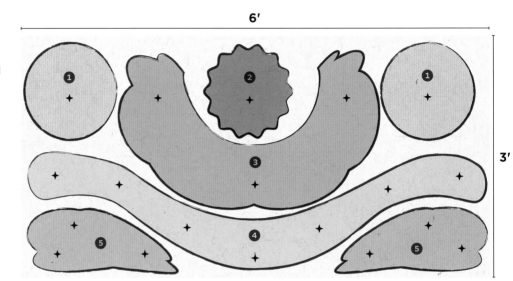

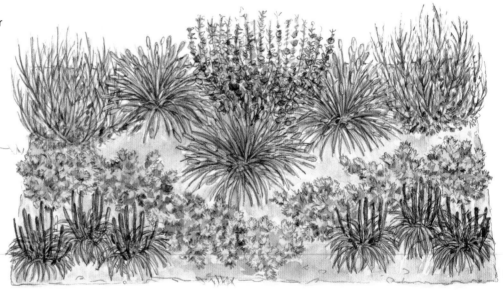

Season by Season

Spring: Early color in this garden comes mostly from foliage: the lacy, aromatic, gray-green leaves of 'Little Spire' Russian sage, the bright yellow shoots of Sunshine Blue bluebeard and 'Angelina' sedum, and the strappy, deep green leaves of blue lilyturf. In mild climates you might also be enjoying the airy, branching spikes of small, purple-blue blooms of the Russian sage in late spring.

A simple spring cleanup will get this garden into good shape for the growing season. In early to mid spring, cut any remaining dead growth on the fountain grass, cut the lilyturf leaves back to about 2 inches above the ground, and trim out any winter-damaged shoots on the sedum. This is also a good time to divide the fountain grass, sedum, and lilyturf, if needed. Once you see new growth starting, cut the Russian sage back to about 6 inches, and trim the bluebeard back by about half its height, or even closer to the ground if new growth is only at the base. Finish up by spreading a fresh layer of organic mulch over the soil.

Summer: Foliage continues to be a key feature of this foundation border in summer, but there are plenty of flowers, too. 'Angelina' sedum produces clusters of yellow flowers, which are pretty, though they're not very noticeable against the yellow leaves. In southern gardens the 'Little Spire' Russian sage is in full glory in early to midsummer; in northern gardens, the peak is usually mid to late summer. Late summer brings the purple-blue spikes of blue lilyturf, the brushy greenish tan spikes of 'Cassian' fountain grass, and the beginning of the clustered, purplish blue blooms on the Sunshine Blue bluebeard.

Summer care is minimal: just snip off the dead flowers on the sedum, cut the Russian sage back by about half if it gets floppy in midsummer, and water the garden during extended dry spells.

Fall and Winter: Autumn brings loads of color, with the bright yellow leaves of the Sunshine Blue bluebeard and 'Angelina' sedum and the purple-blue flowers of the 'Little Spire' Russian sage, bluebeard, and blue lilyturf. The 'Cassian' fountain grass spikes gradually turn tan and last well into winter. The whitish stems of the Russian sage, too, stick around after frost, along with the evergreen leaves of the blue lilyturf, which may also produce some near-black berries in fall. 'Angelina' sedum is especially striking in winter, when its bright yellow foliage often takes on rich orange tones.

Other than dividing the sedum in early fall, if it's outgrowing its spot, leave the garden cleanup until spring so you can enjoy the interesting leaves and stems for winter.

Digging Deeper

A RECTANGULAR BORDER like this one fits neatly into the narrow strip of ground along the front of a house. Use it as is, or repeat the plan end to end if you have a longer space to fill. It's a good idea to leave a bit of space behind the border — an unplanted strip about 18 inches wide — so you can get to the wall or shrubs behind the garden for maintenance.

It's nice to see loads of flowers early in the spring, but for the most part, perennials that are in peak bloom in spring can look tired by midsummer and add little to the garden for the rest of the year. To bring more spring color to this foundation planting while keeping the later-flowering perennials, tuck in loads of early blooming bulbs, such as snowdrops (*Galanthus*), crocuses (*Crocus*), daffodils (*Narcissus*), and hyacinths (*Hyacinthus*). These early risers add plenty of cheery color while their bedmates are just getting started; then, they die back to the ground for the rest of the season as the perennials fill out to play their part.

If you're new to gardening, you may be amazed to find that leaves come in all kinds of colors besides green, including yellows, reds, blues, grays, silvers, and even near blacks. Anything-but-green foliage is invaluable for adding season-long color to borders while the flowers come and go, a trick that's especially important for gardens in high-visibility areas, such as by a door or along a commonly used path.

On the Edge

A simple edging garden turns an ordinary path into a delightful journey. Try a pretty perennial planting along the walkway to your front door to welcome visitors, next to your driveway to cheer your arrival home in the evening, or along a sidewalk to delight passersby. Lining paved surfaces with planting strips rather than turf grass serves a practical purpose, too: you eliminate the tedious trimming that's necessary to keep lawn-lined edges looking tidy.

● Full sun

◆ Average soil

⌄ 'Bath's Pink' dianthus (*Dianthus*)

◄ Rozanne geranium (*Geranium* 'Gerwat')

◄ 'Caradonna' ornamental sage (*Salvia*)

⌄ 'Vera Jameson' sedum (*Sedum*)

⌃ 'Moonbeam' coreopsis (*Coreopsis*)

The Garden Plan

Shopping List

❶ Rozanne GERANIUM
Geranium 'Gerwat' | **3 plants**
Zones 5-8
Alternates: Another 6- to 18-inch-tall perennial with blue or purple-blue flowers, such as 'Sentimental Blue' balloon flower (*Platycodon grandiflorus*) [3 plants] or 'Blue Clips' bellflower (*Campanula carpatica*) [3 plants]

❷ 'BATH'S PINK' DIANTHUS
Dianthus | **2 plants**
Zones 3-8
Alternates: 'Firewitch' or 'Frosty Fire' dianthus or another 6- to 18-inch-tall perennial with spiky gray-blue or green leaves, such as a thrift (*Armeria*) [6 plants] or a blue fescue (*Festuca*) [6 plants]

❸ 'MOONBEAM' COREOPSIS
Coreopsis | **3 plants**
Zones 6-9
Alternates: 'Creme Brulee' or another yellow coreopsis, or another 1- to 2-foot-tall perennial with yellow flowers or leaves, such as lady's mantle (*Alchemilla mollis*) [3 plants] or golden oregano (*Origanum vulgare* 'Aureum') [3 plants]

❹ 'CARADONNA' ORNAMENTAL SAGE
Salvia | **3 plants**
Zones 4-8
Alternates: 'May Night' ornamental sage, or another 1- to 2-foot-tall perennial with blue or purple flowers and/or aromatic leaves, such as a culinary sage (*S. officinalis*) [3 plants] or a lavender (*Lavandula*) [3 plants]

❺ 'VERA JAMESON' SEDUM
Sedum | **3 plants**
Zones 4-8
Alternates: 'Lynda Windsor' sedum or other dark-leaved sedum, or another 1- to 2-foot-tall perennial with dark leaves, such as Chocolate Chip ajuga (*Ajuga reptans* 'Valfredda') [9 plants] or 'Obsidian' heuchera (*Heuchera*) [3 plants]

Planting Plan

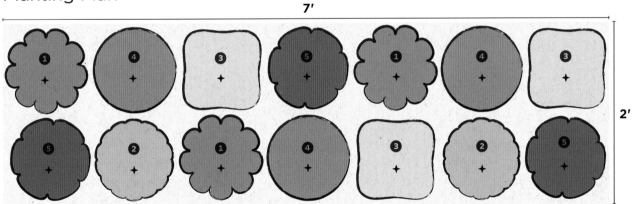

Season by Season

Spring: This border jumps into the growing season with new leafy growth: slender, blue-gray leaves on the 'Bath's Pink' dianthus, tight mounds of deep green leaves on the 'Caradonna' ornamental sage, and rosettes of thick, purple-tinged, blue-green leaves on the 'Vera Jameson' sedum. Light green ROZANNE geranium and bright green 'Moonbeam' coreopsis leaves usually come up a bit later, in mid or even late spring. There are also flowers by late spring: fragrant pink blooms on the dianthus and rich purple-blue spikes on the ornamental sage.

In early to mid spring, cut down any remaining dead stems and clip any winter-damaged leaves off the dianthus. This is also a good time to divide any of the perennials that were starting to outgrow their space last year. Spread a fresh layer of organic mulch over the soil, and your job is done for the spring.

Summer: 'Bath's Pink' dianthus is generally smothered in blooms through early summer, and 'Caradonna' ornamental sage and light yellow 'Moonbeam' coreopsis are at their best in early to midsummer; all of these may produce a few new blooms later in the summer, too. ROZANNE geranium joins in with bowl-shaped, purple-blue blooms through the summer. The leaves of 'Vera Jameson' sedum may gradually darken to deep purple, and the stems are topped with clusters of rosy pink flowers in mid and late summer.

Snip off the dead flowers of the dianthus, coreopsis, and ornamental sage individually, or shear them all off at once when most or all of the blooms are done. If the geranium looks straggly or stops flowering, cut off all the trailing stems close to the center of the plant, where new growth will quickly appear if it isn't already there. Water the garden during extended summer dry spells.

Fall and Winter: ROZANNE geranium, 'Bath's Pink' dianthus, 'Moonbeam' coreopsis, and 'Caradonna' ornamental sage may continue to produce new flowers from early fall to heavy frost. Through this period, the clustered flowers of 'Vera Jameson' sedum gradually age to deep red, gradually drying in place and holding their form through much or all of the winter. Other late-season features of this edging garden include the orange to red fall leaf color of the ROZANNE geranium, and the "ever-blue" carpets of 'Bath's Pink' dianthus leaves.

Trim off the dead stems of the geranium in mid to late fall, if desired, or leave them in place with the other perennials and wait until spring to tidy up the garden.

Digging Deeper

PLANTING A PERENNIAL EDGING along one side of a path is fine, but why not go all out and repeat it on the other side too? It's simple enough to line both sides of any length of path by repeating the plan as many times as needed. This edging strip would also work well around a deck or patio, or as a simple foundation planting around your house, garage, or garden shed.

Perennials are a great choice for plantings right next to sidewalks, driveways, and other paved surfaces in cold-winter areas. Unlike shrubbery, perennials die back to the ground each year, so they won't be damaged if you need to pile snow, slush, or ice on them when you're shoveling, snowblowing, or plowing.

Plantings that line pathways or sitting areas are a fun place to experiment with unusual flower forms — frilly doubles, amazing multicolors, extra-large blossoms, and so on — because you can easily admire them up close. Fragrant flowers and foliage work well in settings like this for the same reason, so don't hesitate to tuck in scented blossoms and aromatic herbs to give your sense of smell a treat, too.

It's nice to have plants spill over the edge of a path a little bit, but you don't want visitors to trip through a tangle of leaves to get where they're going. Stick with relatively low-growing perennials — maybe 18 to 24 inches maximum — and you won't have to bother with staking or pruning to keep them from sprawling into the walkway. It also helps to make sure the path itself is wide enough for easy access. A path that's 24 to 30 inches wide is fine for lesser-traveled trails through your yard, but for high-traffic paths, such as a front walkway, 4 feet is a better width.

A Salt Solution

You generally can't see salt in your soil, and you might not notice it on leaves, but it can drastically affect how plants grow, causing problems such as browned leaf edges, damaged roots, and stunted growth. Salt accumulation can be a real problem along roadsides, driveways, sidewalks, and other paved surfaces that are treated with deicing salt in winter, as well as in coastal areas that are subject to salt spray from the ocean. If you're having bad luck with gardens in sites like these, or if you're planting a garden there for the first time, choosing perennials that can naturally tolerate higher-than-normal salt levels can greatly improve your odds of getting great results.

◄ 'Silver Brocade' beach wormwood (*Artemisia stelleriana*)

➤ 'Little Grapette' daylily (*Hemerocallis*)

➤ 'Creme Brulee' coreopsis (*Coreopsis*)

▼ Cushion spurge (*Euphorbia polychroma*)

▲ 'Autumn Fire' sedum (*Sedum*)

75

The Garden Plan

Shopping List

❶ 'LITTLE GRAPETTE' DAYLILY
Hemerocallis | **3 plants**
Zones 3–9
Alternates: Another 12- to 18-inch-tall, purple-, blue-, or pink-flowered, salt-tolerant perennial, such as 'Blue Hobbit' sea holly (*Eryngium*) [9 plants] or 'Goodness Grows' or 'Hocus Pocus' speedwell (*Veronica*) [3 plants]

❷ 'CREME BRULEE' COREOPSIS
Coreopsis | **3 plants**
Zones 4–9
Alternates: 'Moonbeam', 'Moonlight', or other coreopsis or another 12- to 18-inch-tall, yellow-flowered, salt-tolerant perennial, such as 'Mesa Yellow' blanket flower (*Gaillardia* × *grandiflora*) [3 plants] or a lavender cotton (*Santolina*) [3 plants]

❸ 'SILVER BROCADE' BEACH WORMWOOD
Artemisia stelleriana | **2 plants**
Zones 3–8
Alternates: Another 6- to 18-inch-tall, silver-leaved or white-flowered, salt-tolerant perennial, such as silvermound (*Artemisia schmidtiana*) [2 plants] or perennial candytuft (*Iberis sempervirens*) [6 plants]

❹ 'AUTUMN FIRE' SEDUM
Sedum | **2 plants**
Zones 3–9
Alternates: 'Vera Jameson' sedum or another 6- to 24-inch-tall, salt-tolerant perennial, such as 'Obsidian' heuchera (*Heuchera*) [6 plants] or red-leaved thrift (*Armeria maritima* 'Rubrifolia') [6 plants]

❺ CUSHION SPURGE
Euphorbia polychroma | **2 plants**
Zones 4–9
Alternates: Another 12- to 18-inch-tall, yellow-flowered, salt-tolerant perennial, such as woolly yarrow (*Achillea tomentosa*) [6 plants] or Kamschatka sedum (*Sedum kamtschaticum*) [6 plants]

Planting Plan

2'   2'

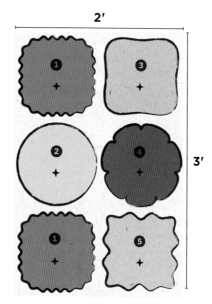 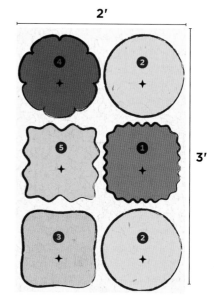

3'   3'

Season by Season

Spring: Color comes along quickly in this garden, with yellow tips on the emerging shoots of cushion spurge in early spring and peak color in mid to late spring. The strappy green leaves of 'Little Grapette' daylily and lacy silver foliage of 'Silver Brocade' beach wormwood appear in early to mid spring, with the bright green leaves of 'Creme Brulee' coreopsis and light green rosettes of 'Autumn Fire' sedum generally coming along in mid to late spring.

To get your garden ready for the growing season, cut down all of the remaining dead stems and leaves in early to mid spring. Divide the daylily, coreopsis, beach wormwood, and sedum then, too, if they were starting to outgrow their space by the end of last year. Apply a fresh layer of organic mulch around the plants.

Summer: Cushion spurge is finished by early summer, but by then, the 'Creme Brulee' coreopsis is beginning to open its butter yellow blooms. The rosy purple trumpets of 'Little Grapette' daylily usually start opening in early to midsummer, with some rebloom possible in late summer. The stems of 'Autumn Fire' are topped with clusters of rosy pink flowers by the end of the summer. 'Silver Brocade' beach wormwood produces clusters of tiny, greenish yellow flowers at the shoot tips, but its main summer feature is its bright silvery white foliage.

Cut the mounds of cushion spurge and sedum back by half in early summer to encourage bushy, non-sprawling new growth. (Wear gloves when working with the cushion spurge to protect your skin from the plant's irritating milky sap.) Shear the shoot tips off the beach wormwood then, too. Pick or clip off the dead daylily flowers regularly. Once all of the buds on a stem have opened, clip off the stem at the base of the plant. On the coreopsis, snip off individual flowers as they finish or shear the clumps back by a third to a half when flowering slows in mid to late summer. Water the garden during extended dry spells.

Fall and Winter: 'Autumn Fire' sedum keeps flowering into fall, with the blooms gradually turning deep red as the seed heads form. After frost, the leaves drop, but the stems and seed heads dry in place and remain for winter interest. 'Little Grapette' daylily and 'Creme Brulee' coreopsis may produce some new blooms in fall. The leaves of cushion spurge can turn shades of orange, red, and purple in fall, and those of 'Silver Brocade' continue to be silvery through fall and into winter.

If the daylily, coreopsis, or beach wormwood clumps are crowding their companions, divide them in early fall. Leave the tops of the perennials in place until spring cleanup to provide some winter protection.

Digging Deeper

THIS PAIR OF SHORT BORDERS would fit perfectly at the start of a walkway, or as an edging for a set of steps. Repeat the plan as many times as you'd like to extend the borders along a longer walkway. Or use only one side of the plan, repeated as needed, to edge just one side of a driveway, or to fill in that awkward strip of ground between the sidewalk and the street.

Perennials are much less likely to be damaged by deicing salts than evergreen shrubs and groundcovers, because the tops of most perennials are already dead by the time winter snow and ice is a problem. To counteract salt buildup in the soil, give the area a few thorough waterings in early spring to wash the salt down below the root zone. If your plants still aren't growing as well as you'd hoped, consider trying some of the suggested alternate plants to see if they are better adapted to your particular conditions.

Minimize salt use by clearing as much snow and ice off paved surfaces as you can *before* applying a deicer. Instead of regular rock salt (sodium chloride), consider using a "plant safe" deicing material such as calcium chloride or calcium magnesium acetate (CMA). Or use coarse sand: it won't melt the ice, but it will provide traction to prevent slipping.

In coastal areas, tall hedges and other windbreaks may help protect your garden from salt spray. If you do notice a dusty white coating on the leaves, try rinsing it off with a gentle spray of water from a hose or overhead sprinkler.

For the Birds

Every time you replace boring lawn grass with a perennial garden, you do more than add color and texture — you also make your yard more enticing to birds. The bushy plants provide shelter, and their seeds provide food for fall and winter. Perennials also attract a wide variety of insects for birds to feed on during the growing season. And in return, birds bring their own charm to the garden, with interesting antics, delightful songs, and colorful feathers for beauty all year long.

◑ ◐ Full sun to partial shade

◆ Average soil

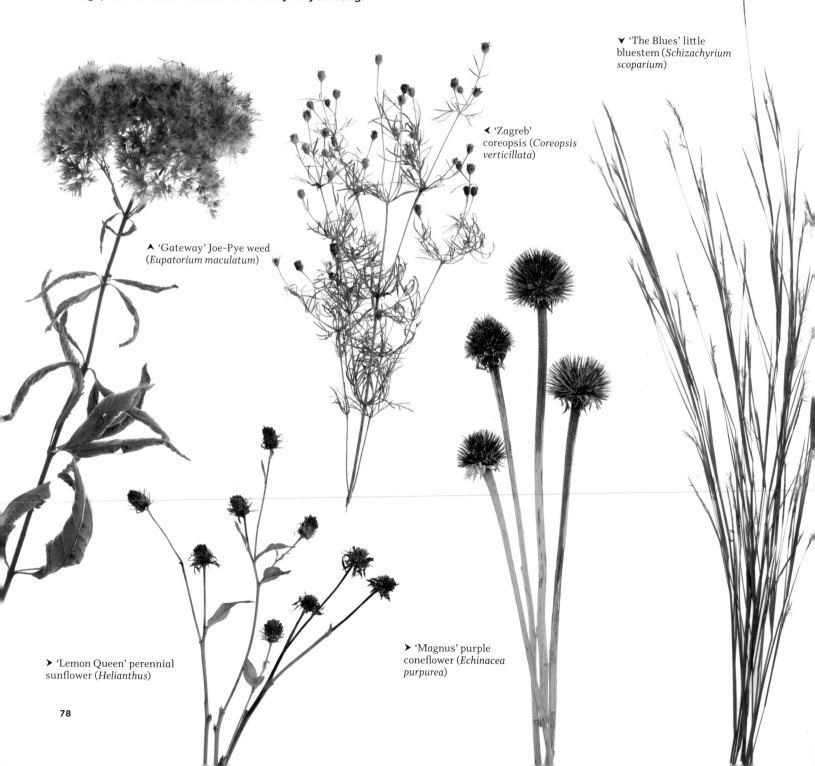

▼ 'The Blues' little bluestem (*Schizachyrium scoparium*)

◄ 'Zagreb' coreopsis (*Coreopsis verticillata*)

▲ 'Gateway' Joe-Pye weed (*Eupatorium maculatum*)

➤ 'Magnus' purple coneflower (*Echinacea purpurea*)

➤ 'Lemon Queen' perennial sunflower (*Helianthus*)

The Garden Plan

Shopping List

❶ 'GATEWAY' JOE-PYE WEED

Eupatorium maculatum | **3 plants**
Zones 4–8
Alternates: 'Little Joe' Joe-Pye weed
(*E. dubium*) or another 4- to 6-foot-tall
perennial that produces lots of seeds for birds,
such as 'Harrington's Pink' New England aster
(*Aster novae-angliae*) [3 plants] or an ironweed
(*Vernonia*) [3 plants]

**❷ 'LEMON QUEEN' PERENNIAL
SUNFLOWER**

Helianthus | **1 plant**
Zones 4–9
Alternates: Another 5- to 7-foot-tall perennial
sunflower or other perennial that produces lots
of seeds for birds, such as giant coneflower
(*Rudbeckia maxima*) [1 plant], 'Cloud Nine'
switch grass (*Panicum virgatum*) [1 plant], or
'Sioux Blue' Indian grass (*Sorghastrum nutans*)
[1 plant]

❸ 'THE BLUES' LITTLE BLUESTEM

Schizachyrium scoparium | **6 plants**
Zones 3–9
Alternates: 'Prairie Blues' or another little
bluestem, or another 2- to 4-foot-tall perennial
that produces lots of seeds for birds, such as
a blazing star (*Liatris*) [6 plants] or orange
coneflower (*Rudbeckia fulgida*) [2 plants]

❹ 'ZAGREB' COREOPSIS

Coreopsis verticillata | **2 plants**
Zones 4–9
Alternates: Another coreopsis or other 1- to
2-foot-tall perennial that produces lots of
seeds for birds, such as 'Low Down' perennial
sunflower (*Helianthus*) [2 plants] or 'Wood's
Purple' aster (*Aster*) [2 plants]

**❺ 'MAGNUS' PURPLE
CONEFLOWER**

Echinacea purpurea | **9 plants**
Zones 3–8
Alternates: Another 2- to 3-foot-tall purple
coneflower or other perennial that produces
lots of seeds for birds, such as 'Summerwine'
or other reddish or pinkish yarrow (*Achillea*)
[9 plants] or 'Burgundy' blanket flower
(*Gaillardia × grandiflora*) [9 plants]

Planting Plan

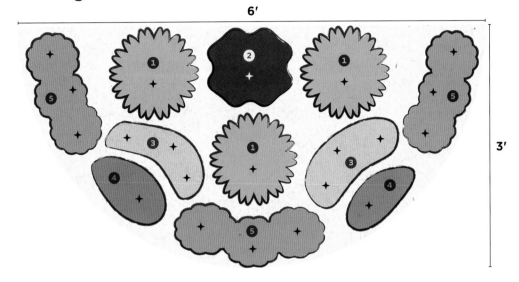

Season by Season

Spring: 'Magnus' purple coneflower jumps into leafy growth relatively early and may even be in bloom by mid spring in mild-winter areas. The sturdy, bright green sprouts of 'Lemon Queen' perennial sunflower usually show up in early to mid spring, joined by the whorled shoots of 'Gateway' Joe-Pye weed, gray-blue blades of 'The Blues' little bluestem, and feathery, bright green shoots of 'Zagreb' coreopsis in mid to late spring.

In early to mid spring, cut down all of the remaining stems, and divide any of the perennials that were starting to outgrow their space by last fall. ('Lemon Queen' perennial sunflower grows very quickly, so figure on dividing it every 2 or 3 years. The others can usually go 3 to 5 years without needing division.)

Summer: 'Magnus' purple coneflower is generally in peak bloom in early to midsummer in southern gardens and mid to late summer in northern areas, with large, rosy pink, daisy-form flowers. Its color is repeated in the fluffy, domed flower clusters of 'Gateway' Joe-Pye weed in mid to late summer. 'Zagreb' coreopsis comes along in early to midsummer, and 'Lemon Queen' perennial sunflower is usually in bloom by mid or late summer; both produce bright yellow daisies. The pinkish stems and blue-gray leaves of 'The Blues' little bluestem contribute foliage color all through the summer, with the addition of small, tufted, silvery seed clusters in late summer.

Cutting back the Joe-Pye weed and perennial sunflower by about half their height in early summer will reduce their later height a bit and delay the start of their bloom period for a few weeks: a plus if you'd like to keep them a bit shorter, or if you'd like to have more late-season blooms in your bird garden. There's no need to clip off any of the faded flowers, because you want to leave the developing seed heads for your feathered friends.

Fall and Winter: 'Gateway' Joe-Pye weed and 'Lemon Queen' perennial sunflower can flower into early fall, especially if you cut them back in early summer. 'Zagreb' coreopsis and 'Magnus' purple coneflower, too, might produce a few new flowers until frost. Once they're done flowering, their developing seed heads last through much of the winter. The leaves and stems of 'The Blues' little bluestem turn reddish orange in fall and then age to coppery pink for winter, holding their silvery seed tufts into winter, too.

No need for any end-of-the-season maintenance in this garden. Leave the stems and seed heads standing for the winter, and enjoy the visits of birds seeking food and shelter.

Digging Deeper

THIS HALF-CIRCLE GARDEN could work well as a border, with the flat side set against a wall, fence, hedge, or other vertical surface. If space allows, you could instead turn it into a circle by flipping the plan along the flat side. Set the two parts right next to each other, or leave a bit of space between them for a path that leads to an arbor, bench, birdhouse, birdbath, or bird feeder.

Perennials that produce clusters of many small flowers, including those with daisy-form blooms, are especially good for bird gardens, because they attract a wide variety of insects for your winged visitors to feed on.

A few simple changes to your gardening routine will help you to get the best from your bird garden. First, don't clip off the faded flowers, because you want the plants to form the nutrient-rich seeds that many birds like to feed on. Hold off on garden cleanup until spring, too, so winter birds can feed and take shelter there. Also, don't use any sort of sprays to control insects, because you want to keep this additional supply of food available for the birds. Perennials aren't especially prone to pest problems anyway, but if you notice a large number of pests on any of your plants, squash them with your fingers or pick them off by hand to reduce their numbers until the birds arrive to take care of the problem for you.

One maintenance step that's especially important in a bird garden is applying a new layer of organic mulch every spring. Hungry birds will eat many of the seeds of the winter, but it's inevitable that they'll miss some, which means that you can end up with a lot of seedlings coming up next spring. Spreading a fresh layer of mulch over the soil or existing mulch in early to mid spring may discourage many of the dropped seeds from sprouting, minimizing maintenance time later.

Hummingbird Heaven

◐◐ Full sun to partial shade

◆ Average soil

Flower-filled gardens have a wonderful way of attracting many kind of interesting wildlife, simply by providing lots of pollen and nectar for critters to feed on. By tweaking your plant choices a bit, you can make your yard especially enticing to one particularly exciting type of visitor: hummingbirds. It's true that hummingbirds are particularly drawn to red and orange, so color is an obvious thing to consider when planning a hummingbird garden. It's also important to consider the flower shape. Nectar-rich blooms that have a tubular or trumpet-like form tend to be most attractive to hungry hummers.

∨ 'Flamenco' torch lily
(*Kniphofia*)

◄ 'Jacob Cline' bee balm
(*Monarda didyma*)

▲ 'Walker's Low'
catmint (*Nepeta*)

➤ Wild columbine
(*Aquilegia canadensis*)

➤ Cardinal flower
(*Lobelia cardinalis*)

The Garden Plan

Shopping List

❶ 'JACOB CLINE' BEE BALM
Monarda didyma | 1 plant
Zones 3–9
Alternates: 'Raspberry Wine' or other bee balm, or another 3- to 5-foot-tall perennial with red and/or nectar-rich flowers, such as hummingbird mint (*Agastache cana*) [1 plant] or blue anise sage (*Salvia guaranitica*) [1 plant]

❷ 'FLAMENCO' TORCH LILY
Kniphofia | 2 plants
Zones 5–9
Alternates: Another 3- to 4-foot-tall perennial with red and/or nectar-rich flowers, such as Maltese cross (*Lychnis chalcedonica*) [2 plants] or beardlip penstemon (*Penstemon barbatus*) [2 plants]

❸ 'WALKER'S LOW' CATMINT
Nepeta | 3 plants
Zones 4–8
Alternates: Another catmint, or another 18- to 30-inch-tall perennial with red and/or nectar-rich flowers, such as 'Caradonna' or 'May Night' ornamental sage (*Salvia*) [3 plants] or blue lobelia (*Lobelia siphilitica*) [3 plants]

❹ CARDINAL FLOWER
Lobelia cardinalis | 3 plants
Zones 3–9
Alternates: Another 2- to 4-foot-tall perennial with red and/or nectar-rich flowers, such as 'Lucifer' crocosmia (*Crocosmia*) [3 plants] or foxglove penstemon (*Penstemon digitalis*) [3 plants]

❺ WILD COLUMBINE
Aquilegia canadensis | 6 plants
Zones 3–9
Alternates: Another columbine or other 1- to 2-foot-tall perennial with red and/or nectar-rich flowers, such as coral bells (*Heuchera sanguinea*) [6 plants] or fire pink (*Silene virginica*) [6 plants]

Planting Plan

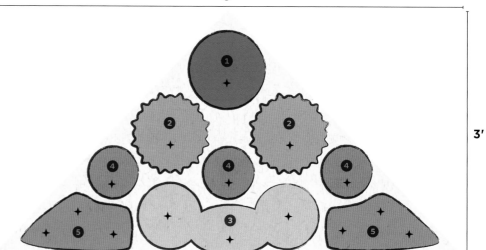

Season by Season

Spring: The upright shoots of 'Jacob Cline' bee balm, spiky foliage of 'Flamenco' torch lily, multipart leaves of wild columbine, and dense rosettes of cardinal flower add a wide range of greens to this garden in spring, along with the gray-green mounds of 'Walker's Low' catmint. By late spring, the catmint comes into bloom with loose spikes of small, purple-blue flowers, and the wild columbine is topped with nodding red-and-yellow blooms.

In early to mid spring, cut down the dead tops of the bee balm, catmint, cardinal flower, and wild columbine, and cut the leaves of the torch lily back to about 6 inches above the ground. Every 3 years or so, divide the clumps of bee balm, catmint, and cardinal flower. Finish the spring maintenance by applying a fresh layer of organic mulch.

Summer: 'Walker's Low' catmint and wild columbine continue flowering through early summer, gradually slowing in midsummer. 'Flamenco' torch lily is in full glory in early to midsummer, with spiky clusters of red buds that open orange and age to creamy yellow. And for mid to late summer color, there's 'Jacob Cline' bee balm, with shaggy-looking clusters of rich red flowers at the shoot tips, and cardinal flower, with spikes of bright red blooms.

In midsummer, shear the catmint clumps back by one-half to two-thirds, and cut off the finished flower stems of the wild columbine at the base. (Columbine plants often die out after a few years, so leave one or two stems in place to set seed so you can get a few seedlings for replacements.) Cut the dead flower stalks of the torch lily at the base, and snip off the finished flower heads of the bee balm just above a set of leaves. And on the cardinal flower, cut the spent spikes back to the leafy part of the stems, leaving one or two in place to set seed.

Fall and Winter: 'Jacob Cline' bee balm and wild columbine stay green into fall, and the columbine leaves may remain for at least part of the winter. 'Flamenco' torch lily occasionally produces a few new blooms in early fall, and its leaves remain green through the winter in mild-winter areas. 'Walker's Low' catmint and cardinal flower may also rebloom in fall; and the catmint leaves hang on into early winter, or even longer.

Cut down the dead stems in late fall, if you wish, but leave any live foliage untrimmed. Or, simply leave everything in place for spring cleanup.

Digging Deeper

A HUMMINGBIRD GARDEN DOESN'T NEED TO BE BIG; even a small planting like this one can keep a resident hummer happy for months. By itself, this triangular garden fits easily into a corner. Or, flip the design along one of the shorter sides to create a mirror image, and use the two versions to flank an arbor, a bench, a gate, a set of steps, or the start of a walkway.

Wild columbine (*Aquilegia canadensis*) is a great addition to hummingbird gardens because it's one of the earliest flowering favorites, providing a welcome source of nectar for the hummers as they return from their winter quarters. You might also want to add a hummingbird feeder to your garden as an extra enticement for the hummers to hang around.

Cardinal flower (*Lobelia cardinalis*), with its tall spikes of brilliant red blooms, is a magnet for hummingbirds, and butterflies, too. This beautiful perennial grows in full sun in cooler areas, especially if the soil is on the moist side, but often performs better in a site with morning sun and afternoon shade. Even in ideal conditions, the clumps tend to die out after 3 or 4 years. To keep them vigorous, divide them every 2 or 3 years in spring or fall. They'll also self-sow (produce seeds that fall to the ground, sprout, and grow into new clumps) if you leave the stalks in place after the flowers have finished. Leave some bare (unmulched) earth around the plants too, so the tiny seeds can reach the soil to sprout.

Butterfly Banquet

Any time you plant flowers in your yard, you increase the chances that butterflies will visit your yard to check them out. But if you really want to draw in these "floating flowers" and encourage them to linger longer, planting a garden filled with their favorite food sources is the way to go. Butterflies are especially fond of blooms that are made up of many small blossoms, such as daisy-form flowers, which are packed with nectar and pollen for the adults to eat. It's also smart to include perennials with leaves that the caterpillars like to feed on, so you're supporting the next generation, too.

◄ 'Butterfly Blue' pincushion flower (*Scabiosa*)

➤ 'White Swan' purple coneflower (*Echinacea purpurea*)

◄ Swamp milkweed (*Asclepias incarnata*)

➤ 'Coronation Gold' yarrow (*Achillea*)

➤ 'Little Spire' Russian sage (*Perovskia*)

84

The Garden Plan

Shopping List

❶ SWAMP MILKWEED
Asclepias incarnata | 3 plant
Zones 3–9
Alternates: Another 3- to 4-foot-tall perennial with pink, butterfly-attracting flowers, such as 'Marshall's Delight' or other pink-flowered bee balm (*Monarda*) [3 plant] or 'Little Joe' Joe-Pye weed (*Eupatorium dubium*) [1 plant]

❷ 'WHITE SWAN' PURPLE CONEFLOWER
Echinacea purpurea | 6 plants
Zones 3–8
Alternates: Another 30- to 40-inch-tall perennial with white, butterfly-attracting flowers, such as 'David' phlox (*Phlox paniculata*) [4 plants] or 'Black Ace' turtlehead (*Chelone glabra*) [4 plants]

❸ 'LITTLE SPIRE' RUSSIAN SAGE
Perovskia | 2 plants
Zones 5–9
Alternates: Another 3- to 4-foot-tall perennial with blue, butterfly-attracting flowers, such as globe thistle (*Echinops ritro*) [2 plants] or 'Longwood Blue' blue mist shrub (*Caryopteris × clandonensis*) [2 plants]

❹ 'CORONATION GOLD' YARROW
Achillea | 3 plants
Zones 3–8
Alternates: Another 2- to 3-foot-tall perennial with yellow, butterfly-attracting flowers, such as 'Prairie Sun' Gloriosa daisy (*Rudbeckia hirta*) [3 plants] or 'Sonnenschein' Shasta daisy (*Leucanthemum × superbum*) [3 plants]

❺ 'BUTTERFLY BLUE' PINCUSHION FLOWER
Scabiosa | 5 plants
Zones 3–8
Alternates: Another 1- to 2-foot-tall perennial with blue or purple-blue, butterfly-attracting flowers, such as 'Kit Cat' catmint (*Nepeta × faassenii*) [5 plants] or English lavender (*Lavandula angustifolia*) [5 plants]

Planting Plan

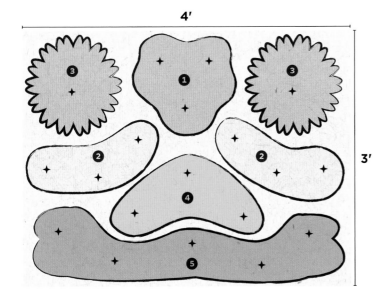

Season by Season

Spring: Along with lots of leafy growth, this garden offers some blooms for early arriving butterflies. The orange-centered white daisies of 'White Swan' purple coneflower may appear by mid spring in mild climates, and the lavender-blue blooms of 'Butterfly Blue' pincushion flower may begin in late spring.

To get your butterfly garden ready for the growing season, cut down any dead or winter-damaged stems and leaves on the swamp milkweed, coneflower, yarrow, and pincushion flower in early to mid spring. This is also the time to divide any of those perennials if they were starting to outgrow their space last year. Wait until the 'Little Spire' Russian sage starts growing; then, cut it back to about 6 inches. Apply a fresh layer of organic mulch around all of the plants.

Summer: 'White Swan' purple coneflower is generally in peak bloom in early to midsummer in southern gardens and in mid to late summer in northern regions. The golden yellow clusters of 'Coronation Gold' yarrow and lavender-blue 'Butterfly Blue' pincushion flower appear throughout the summer. Pink swamp milkweed usually joins the show in mid to late summer. In southern gardens, the 'Little Spire' Russian sage is in full bloom in early to midsummer; in northern gardens, the peak flowering period is usually mid to late summer.

Throughout the summer, clip off the faded flowers, if desired; it helps to keep the garden looking tidy and can extend the bloom period on the coneflower and pincushion flower. Cut back the Russian sage by about half if it gets floppy in midsummer. Water the garden during summer dry spells.

Fall and Winter: 'Butterfly Blue' pincushion flower continues to flower into fall, along with some rebloom possible on the 'White Swan' purple coneflower and 'Coronation Gold' yarrow. These plants also offer attractive seed heads for winter interest. The leaves of yarrow and the pincushion flower can stay green through the winter.

Stop clipping off the faded flowers in early fall (or even late summer) if you want the seed heads for winter, and wait until spring to clean up the frost-killed tops. Otherwise, it's fine to cut down the dead stalks of the swamp milkweed, coneflower, yarrow, and pincushion flower in late fall.

Digging Deeper

THIS SIMPLE RECTANGULAR GARDEN could work well in just about any spot: at the base of a lamppost, in a sunny corner, or on either side of a gate, arbor, doorway, or set of steps. Repeat the plan end to end as many times as needed if you want to extend it as a foundation planting around your house or an edging for a path or driveway. A site that's sheltered from strong wind is ideal, because strong breezes make it tough for butterflies to land and feed on your flowers.

There's little need for insecticide sprays in flower gardens, because perennials that are basically healthy and vigorous can withstand a fair bit of insect damage with no permanent harm. Avoiding pesticides (even organic ones) is especially important in butterfly gardens, because you don't want to harm the very creatures you're trying to attract. If you find caterpillars chewing on the leaves here, it's cause for celebration, not worry!

Milkweeds (*Asclepias*) are a favorite food source for the larvae of monarch butterflies (queen butterflies, too), but they're not the only perennials that provide food for butterfly larvae. Some other great "host plants" include asters (*Aster*), coreopsis (*Coreopsis*), false indigos (*Baptisia*), hollyhocks (*Alcea*), and turtleheads (*Chelone*).

Don't Stop Here, Deer!

Few things are more disappointing than putting time, money, and effort into creating a beautiful garden and then having it be destroyed by marauding deer. If you know that these critters already hang around your neighborhood, it's smart to start with "deer-resistant" perennials: plants that are known to be less than enticing to deer. There's no guarantee that deer will *never* nibble on these plants, but they're more likely to move on to tastier fare, and it may keep them from getting in the habit of treating your yard as their own private salad bar.

◑ Full sun to partial shade

◆ Average soil

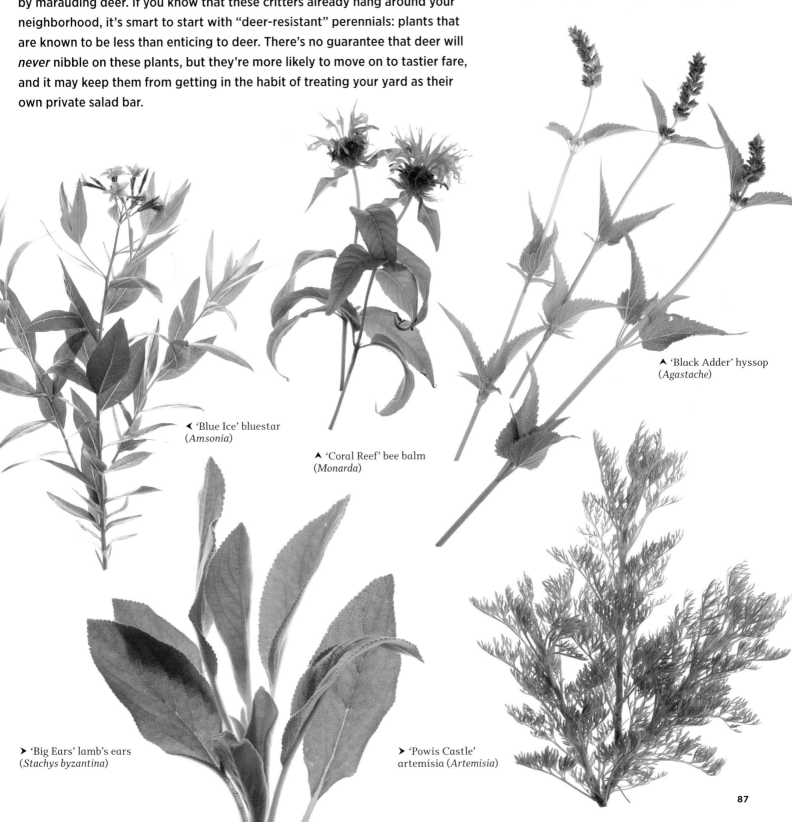

◀ 'Blue Ice' bluestar
(*Amsonia*)

▲ 'Coral Reef' bee balm
(*Monarda*)

▲ 'Black Adder' hyssop
(*Agastache*)

➤ 'Big Ears' lamb's ears
(*Stachys byzantina*)

➤ 'Powis Castle'
artemisia (*Artemisia*)

The Garden Plan

Shopping List

1 'BLACK ADDER' HYSSOP
Agastache | **3 plants**
Zones 6-9
Alternates: Another hyssop or other 3- to 5-foot-tall, deer-resistant perennial, such as globe thistle (*Echinops ritro*) [3 plants] or 'Longin' Russian sage (*Perovskia*) [3 plants]

2 'CORAL REEF' BEE BALM
Monarda | **3 plants**
Zones 3-9
Alternates: Another bee balm or other 3- to 4-foot-tall, deer-resistant perennial, such as swamp milkweed (*Asclepias incarnata*) [3 plants] or purple coneflower (*Echinacea purpurea*) [3 plants]

3 'POWIS CASTLE' ARTEMISIA
Artemisia | **4 plants**
Zones 6-9
Alternates: Another 2- to 3-foot-tall, deer-resistant perennial, such as blue mist shrub (*Caryopteris × clandonensis*) [4 plants] or 'Hameln' fountain grass (*Pennisetum alopecuroides*) [4 plants]

4 'BLUE ICE' BLUESTAR
Amsonia | **3 plants**
Zones 5-9
Alternates: Another 1- to 2-foot-tall, deer-resistant perennial, such as a catmint (*Nepeta*) [3 plants] or a coreopsis (*Coreopsis*) [3 plants]

5 'BIG EARS' LAMB'S EARS
Stachys byzantina | **4 plants**
Zones 4-8
Alternates: Another 6- to 12-inch-tall, deer-resistant perennial, such as 'Berggarten' culinary sage (*Salvia officinalis*) [4 plants] or 'Bath's Pink' dianthus (*Dianthus*) [4 plants]

Planting Plan

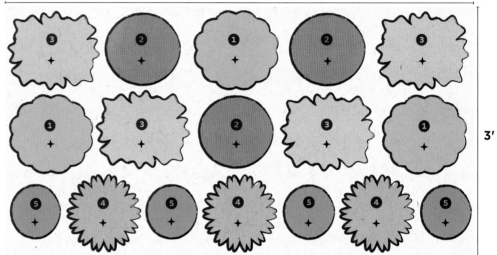

Season by Season

Spring: Interest builds slowly in this garden, with early color coming mostly from emerging leaves: the greens of the 'Black Adder' hyssop, 'Coral Reef' bee balm, and 'Blue Ice' bluestar and the silvers of lacy 'Powis Castle' artemisia and fuzzy 'Big Ears' lamb's ears. In mid to late spring, they're joined by the starry, medium blue flowers of the bluestar.

Take care of cleanup in early to mid spring, starting with cutting down any remaining dead top growth. Once new growth appears on the artemisia, cut the stems back to 6 to 12 inches tall. Divide the bee balm and lamb's ears if they are starting to outgrow their space. Finish the cleanup by applying a fresh layer of organic mulch.

Summer: 'Blue Ice' bluestar generally finishes flowering by early summer, about the time that 'Black Adder' hyssop begins its summer-long show of spiky blue-purple flowers. 'Coral Reef' bee balm jumps in for mid to late summer, with shaggy-looking clusters of lavender-pink flowers at the shoot tips. Throughout the summer, the bushy artemisia and carpeting lamb's ears complement their flowering partners with silvery to gray-green foliage.

Snip the dead flower heads off the bee balm to prevent self-sowing and get more blooms, or leave them on the plant for winter interest. 'Big Ears' lamb's ears usually doesn't bloom, but if it does send up one or more stalks, clip them off at the base to keep the plants tidy. In humid or rainy weather, the lamb's ears' fuzzy leaves may rot where they're crowded close to the ground. If this happens, cut back the clumps close to the ground and remove all of the leaves, so the plants can sprout fresh foliage that looks good for the rest of the growing season. Cutting back the hyssop lightly (by about a quarter) in late summer makes the plant look neater and encourages it to produce more flowers for fall. Water the garden during extended summer dry spells.

Fall and Winter: 'Black Adder' hyssop continues to bloom until frost, and then its dried stalks and flower heads stay for winter interest, along with those of the bee balm. The silver leaves of the artemisia and lamb's ears also look good through most or all of the winter. 'Blue Ice' bluestar's foliage turns yellow in fall, and then drops off in mid to late fall.

If the bluestar or lamb's ears are crowding their companions, divide them in early fall. Cut down the frost-killed stems of the bluestar; leave the rest of the perennials standing until spring cleanup.

Digging Deeper

THIS RECTANGULAR BORDER is planned with tall plants at the back and shorter companions toward the front, so it's best suited for a spot where you'll see it mainly from one side. Set it against a vertical surface, such as a wall, fence, or hedge, or use it to dress up the area around a raised deck or porch. If you need to fill a longer space, repeat the plan end to end as many times as needed, replacing some of the main plants with their suggested alternates to mix things up a bit.

The plants that deer find tasty and those that they avoid vary widely from region to region, so if you find that your supposedly deer-resistant perennials are getting eaten, experiment with some of the alternate plants. Or try making one (or a few) applications of Plantskydd or another repellent spray to give your garden an extra level of protection against deer damage. Also, avoid planting "deer candy", such as daylilies (*Hemerocallis*), true lilies (*Lilium*), hostas (*Hosta*), and tulips (*Tulipa*), which deer pretty much everywhere seem to love.

If you want more options for deer-resistant perennials, look to the leaves. Deer seem to dislike plants that have fuzzy, spiny, or strongly scented foliage. Ornamental grasses, as a group, also seem to be less enticing than other perennials.

Fabulous Fragrance

This garden is a delight to more than the eyes; it's a treat for your sense of scent as well. Perennials with fragrant flowers are a wonderful choice for plantings along a path or walkway, where you can get up close to enjoy the perfumed blooms. They're also lovely outside of a window, where the fragrance can drift indoors in summer, or near a porch, patio, deck, or other outdoor sitting area.

◐◑ Full sun to partial shade

◆ Average soil

➤ 'David' phlox (*Phlox paniculata*)

➤ Variegated meadowsweet (*Filipendula ulmaria* 'Variegata')

➤ 'Festiva Maxima' peony (*Paeonia*)

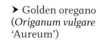

➤ Golden oregano (*Origanum vulgare* 'Aureum')

◄ Cheddar pink (*Dianthus gratianopolitanus*)

The Garden Plan

Shopping List

❶ 'FESTIVA MAXIMA' PEONY
Paeonia | 1 plant
Zones 3–8
Alternates: Another fragrant peony or other
2- to 5-foot-tall perennial with scented flowers
or leaves, such as a hyssop (*Agastache*) [1 plant]
or 'Silk Road' or another Orienpet lily [3 bulbs]

❷ VARIEGATED MEADOWSWEET
Filipendula ulmaria 'Variegata' | 2 plants
Zones 3–9
Alternates: Another 2- to 4-foot-tall perennial
with scented flowers or leaves, such as
variegated sweet iris (*Iris pallida* 'Variegata')
[6 plants] or a bee balm (*Monarda*) [2 plants]

❸ 'DAVID' PHLOX
Phlox paniculata | 3 plants
Zones 4–9
Alternates: Another 3- to 4-foot-tall perennial
with scented flowers or leaves, such as 'Ice
Ballet' swamp milkweed (*Asclepias incarnata*)
[3 plants] or 'White Swan' purple coneflower
(*Echinacea purpurea*) [3 plants]

❹ CHEDDAR PINK
Dianthus gratianopolitanus | 2 plants
Zones 3–8
Alternates: Another fragrant dianthus or other
6- to 12-inch-tall perennial with scented flowers
or leaves, such as wall rock cress (*Arabis
caucasica*) [2 plants] or calamint (*Calamintha
nepeta*) [2 plants]

❺ GOLDEN OREGANO
Origanum vulgare 'Aureum' | 3 plants
Zones 4–8
Alternates: Another 9- to 18-inch-tall
perennial with scented flowers or leaves,
such as 'Berggarten' sage (*Salvia officinalis*)
[3 plants] or variegated lemon thyme (*Thymus* ×
citriodorus 'Aureus') [5 plants]

Planting Plan

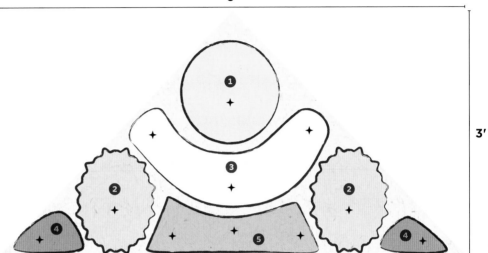

Season by Season

Spring: The peony and cheddar pink generally start sharing their scents in late spring. 'Festiva Maxima' peony produces bushy clumps of rich green, glossy leaves topped with large, fully double white flowers, while the cheddar pink creates carpets of slender, blue-gray leaves that are covered with an abundance of single pink blooms. The phlox's bright green foliage isn't especially interesting now, but the variegated meadowsweet's yellow-splashed, deep green leaves are quite eye-catching, and the golden oregano contributes bright yellow leaves that release their rich, spicy scent when you rub or brush against them.

In early to mid spring, cut down any dead or winter-damaged top growth, and divide any of the perennials that were starting to outgrow their space by the end of the previous year. The peony's flowers can be very heavy and tend to flop, so you may want to place a hoop-type or grid-type support over the emerging shoots in spring so they'll be supported as they grow. Finish up by spreading a fresh layer of organic mulch over the soil to get the garden off to a great start for the growing season.

Summer: 'Festiva Maxima' peony finishes flowering in early summer, if not before, but the cheddar pink usually reaches its peak bloom then. (It takes a break in midsummer but may send up some more flowers in late summer.) Early to midsummer also brings on the variegated meadowsweet, with its plume-like clusters of creamy white blooms over leaves that are now solid green. It often overlaps with the mid- to late-summer bloom season of 'David' phlox, which produces domed clusters of bright white flowers. Golden oregano blooms, too, with tiny pinkish white blossoms, but it's still the leaves that provide great scents to the garden.

Summer care for this garden is mostly a matter of removing the dead flowers to keep the plants looking neat, prevent them from producing unwanted seedlings, and possibly encourage the phlox and cheddar pink to rebloom. On the peony, snip off each spent bloom just above the uppermost leaf on the stem. On the variegated meadowsweet, cut off the finished flowering stalks near the base of the plant. On the phlox, clip off the entire flower cluster on each stem. And on the cheddar pink and golden oregano, trim off the finished flower stems individually or shear them off as a group just above the leaves. Water the garden during extended summer dry spells.

Fall and Winter: A bit of fragrance continues into fall, with some flowers possible on both the 'David' phlox and the cheddar pink. The golden oregano's leaves continue to be aromatic through the fall and also last into winter.

If any of the perennials are crowding out their companions, you can divide them in early fall or wait until spring. Cut the peony, meadowsweet, and phlox stems to the ground in mid to late fall, but leave the rest of the cleanup until spring.

Digging Deeper

A TRIANGULAR PLAN like this is an obvious choice for fitting into a corner. Or, use it twice (flip the plan along one of the shorter sides to make one of the triangles a mirror image) and use the two parts to flank a short path leading to a cozy garden bench, where you and your guests can sit and enjoy the fragrance. If possible, site your scented garden in a place that's sheltered from winds, because breezes tend to blow away some of the fragrance.

Keep in mind that scents are very subjective: what smells wonderful to one person may be uninteresting or even unpleasant to someone else. Even among plants that most people enjoy, such as peonies (*Paeonia*), the type and strength of scent can vary quite a bit. So, if you want to enjoy your scented perennials to the fullest, try to shop for them when they are in bloom; that way, you can take a test smell before you buy.

A planting of fragrant perennials already does double duty, adding beauty to your yard as well as wonderful scents to sniff. It doesn't stop there, though, because fragrant flowers and leaves are also a joy to bring indoors for bouquets and arrangements. And if you incorporate aromatic herbs such as culinary sage (*Salvia officinalis*), oreganos (*Origanum*), winter savory (*Satureja montana*), lemon balm (*Melissa officinalis*), and lavenders (*Lavandula*), you can harvest them for use in cooking or crafts as well.

Cut Flowers for Free

◗ ◑ Full sun to partial shade

◆ Average soil

When you plant a perennial garden in your yard, you're doing more than beautifying the outside of your home — you're also treating yourself to a steady supply of fresh flowers for indoor bouquets. Snipping a few blooms here and there won't harm the plants, and turning your harvest into mini-arrangements is a fun way to unleash your creativity. If you find that your existing plantings aren't providing all the flowers you'd like, consider growing a garden filled with perennials specifically for cut flowers, so you can clip to your heart's content all season long.

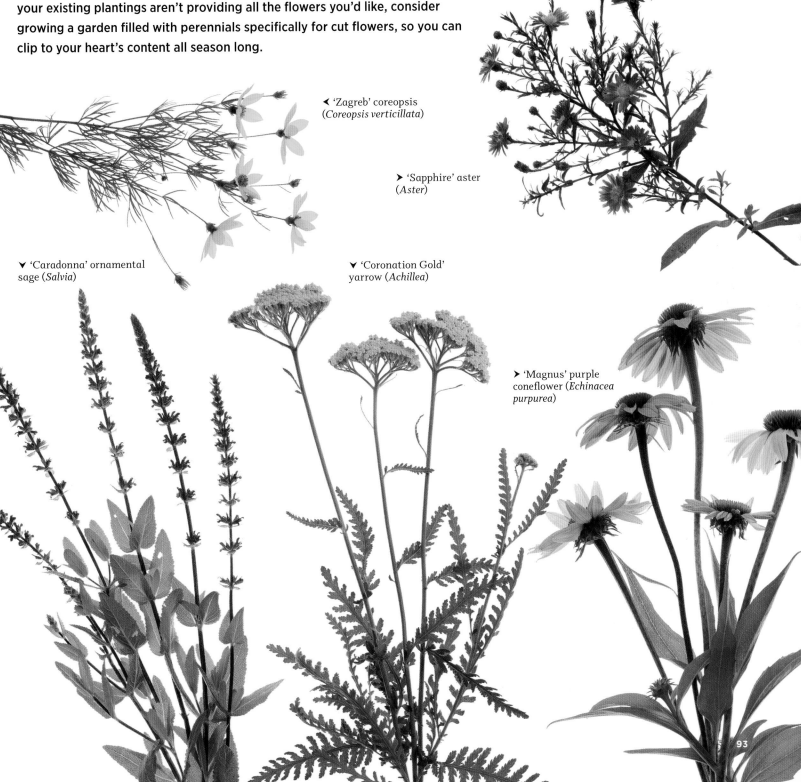

◄ 'Zagreb' coreopsis (*Coreopsis verticillata*)

➤ 'Sapphire' aster (*Aster*)

▼ 'Caradonna' ornamental sage (*Salvia*)

▼ 'Coronation Gold' yarrow (*Achillea*)

➤ 'Magnus' purple coneflower (*Echinacea purpurea*)

93

The Garden Plan

Shopping List

❶ 'MAGNUS' PURPLE CONEFLOWER
Echinacea purpurea | **3 plants**
Zones 3–8
Alternates: Another purple coneflower or other 2- to 3-foot-tall perennial with flowers or foliage for cutting, such as a sea holly (*Eryngium*) [3 plants] or a blazing star (*Liatris*) [3 plants]

❷ 'CORONATION GOLD' YARROW
Achillea | **3 plants**
Zones 3–8
Alternates: Another yarrow or other 2- to 3-foot-tall perennial with flowers or foliage for cutting, such as 'Prairie Sun' Gloriosa daisy (*Rudbeckia hirta*) [3 plants] or an orange coneflower (*Rudbeckia fulgida*) [3 plants]

❸ 'CARADONNA' ORNAMENTAL SAGE
Salvia | **2 plants**
Zones 4–8
Alternates: Another ornamental sage or other 1- to 2-foot-tall perennial with flowers or foliage for cutting, such as 'Blue Charm' speedwell (*Veronica*) [6 plants] or lamb's ears (*Stachys byzantina*) [2 plants]

❹ 'SAPPHIRE' ASTER
Aster | **4 plants**
Zones 4–8
Alternates: Another compact aster or other 1- to 2-foot-tall perennial with flowers or foliage for cutting, such as a lavender (*Lavandula*) [4 plants] or 'Butterfly Blue' pincushion flower (*Scabiosa*) [4 plants]

❺ 'ZAGREB' COREOPSIS
Coreopsis verticillata | **2 plants**
Zones 4–9
Alternates: Another coreopsis or other 1- to 2-foot-tall perennial with flowers or foliage for cutting, such as lady's mantle (*Alchemilla mollis*) [2 plants] or 'Crown of Rays' goldenrod (*Solidago*) [2 plants]

Planting Plan

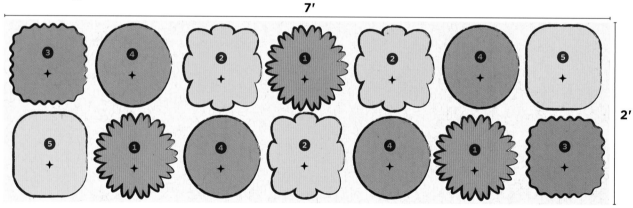

Season by Season

Spring: The return of milder weather brings on lots of leafy new growth. 'Magnus' purple coneflower can start blooming as early as mid spring in southern gardens. 'Caradonna' ornamental sage may be in bloom by late spring, with slender spikes of deep purple-blue flowers.

Cut any remaining dead leaves and stems to the ground in early to mid spring, and divide any of the perennials that were getting too crowded last season. Add a fresh layer of organic mulch to cover the soil, and your garden is ready to get growing.

Summer: The dark-centered pink daisies of 'Magnus' purple coneflower peak in early to midsummer in southern gardens and mid to late summer in northern regions. They look terrific with the golden yellow flowers of the 'Coronation Gold' yarrow, which appear throughout the summer months, and the 'Zagreb' coreopsis, which are most abundant in early to midsummer. 'Caradonna' ornamental sage continues to bloom through early summer, at least, and usually takes a break in mid to late summer. While all this is going on, the aster is forming dense mounds of tiny leaves and, later in the summer, hundreds of buds for fall.

Harvest your cut flowers frequently, clipping their stems just above a leaf or leaf pair or developing flower bud. On the sage and the coreopsis, cut the plants back by about a third when flowering slows in mid to late summer to encourage rebloom later in the growing season. Water the garden during summer dry spells to keep the plants growing and flowering freely.

Fall and Winter: 'Magnus' purple coneflower and 'Coronation Gold' yarrow may continue to flower into early fall, and the 'Caradonna' ornamental sage and 'Zagreb' coreopsis are also likely to bloom again in the fall, especially if you trimmed them back in summer. 'Sapphire' aster is the star of the garden at this time of year, with densely branched stems practically smothered in purple-blue, daisy-form flowers in early to mid fall.

Instead of cutting down the plants to clean up the garden in mid to late fall, leave them in place so any unharvested blooms can develop into seed heads, which can be useful for holiday decorating. (To spruce them up a bit, spritz the seed heads with a bit of colorful or metallic spray paint.)

Digging Deeper

THIS CUTTING GARDEN is pretty enough to be a front-yard or foundation planting, but it's better to give it a lower-visibility spot in the backyard or a sunny side yard, so you won't hesitate to cut all the flowers you want. Narrow beds like this are ideal for harvesting, because you can readily see and reach all of the blooms without stretching too much. If you want even more flowers for cutting, repeat the plan multiple times, with the strips parallel to each other and separated by 2-foot paths for easy access.

To give your bouquets more variety, choose some of the suggested alternate plants to replace some of the main plant suggestions. Instead of planting four 'Sapphire' asters, for instance, you might plant only two and fill the other two spots with clumps of lavender. Speaking of herbs, keep in mind that fragrant flowers and foliage add an extra level of enjoyment to your indoor arrangements.

Summer- and fall-blooming flowers tend to be on the tall side, which is great because they give you long stems for large bouquets. Don't hesitate to add spring bulbs for cutting, too. Some hybrid tulips, for instance, can easily produce 2-foot stems, while lower growers like grape hyacinths (*Muscari*) and snowdrops (*Galanthus*) are adorable in miniature arrangements.

Miniature Meadow

Bring the country charm of rural fields to your yard with one or more mini-meadow plantings. These simple combinations of trouble-free grasses and perennials provide months of easy-care color and texture, making them great for replacing unneeded lawn areas. The plants in the plan featured here also attract birds (with seeds) and butterflies (with pollen and nectar), so you get a wonderful wildlife-attracting garden, too!

◄ 'Raspberry Wine' bee balm (*Monarda*)

▲ 'Pink Grapefruit' yarrow (*Achillea*)

▼ 'Ruby Star' purple coneflower (*Echinacea purpurea*)

➤ 'Karley Rose' Oriental fountain grass (*Pennisetum orientale*)

▼ 'Vivid' obedient plant (*Physostegia virginiana*)

The Garden Plan

Shopping List

❶ 'KARLEY ROSE' ORIENTAL FOUNTAIN GRASS
Pennisetum orientale | **1 plant**
Zones 5–9
Alternates: Another 2- to 3-foot-tall ornamental grass, such as pink muhly grass (*Muhlenbergia capillaris*) [1 plant] or 'Overdam' feather reed grass (*Calamagrostis × acutiflora*) [1 plant]

❷ 'RUBY STAR' PURPLE CONEFLOWER
Echinacea purpurea | **2 plants**
Zones 3–8
Alternates: Another purple coneflower or other 18- to 30-inch-tall perennial, such as 'Mohrchen' sedum (*Sedum*) [2 plants] or 'Ping Pong' phlox (*Phlox × arendsii*) [2 plants]

❸ 'RASPBERRY WINE' BEE BALM
Monarda | **2 plants**
Zones 4–9
Alternates: Another pink bee balm or other 18- to 30-inch-tall perennial, such as 'Rose Queen' ornamental sage (*Salvia*) [2 plants] or 'Pink Mist' pincushion flower (*Scabiosa*) [2 plants]

❹ 'VIVID' OBEDIENT PLANT
Physostegia virginiana | **2 plants**
Zones 3–9
Alternates: Another 18- to 30-inch-tall perennial, such as 'Star Cluster' coreopsis (*Coreopsis*) [2 plants] or 'September Charm' anemone (*Anemone × hybrida*) [2 plants]

❺ 'PINK GRAPEFRUIT' YARROW
Achillea | **2 plants**
Zones 3–8
Alternates: Another pink yarrow or other 18- to 30-inch-tall perennial, such as 'Crimson Butterflies' gaura (*Gaura lindheimeri*) [2 plants] or 'Rosenkuppel' ornamental oregano (*Origanum*) [2 plants]

Planting Plan

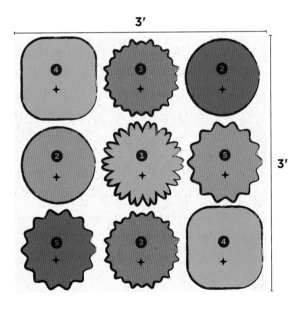

Season by Season

Spring: 'Ruby Star' purple coneflower, 'Raspberry Wine' bee balm, 'Vivid' obedient plant, and 'Pink Grapefruit' yarrow jump into leafy growth in early to mid spring, followed by 'Karley Rose' Oriental fountain grass in mid to late spring. Purple coneflowers may begin blooming by mid spring in mild-winter areas.

Meadow maintenance is easy: simply cut down all of the dead stems in early to mid spring. Divide all of the plants now every 3 to 5 years, if you wish, or let them grow undisturbed. Apply a fresh layer of organic mulch around the plants; then, stand back and watch your mini-meadow come to life.

Summer: 'Ruby Star' purple coneflower is usually in full bloom in early to midsummer in southern gardens and mid to late summer in northern areas, with large, pink-petaled, daisy-form flowers. 'Pink Grapefruit' yarrow generally blooms through the summer, with clustered deep pink flowers that age to light pink. 'Karley Rose' Oriental fountain grass joins the show in mid and late summer, with fluffy, arching, pinkish spikes, and so does 'Raspberry Wine', with shaggy-looking clusters of rosy red flowers at the shoot tips. 'Vivid' obedient plant might be in bloom by late summer.

Water your mini-meadow during extended summer dry spells; there's no need for other maintenance.

Fall and Winter: 'Karley Rose' Oriental fountain grass keeps flowering into fall. 'Ruby Star' purple coneflower and 'Pink Grapefruit' yarrow may produce some new blooms now, too, and 'Vivid' obedient plant is in full glory in early to mid fall, with spikes of rosy-pink flowers. The purple coneflower, 'Raspberry Wine' bee balm, obedient plant, and yarrow also have interesting seed heads that linger into winter.

There's no need to spend any time on your mini-meadow in fall or winter. Leave the cleanup until spring so hungry birds can feed on the seeds and shelter among the dead stems and leaves.

Digging Deeper

STARTING WITH A SMALL PLOT like this one is a great way to see if you enjoy the mini-meadow effect before you go all out. If you do like the look, it's easy to fill more space by repeating the plan as many times as you like, leaving about 2 feet of space between the squares for paths. Besides giving you the delightful opportunity to stroll through your meadow, these paths make it easy for you to reach all parts of the plantings for easy cleanup. The space taken up by the paths also cuts down on the amount of plants you need to buy: a big plus if you have a lot of space to fill.

This simple plan is based on a pink color theme — both in the main plants and their suggested substitutes. If you want to mix things up a bit, or perhaps choose an entirely different color scheme, feel free to experiment. Green-leaved ornamental grasses work well with all kinds of other colors. For ideas of perennials in other color themes, check out the plans at the beginning of this part, such as "Bright White Garden" on page 18 or "Touch of Gold" on page 33. The trick to keeping the meadow effect is to combine flowers and grasses that are all similar in height: in the 12- to 24-inch-tall range for a low meadow, and the 18- to 36-inch-tall range for a medium-height meadow.

Part of the charm of a mini-meadow is its less-than-perfect look: no need for staking, cutting back stems to control their height, or trimming off the flowers as they fade. The plants are set close together, so they can mingle and lean on each other, and their finished flowers turn into interesting seed heads that provide fascinating forms into the winter months. Over time, some of the plants may get crowded out, but you can simply let the successful survivors fill the space that's left. A once-a-year cleanup and mulching is pretty much all it needs!

Cottage Charm

If you're drawn to the charm of classic garden perennials, a cottage-style planting could be a perfect choice for you. Traditional favorites such as catmints, foxgloves, and lady's mantle add loads of color and the charm of an old-fashioned English garden. With the addition of perennials that produce fragrant flowers, you have a garden that's a treat to smell as well as to see.

◖◑ Full sun to partial shade

◆ Average soil

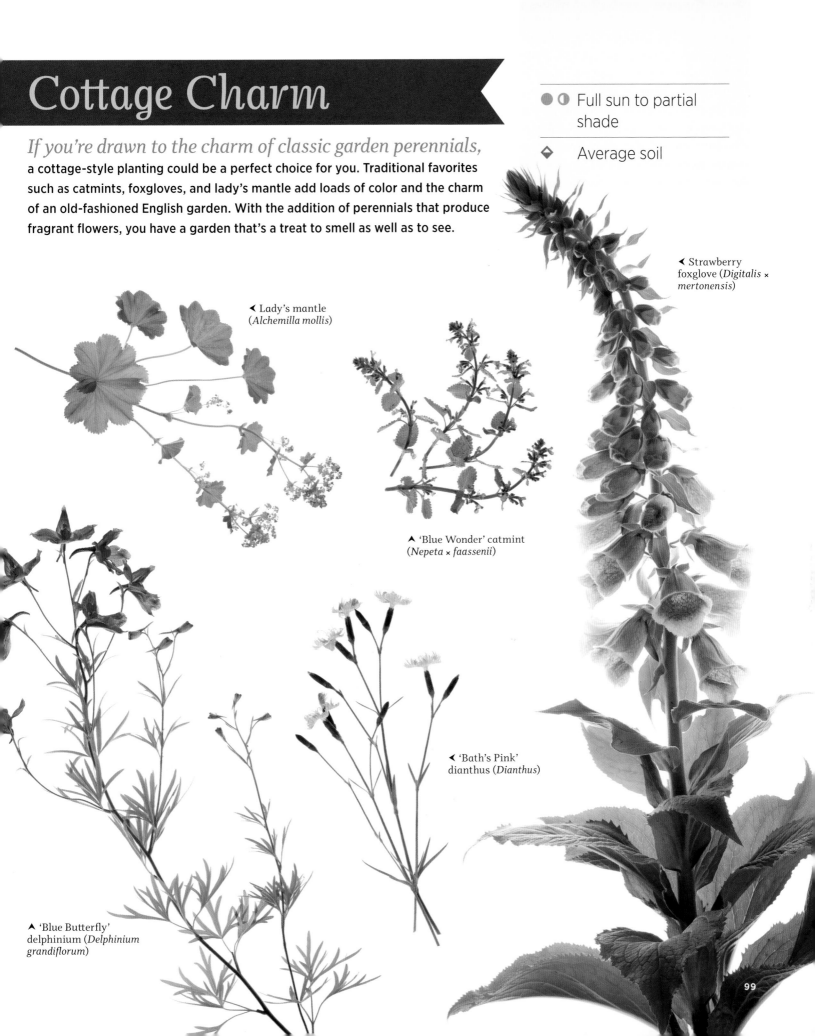

◄ Strawberry foxglove (*Digitalis × mertonensis*)

◄ Lady's mantle (*Alchemilla mollis*)

▲ 'Blue Wonder' catmint (*Nepeta × faassenii*)

◄ 'Bath's Pink' dianthus (*Dianthus*)

▲ 'Blue Butterfly' delphinium (*Delphinium grandiflorum*)

The Garden Plan

Shopping List

❶ 'BLUE WONDER' CATMINT
Nepeta × faassenii | **2 plants**
Zones 4–8
Alternates: Another catmint or other 1- to 2-foot-tall perennial with blue flowers, such as 'Sarastro' bellflower (*Campanula*) [6 plants] or 'Butterfly Blue' pincushion flower (*Scabiosa*) [6 plants]

❷ LADY'S MANTLE
Alchemilla mollis | **2 plants**
Zones 3–9
Alternates: Another 1- to 2-foot-tall perennial with yellow or white flowers, such as 'Moonlight' or other coreopsis (*Coreopsis*) [2 plants] or 'Susanna Mitchell' marguerite daisy (*Anthemis*) [2 plants]

❸ 'BATH'S PINK' DIANTHUS
Dianthus | **2 plants**
Zones 3–8
Alternates: Another dianthus or other 6- to 18-inch-tall perennial with pink flowers, such as striped bloody cranesbill (*Geranium sanguineum* var. *striatum*) [2 plants] or 'Pink Grapefruit' yarrow (*Achillea*) [2 plants]

❹ STRAWBERRY FOXGLOVE
Digitalis × mertonensis | **3 plants**
Zones 4–9
Alternates: Another foxglove or other 3- to 4-foot-tall perennial with pink, yellow, or white flowers, such as hybrid lupines (*Lupinus*) [3 plants] or meadowsweet (*Filipendula ulmaria*) [3 plants]

❺ 'BLUE BUTTERFLY' DELPHINIUM
Delphinium grandiflorum | **3 plants**
Zones 3–7
Alternates: Another dwarf delphinium or other 18- to 36-inch-tall perennial with pink or blue flowers, such as a Siberian iris (*Iris sibirica*) [3 plants] or a Japanese anemone (*Anemone × hybrida*) [3 plants]

Planting Plan

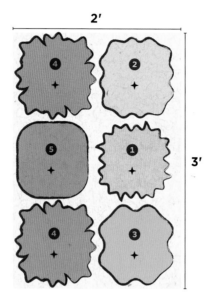
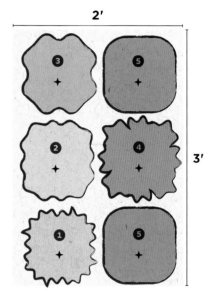

Season by Season

Spring: Excitement builds gradually through the spring in this simple cottage garden, but it comes into full glory by late spring, with the airy purple-blue spikes of 'Blue Wonder' catmint, the greenish yellow clouds of lady's mantle, and the fragrant, light pink blooms of 'Bath's Pink' dianthus.

Plan on doing a bit of cleanup in early to mid spring to get ready for this late-spring spectacle. Cut off any remaining dead top growth on the catmint and delphinium, and trim away any winter-damaged parts on the lady's mantle, dianthus, and foxglove. This is also a fine time to divide the catmint, lady's mantle, and dianthus if they were outgrowing their spaces last year. Then, apply a fresh layer of organic mulch over the soil.

Summer: The extravaganza of color and fragrance continues into early summer, with the addition of strawberry foxglove's rosy pink bells and the brilliant blue flowers of 'Blue Butterfly' delphinium. The catmint, lady's mantle, and dianthus are pretty much done by the end of early summer, but the foxglove and delphinium often continue into midsummer.

Once the flowers are finished, remove them to tidy the plants. On the catmint, shearing the whole plant back by one-half to two-thirds will remove the old blooms and promote bushy new growth. Cutting all of the top growth back to about 2 inches will have the same effect on the lady's mantle. On the dianthus, clip off individual flower stems or shear them off all at once, down to the leaves. Trim off the delphinium's flowering tops back to the uppermost leaf on the stem, and cut off the foxglove's flowering stems close to the base of the plant.

Fall and Winter: Late-season interest in this garden comes mostly from the foliage — especially the velvety, scalloped-edged leaves of the lady's mantle and the spiky, gray-green carpets of the dianthus — but there may also be some scattered fall flowers on the catmint, lady's mantle, dianthus, and delphinium until frost.

Keep clipping off the dead flowers on the late bloomers through autumn. In early to mid fall, divide the catmint and lady's mantle clumps if they are crowding their companions. After frost, clip off the old delphinium stems close to the base of the plant, but leave the rest of the perennials alone until spring cleanup.

Digging Deeper

THERE ARE LOTS OF WAYS YOU COULD ENJOY this simple plan in your yard. Tuck just one of the beds into a corner, or use the two beds to flank a bench, arbor, doorway, or set of steps. They'd also be lovely for edging a longer path; simply repeat the plans end to end as many times as needed to extend all along the length of the path, replacing some of the plants with their suggested alternates to add some variety.

Herbs have long been a part of cottage gardens, and this one includes two herbs that are also well known as flowering perennials: catmints (*Nepeta*) and lady's mantle (*Alchemilla mollis*). Some other perennials that do double-duty as herbs include bee balms (*Monarda*), purple coneflower (*Echinacea purpurea*), hyssops (*Agastache* and *Hyssopus*), and yarrows (*Achillea*). If you'd like to incorporate flowering herbs that you could harvest for cooking as well, consider culinary sage (*Salvia officinalis*), oreganos (*Origanum*), and thymes (*Thymus*).

The towering spires of hybrid delphiniums are a common part of classic cottage gardens, but growing those English-garden favorites successfully can be a challenge unless you live in an area with relatively cool summers. Chinese delphiniums (*Delphinium grandiflorum*), such as 'Blue Butterfly' tend to be shorter than the hybrids, but they also tend to be more heat-tolerant. Any of these delphiniums may be very short-lived in less-than-ideal climates, so plan on replacing them every year or two and you won't be disappointed.

Five-Plant Gardens

for Partial to Full Shade

Just White for Shade

White shines in the shade, brightening the gloom and catching your eye without being unpleasantly glaring, as it can be in full-sun gardens. Lots of shade-loving perennials have white flowers, so you have plenty of options to choose from. Don't forget to add some variegated foliage, too: green or blue leaves that are spotted, edged, or striped with white add interest all season long while the flowers come and go.

◄ 'Niveum' barrenwort (*Epimedium* × *youngianum*)

▲ Foamflower (*Tiarella wherryi*)

▲ Variegated Solomon's seal (*Polygonatum odoratum* 'Variegatum')

▲ 'Bridal Veil' astilbe (*Astilbe*)

➤ 'Patriot' hosta (*Hosta*)

The Garden Plan

Shopping List

❶ 'BRIDAL VEIL' ASTILBE
Astilbe | **5 plants**
Zones 4–9
Alternates: 'Deutschland' or other white
astilbe, or another 2- to 4-foot-tall, shade-
tolerant perennial with white flowers, such as
'White Pearl' bugbane (*Cimicifuga*) [3 plants]
or 'White Towers' toad lily (*Tricyrtis*) [5 plants]

❷ 'PATRIOT' HOSTA
Hosta | **1 plant**
Zones 3–9
Alternates: Another 18- to 30-inch-tall hosta
or other broad-leaved, shade-tolerant perennial
with white-and-green, gray-blue, or silvery
leaves, such as variegated Siberian bugloss
(*Brunnera macrophylla* 'Variegata') [1 plant]

❸ VARIEGATED SOLOMON'S SEAL
Polygonatum odoratum 'Variegatum' |
1 plant
Zones 4–8
Alternates: Another 1- to 2-foot-tall, shade-
tolerant perennial with white-and-green or
silver-and-green leaves, such as 'Stairway to
Heaven' or 'Touch of Class' creeping Jacob's
ladder (*Polemonium reptans*) [1 plant] or
'Sissinghurst White' lungwort (*Pulmonaria*)
[1 plant]

❹ 'NIVEUM' BARRENWORT
Epimedium × youngianum | **9 plants**
Zones 4–8
Alternates: Another 6- to 12-inch-tall, shade-
tolerant perennial with white flowers, such
as 'Fuller's White' woodland phlox (*Phlox
divaricata*) [9 plants] or 'Bruce's White' creeping
phlox (*Phlox stolonifera*) [9 plants]

❺ FOAMFLOWER
Tiarella wherryi | **9 plants**
Zones 4–9
Alternates: Another foamflower or other
6- to 12-inch-tall, shade-tolerant perennial
with white flowers, such as white crested iris
(*Iris cristata* 'Alba') [9 plants] or 'Ivory Hearts'
dwarf bleeding heart (*Dicentra*) [9 plants]

Planting Plan

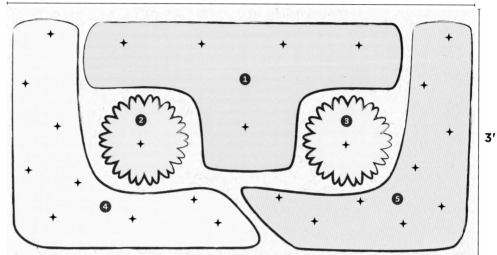

Season by Season

Spring: Spring tends to be prime bloom time in shady gardens, and this one is no exception, with 'Niveum' barrenwort and foamflower usually starting their show of white blossoms in mid spring. The other perennials are coming up now, too: the lacy, light green leaves of 'Bridal Veil' astilbe with the plump, pinkish shoots of variegated Solomon's seal, and, finally, the stout 'Patriot' hosta shoots. The Solomon's seal sprouts up quickly, so it too is in bloom by late spring, though you may not notice the small white bells because they're mostly hidden by the leaves.

If any of the plants were getting too crowded last year and you didn't have time to divide them last fall, early spring — just as the new growth appears — is a fine time to dig up and divide them. This is also a good time to cut off any remaining dead leaves and stems. Applying an organic mulch at some point during the spring (being careful not to mound it over the emerging sprouts) gives a tidy setting for the showy blooms and gets your white garden off to a good start for the growing season.

Summer: 'Niveum' barrenwort is finished flowering by early summer, but there is still plenty to look forward to, as the green-and-white 'Patriot' hosta leaves unfurl and expand and the plumy white 'Bridal Veil' astilbe blooms in early to midsummer. The foamflower's main flush of bloom usually finishes in early summer, but it often sends up scattered flower spikes through the summer. The cream- to white-striped leaves of variegated Solomon's seal are a dependable presence through the summer months, and so are those of the hosta. 'Patriot' hosta also produces pale purple flowers in midsummer; leave them on or trim them off, as you like.

Snip off the bloom stalks of the foamflower and the hosta after the blossoms have dropped off, if you want to tidy the plants. Do the same for the astilbe plumes, if desired. Otherwise, this garden needs little summer care, other than occasional watering during extended dry spells.

Fall and Winter: Leaves provide most of the autumn color in your white garden. 'Patriot' hosta and variegated Solomon's seal stay green-and-white into fall, eventually turning yellow and then withering away for the winter. Foamflower leaves take on a reddish tinge in fall and often remain through the winter. (The foamflower plants may send up some late-season blooms, as well.) The leaves of 'Niveum' barrenwort also turn red in fall. If you didn't cut off the 'Bridal Veil' astilbe seed heads, you'll have them for fall and winter interest.

Early to mid fall is a good time to lift and divide plants that are getting too big for their space. Clip off the dead tops of the hosta and Solomon's seal any time or leave them until spring. Wait until late winter or early spring to cut down the dead top growth of the astilbe.

Digging Deeper

PLANNED AS A BORDER, with taller plants at the back, this rectangular garden would work well as a foundation planting or against a fence or wall. If you want to expand it, repeat it end to end as many times as needed to fill the available space; keep the plants the same in each repetition, or incorporate some of the alternate plants to mix things up a bit.

If you'd like additional color for spring, add some white-flowered spring bulbs in fall. Tuck snowdrops (*Galanthus*) or white crocuses (*Crocus*) around the clumps of 'Bridal Veil' astilbe (*Astilbe*), and maybe some white daffodils (*Narcissus*), such as 'Ice Wings', around the 'Patriot' hosta (*Hosta*). The bulbs will bloom early, and then the emerging perennials will cover up their yellowing leaves by early summer.

Want a bit more than just white? Replace the white-and-green foliage with silvery, gray, or blue leaves for an equally elegant effect. Blue or yellow flowers add a bit of zip to mostly white gardens.

Silver Celebration

Plants need a lot of energy to produce flowers, so where sunlight is lacking, their blooms tend to be sparse, too. That doesn't mean you can't have a pretty perennial garden in the shade, though: just look to perennials that have showy leaves for color you can count on from spring to frost. Plants with silvery, gray, or powder-blue foliage are especially good for adding the illusion of light to shady spaces.

❯ Lamb's ears (*Stachys byzantina*)

❯ 'Jack Frost' Siberian bugloss (*Brunnera macrophylla*)

❯ Japanese painted fern (*Athyrium niponicum* var. *pictum*)

❯ 'Krossa Regal' hosta (*Hosta*)

❯ 'White Nancy' spotted deadnettle (*Lamium maculatum*)

107

The Garden Plan

Shopping List

❶ 'KROSSA REGAL' HOSTA
Hosta | 1 plant
Zones 3–8
Alternates: 'Big Daddy', 'Blue Angel', or
another 2- to 3-foot-tall hosta with blue leaves
or other shade-tolerant perennial with deep
green leaves, such as bearsfoot hellebore
(*Helleborus foetidus*) [1 plant]

**❷ 'JACK FROST' SIBERIAN
BUGLOSS**
Brunnera macrophylla | 2 plants
Zones 3–8
Alternates: 'Langtrees' or 'Looking Glass'
Siberian bugloss, or another 1- to 2-foot-tall,
broad-leaved, shade-tolerant perennial with
silver or silver-spotted leaves, such as 'Mrs.
Moon' or other lungwort (*Pulmonaria*) [6 plants]

❸ JAPANESE PAINTED FERN
Athyrium niponicum var. *pictum* | 2 plants
Zones 4–9
Alternates: 'Ghost', 'Ursula's Red', or another
silver-gray painted fern, or another 1- to 3-foot-
tall, shade-tolerant perennial with lacy or grassy
blue or white-striped leaves, such as 'River Mist'
sea oats (*Chasmanthium latifolium*) [2 plants] or
'Ice Dance' sedge (*Carex*) [2 plants]

**❹ 'WHITE NANCY' SPOTTED
DEADNETTLE**
Lamium maculatum | 6 plants
Zones 3–8
Alternates: Another 9- to 18-inch-tall, shade-
tolerant perennial with silver-and-green leaves,
such as 'Dale's Strain' heuchera (*Heuchera
americana*) [6 plants] or 'Hermann's Pride'
yellow archangel (*Lamiastrum galeobdolon*)
[6 plants]

❺ LAMB'S EARS
Stachys byzantina | 3 plants
Zones 4–8
Alternates: Another 4- to 8-inch-tall, shade-
tolerant perennial with silver or green-and-
silver leaves, such as 'Callaway' mottled wild
ginger (*Asarum shuttleworthii*) [9 plants] or
'Sylettas' violet (*Viola koreana*) [9 plants]

Planting Plan

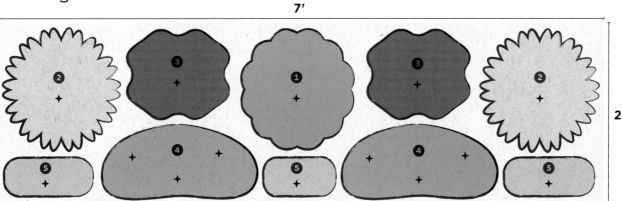

7'

2'

Season by Season

Spring: Planning a perennial garden around plants with attractive leaves doesn't mean you won't get any flowers at all. 'Jack Frost' Siberian bugloss kicks off the season in early to mid spring with sprays of dainty blue blooms, looking much like a super-sized version of forget-me-nots (*Myosotis*). The white flowers of 'White Nancy' spotted deadnettle start a few weeks later, once its silvery leaves have begun to expand. By late spring, the fern and lamb's ears are filling out, too, followed by the 'Krossa Regal' hosta.

In early to mid spring, clean up any debris left from last year; then dig up and divide any too-large perennials that you didn't take care of in the fall. Apply a fresh layer of organic mulch around the plants.

Summer: 'Jack Frost' Siberian bugloss usually finishes blooming in late spring, but the 'White Nancy' spotted deadnettle continues into summer. Lamb's ears and 'Krossa Regal' hosta also flower in summer: the first has fuzzy spikes of tiny pinkish blossoms, and the other has pale purple trumpets. As the flowers come and go, the Japanese painted fern, as well as the leaves of the other perennials, are at their lush and lovely best.

Summer maintenance is minimal, other than watering during extended dry spells. If you like the flowers of the lamb's ears and hostas, wait until the blossoms drop off before trimming off the bloom stalks; if you decide you don't care for them, it's fine to cut them off as soon as they appear.

Fall and Winter: Apart from a few scattered blooms on the 'White Nancy' spotted deadnettle, it's the leaves that keep your silver garden shining into fall, at least. Heavy frost will zap the 'Krossa Regal' hosta and Japanese painted fern, but the other plants in the garden can be quite tough and may continue to look good for a few more weeks.

If any of the perennials have outgrown their space, early to mid fall is a good time to dig up and divide them. Trim off the dead or cold-damaged leaves in late fall, or leave that job until late winter or early spring.

Digging Deeper

THIS SIMPLE SILVER GARDEN needs only the most minimal maintenance: mainly just a yearly mulching and cleanup. Spotted deadnettle and lamb's ears can spread at a good clip in moist, fertile soil, so you may need to divide them every other year to keep them in check. The other perennials in this garden can stay in place for many years without division.

This rectangular bed is planned as an edging for one or both sides of a path, but you could also use it as a narrow border along a fence or wall, with the larger plants along the back. To fill a longer space, repeat the plan end to end, overlapping the Siberian bugloss (*Brunnera macrophylla*) and lamb's ears (*Stachys byzantina*) each time so the hosta-fern-bugloss pattern alternates along the length of the extended planting. It's also easy to wrap this narrow rectangle around a corner in the same way.

Solid silver, silver-and-green, gray, and powder-blue leaves are all fair game for silver gardens, but they're not your only options. Dark green and deep purple to near black foliage can add welcome contrast to pale-leaved partners and give your silver planting even more visual impact.

Blue or white flowers are perfect complements for silvery leaves, and pale pinks and yellows can add a nice touch, too. If you want to spice things up a bit, choose richer flower colors instead, such as bright reds or hot pinks.

Thinking Pink

Perennials that bloom in pastel pinks are tailor-made for the shade, because bright but mostly indirect light keeps their delicate tints from fading. Plus, pink flowers have enough white to make them pop in places where rich reds would blend right into the background. Luckily, there are loads of pink-flowered perennials that thrive in shady sites, so it's easy to create a great-looking garden with them in almost any sort of shade.

‹ 'Luxuriant' dwarf bleeding heart (*Dicentra*)

∨ 'Bressingham Beauty' astilbe (*Astilbe*)

∧ 'Pink Pewter' spotted deadnettle (*Lamium maculatum*)

∧ 'September Charm' anemone (*Anemone* × *hybrida*)

‹ Common bleeding heart (*Dicentra spectabilis*)

The Garden Plan

Shopping List

❶ 'BRESSINGHAM BEAUTY' ASTILBE
Astilbe | **6 plants**
Zones 4–9
Alternates: 'Rheinland', Oꜱᴛʀɪᴄʜ Pʟᴜᴍᴇ ('Straussenfeder') or another pink astilbe or other 2- to 3-foot-tall, shade-tolerant perennial with pink flowers, such as strawberry foxglove (*Digitalis × mertonensis*) [6 plants] or pink turtlehead (*Chelone lyonii*) [6 plants]

❷ 'SEPTEMBER CHARM' ANEMONE
Anemone × hybrida | **3 plants**
Zones 4–8
Alternates: Another pink anemone or other 1- to 3-foot-tall, shade-tolerant perennial with pink flowers, such as hardy begonia (*Begonia grandis*) [3 plants] or 'Rosalie' heucherella (*× Heucherella*) [3 plants]

❸ COMMON BLEEDING HEART
Dicentra spectabilis | **1 plant**
Zones 3–9
Alternates: Another 2- to 4-foot-tall, shade-tolerant perennial with pink flowers, such as 'Pink Profusion' Bowman's root (*Gillenia trifoliata*) [3 plants] or 'Pink Spire' bugbane (*Cimicifuga*) [1 plant]

❹ 'PINK PEWTER' SPOTTED DEADNETTLE
Lamium maculatum | **3 plants**
Zones 3–8
Alternates: Another 6- to 12-inch-tall, shade-tolerant perennial with pink flowers, such as 'Raspberry Splash' lungwort (*Pulmonaria*) [3 plants] or dwarf fleeceflower (*Persicaria affinis*) [3 plants]

❺ 'LUXURIANT' DWARF BLEEDING HEART
Dicentra | **6 plants**
Zones 3–8
Alternates: Another dwarf bleeding heart or other 12- to 18-inch-tall, shade-tolerant perennial with pink flowers, such as 'Winky Double Rose-White' columbine (*Aquilegia*) [6 plants] or bigroot geranium (*Geranium macrorrhizum*) [6 plants]

Planting Plan

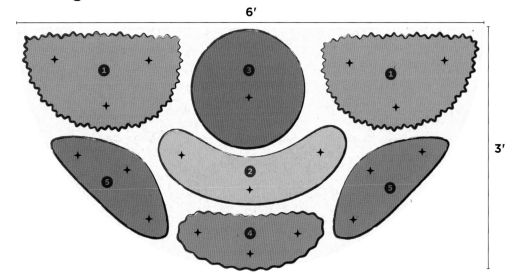

Season by Season

Spring: Excitement builds slowly through the spring in this pink planting, as the perennials begin to poke up and unfurl their leaves. By mid to late spring, though, there's no doubting the theme, when the 'Pink Pewter' spotted deadnettle and the bleeding hearts display their pink blossoms. By this time, you'll also be enjoying the bleeding hearts' ferny foliage, the lacy leaves of the emerging 'Bressingham Beauty' astilbe, and the silvery carpet created by the spotted deadnettle. Like other fall-flowering anemones, 'September Charm' may be late to appear, so don't worry if it doesn't even send up its shoots until its companions are in full flower.

Early to mid spring is a good time to clean up any dead or damaged leaves left from last year and give the whole garden a fresh layer of organic mulch. It's also the ideal time to dig up and divide the anemone, if it's starting to crowd out its companions. You could also divide the others now, if you didn't get to it last fall, but try to get the job done as quickly as possible so they'll have time to get settled in again before bloom time.

Summer: Common bleeding heart usually winds up its display by early summer, but 'Luxuriant' dwarf bleeding heart continues for a few more weeks, at least; in fact, it may continue to send up new flowers through the summer where the weather doesn't get too hot or the soil doesn't dry out. 'Pink Pewter' spotted deadnettle, too, slows down for summer, but by midsummer, 'Bressingham Beauty' astilbe comes into its full glory for the season.

Water your pink garden during dry spells, especially for the first few years, and trim off the astilbe plumes once the flowers are finished, if you don't like the seed heads. Other than that, this simple garden shouldn't need much attention to stay attractive through the summer.

Fall and Winter: As the weather cools off, 'Luxuriant' dwarf bleeding heart and 'Pink Pewter' spotted deadnettle may send up some additional blooms. The real star of the season, though, is the 'September Charm' anemone. By this time, it has pretty much covered up the common bleeding heart behind it — that's fine, because the bleeding heart probably looks pretty tattered by now — and is filled with flowers in early to mid fall. (Keep in mind that it may take a while for the anemone to settle in, so don't be too disappointed if you don't get flowers for the first year or two.)

Early to mid fall is an ideal time to dig up and divide any of your pink perennials that have overgrown their places (except for the anemone; don't disturb it until spring). Clean up any dead stems and leaves in mid to late fall, if you wish, or leave them in place to serve as a winter mulch.

Digging Deeper

APART FROM THE YEARLY MULCHING AND CLEANUP, the main thing you'll need to do is divide the perennials as they outgrow their places. The spotted deadnettle and anemone can spread quickly in ideal conditions, so you may have to divide them every 2 to 3 years. The rest probably will need division only every 3 to 5 years.

With the taller plants at back and short ones toward the front, this half-circle plan is meant as a border to fit against a wall or fence, but there are also ways to adapt or expand it. You could, for example, flip it over to create a circular planting, with a bird bath or ornament in the center for a bit of extra height. Or extend two narrow, rectangular borders (such as the "Silver Celebration" plan) from the straight side, with a path in between, to create a U-shaped, walk-in garden.

Where summers are hot, both full-sized and dwarf bleeding hearts (*Dicentra*) may die back to the ground by midsummer, especially if the soil is dry, too. Consider using some of the suggested alternate plants here instead to avoid having bare spaces in your summer border.

A Study in Blue

◑ ◯ Partial to full shade

◆ Average soil

Blue flowers are a favorite with many gardeners, and there are loads of them to choose from for shady yards. The only problem is that blue flowers tend to blend into the background of green leaves, so they can be hard to see from a distance. The trick to using them effectively is to keep them at close range — right next to a well-used path, by your favorite garden bench, or against your deck or patio.

˅ 'Stairway to Heaven' creeping Jacob's ladder (*Polemonium reptans*)

˄ Blue lobelia (*Lobelia siphilitica*)

˅ 'Fragrant Blue' hosta (*Hosta*)

❯ 'Burgundy Glow' ajuga (*Ajuga reptans*)

❯ 'Pewter Lace' Japanese painted fern (*Athyrium niponicum* var. *pictum*)

113

The Garden Plan

Shopping List

❶ 'FRAGRANT BLUE' HOSTA
Hosta | 1 plant
Zones 3–8
Alternates: 'Hadspen Blue', 'Halcyon', or other hosta with blue leaves, or another 18- to 36-inch-tall shade-tolerant perennial with blue or silvery leaves or blue flowers, such as 'Looking Glass' Siberian bugloss (*Brunnera macrophylla*) [1 plant]

❷ 'STAIRWAY TO HEAVEN' CREEPING JACOB'S LADDER
Polemonium reptans | 3 plants
Zones 3–8
Alternates: 'Touch of Class' or other Jacob's ladder or another 9- to 24-inch-tall, shade-tolerant perennial with blue flowers, such as a columbine (*Aquilegia*) [3 plants] or forget-me-not (*Myosotis sylvatica*) [5 plants]

❸ BLUE LOBELIA
Lobelia siphilitica | 6 plants
Zones 3–8
Alternates: Another 18- to 48-inch-tall, shade-tolerant perennial with blue flowers, such as monkshood (*Aconitum napellus*) [6 plants] or 'Zwanenburg Blue' spiderwort (*Tradescantia*) [2 plants]

❹ 'PEWTER LACE' JAPANESE PAINTED FERN
Athyrium niponicum var. *pictum* | 3 plants
Zones 4–9
Alternates: Another Japanese painted fern or other 12- to 18-inch-tall, shade-tolerant perennial with silvery leaves and/or blue flowers, such as a lungwort (*Pulmonaria*) [3 plants]

❺ 'BURGUNDY GLOW' AJUGA
Ajuga reptans | 2 plants
Zones 3–9
Alternates: Another 6- to 9-inch-tall, shade-tolerant perennial with blue flowers, such as woodland phlox (*Phlox divaricata*) [2 plants] or crested iris (*Iris cristata*) [6 plants]

Planting Plan

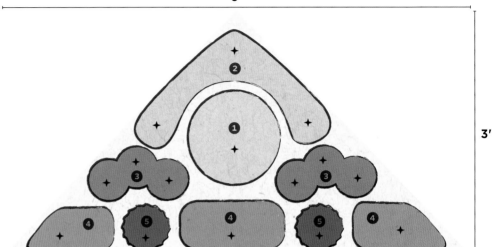

Season by Season

Spring: The blues come along gradually in this garden, starting with the lightly scented, light blue flowers of 'Stairway to Heaven' creeping Jacob's ladder and the more intense purple-blue spikes of 'Burgundy Glow' ajuga, usually in mid to late spring. These two perennials also bear showy green-and-white leaves that are heavily blushed with pink, contributing extra touches of color. The other perennials eventually come along, too, usually sprouting foliage in mid to late spring.

Get your blue garden off to a good start in early to mid spring by cutting down any remaining top growth. This is also a fine time to divide the hosta, Japanese painted fern, and blue lobelia clumps if you noticed that they were getting too big for their allotted spaces last year. Finish up by spreading a fresh layer of mulch over the soil.

Summer: 'Burgundy Glow' ajuga is generally done flowering by early summer, but 'Stairway to Heaven' creeping Jacob's ladder continues for a few more weeks, at least. The foliage of both loses its pink tinge but is still a showy combo of white and green through the summer. 'Fragrant Blue' hosta is splendid now, too, with lightly scented, pale lavender trumpets mostly in midsummer and broad, powder blue to blue-green leaves through the summer. The showy spikes of blue lobelia come along in mid to late summer. And through the whole season, the ghostly silver-gray fronds of 'Pewter Lace' Japanese painted fern provide a cool complement to all of the beautiful blues.

A bit of trimming helps to keep the garden tidy through the summer months. When their flowers are finished, clip off the ajuga spikes at their base, the hosta and Jacob's ladder bloom stalks at their base, and the blue lobelia spikes just above the main leafy part of the stem. To keep the plants looking fresh, water your garden during extended summer dry spells.

Fall and Winter: Fall blue comes mostly from the lingering blooms of blue lobelia and the leaves of the 'Fragrant Blue' hosta, with added color and textural interest from the pale fronds of the Japanese painted ferns and the pink-tinged, variegated leaves of 'Burgundy Glow' ajuga and 'Stairway to Heaven' creeping Jacob's ladder.

Early to mid fall is the time to divide any clumps that are starting to crowd out their companions. Otherwise, you can leave cleanup chores until spring: frost will kill the fern and hosta foliage, but the other perennials generally look respectable through at least part of the winter.

Digging Deeper

A THREE-SIDED PLAN like this one is an obvious choice for filling a corner formed where walls, hedges, fences, or other structures meet. Another option is to flip and repeat the plan along one of the short sides, leaving space between the two parts for an arbor, bench, or path.

When you think of a "blue garden," flowers are the obvious place to start. (To be honest, not many blooms are true blue; most are some tint or shade of purple-blue, but that doesn't make them any less beautiful.) Then, look to leaves to carry through the theme. True blue isn't a feature you'll find in foliage, but there are a variety of choices with gray-blue to blue-green leaves, and from there, it's an easy step to see how all-gray to silvery leaves look great with blue flowers. All of these soft colors are lovely, but if you want to give a blue garden a bit of zip, mix in a few white flowers and white-marked leaves as accents.

"Blue" hostas (*Hosta*) may not have the rich hues of blue flowers, but they're among some of the most stunning foliage plants for the shade garden. Their leaves are actually green, but they have a waxy coating that gives them a blue appearance. (The thicker the wax, the more blue they are.) Strong sun can actually melt off this coating and spoil the beautiful blue look, so it's important to give blue-leaved hostas a site with only morning sun or light to moderate, all-day shade. Touching the leaves can also remove the wax, so avoid handling the leaves as much as possible.

Say Hello to Yellow

Yellow flowers are a cheery addition to any garden, but they're especially welcome in shady places, because their light color makes them so easy to see. You can also enjoy the brightness of yellow in perennial leaves: those that are a solid yellow as well as those that are green and showily striped, edged, or spotted with yellow. There are so many options that you could easily add *too much* yellow, so don't forget to keep some greens, at least, for contrast.

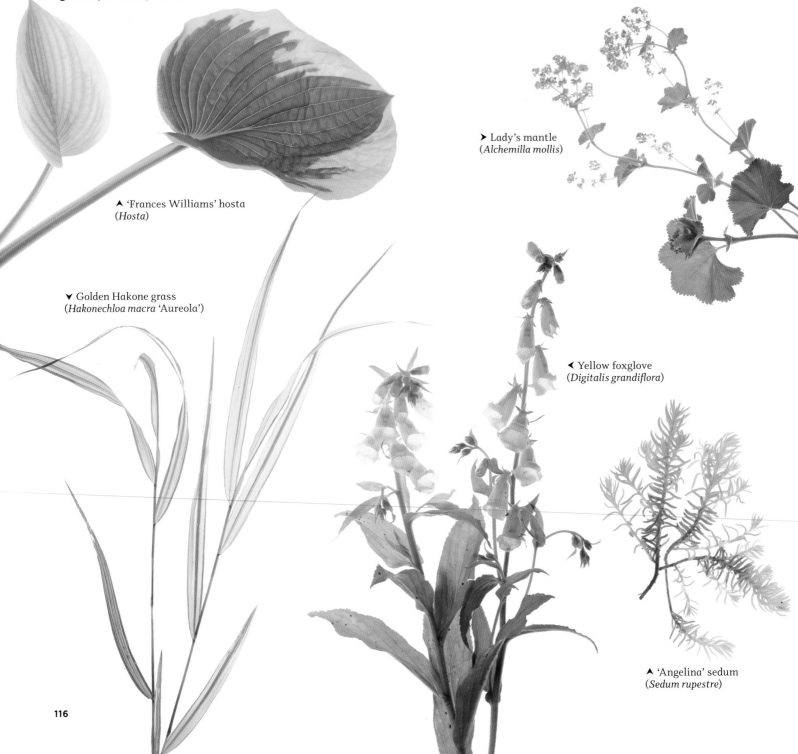

▲ 'Frances Williams' hosta
(*Hosta*)

➤ Lady's mantle
(*Alchemilla mollis*)

▼ Golden Hakone grass
(*Hakonechloa macra* 'Aureola')

◀ Yellow foxglove
(*Digitalis grandiflora*)

▲ 'Angelina' sedum
(*Sedum rupestre*)

Shopping List

❶'FRANCES WILLIAMS' HOSTA
Hosta | **1 plant**
Zones 3–8
Alternates: 'Gold Standard', 'Paul's Glory', 'Sum and Substance', or another 2- to 3-foot-tall hosta or other shade-tolerant perennial with solid yellow, yellow-and-blue, or yellow-and-green leaves or yellow flowers, such as yellow wax bells (*Kirengeshoma palmata*) [3 plants]

❷ GOLDEN HAKONE GRASS
Hakonechloa macra 'Aureola' | **5 plants**
Zones 5–9
Alternates: 'All Gold' Hakone grass or another 1- to 2-foot-tall, shade-tolerant perennial with slender, solid yellow or yellow-and-green leaves, such as 'Sweet Kate' spiderwort (*Tradescantia*) [5 plants] or Bowles' golden sedge (*Carex elata* 'Aurea') [5 plants]

❸ YELLOW FOXGLOVE
Digitalis grandiflora | **3 plants**
Zones 4–8
Alternates: Another yellow-flowered foxglove, such as *Digitalis lutea,* or another 2- to 3-foot-tall, shade-tolerant perennial with yellow flowers, such as 'Denver Gold' columbine (*Aquilegia chrysantha*) [3 plants], 'Lemon Queen' globeflower (*Trollius* × *cultorum*) [3 plants], or merrybells (*Uvularia grandiflora*) [3 plants]

❹ LADY'S MANTLE
Alchemilla mollis | **6 plants**
Zones 3–9
Alternates: Another 12- to 18-inch-tall, shade-tolerant perennial with yellow flowers or yellow-and-green or yellow-and-blue leaves, such as a yellow barrenwort (*Epimedium* × *versicolor*) [6 plants] or 'June', 'Touch of Class', or another compact hosta (*Hosta*) [6 plants]

❺ 'ANGELINA' SEDUM
Sedum rupestre | **5 plants**
Zones 3–8
Alternates: Another 6- to 9-inch-tall, shade-tolerant perennial with yellow leaves and/or flowers, such as golden creeping Jenny (*Lysimachia nummularia* 'Aurea') [5 plants] or green-and-gold (*Chrysogonum virginianum*) [5 plants]

Planting Plan

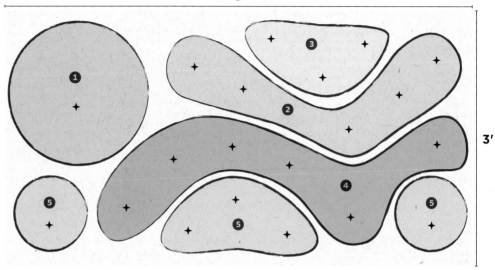

Season by Season

Spring: Sunny yellows abound in this shady spring garden even before flowering begins, with the bright, needlelike leaves of 'Angelina' sedum and the slender yellow sprouts of golden Hakone grass. Lady's mantle, with its frothy greenish-yellow flowers, generally joins the show by late spring, and the spires of yellow foxglove often open then, too.

Early spring is the ideal time to get this garden ready for a season of eye-catching color. Cut down any remaining dead top growth, and clip off any winter-damaged leaves on the lady's mantle and yellow foxglove. If you noticed that the clumps of foxglove, Hakone grass, hosta, or sedum were outgrowing their space last year and you didn't have time to divide them in fall, then divide them now. When you're done, add a fresh layer of organic mulch.

Summer: The fellowship of yellow foxglove and lady's mantle continues in early summer, with the foxglove lingering even into midsummer. The bright yellow-and-green blades of Hakone grass and the broad, heavily textured, yellow-edged blue leaves of the 'Frances Williams' hosta are also around to provide all-summer interest. 'Angelina' sedum produces clusters of yellow summer flowers *and* yellow foliage. (The more shade 'Angelina' gets, the more greenish yellow the leaves will be.) The large, trumpet-shaped flowers of the hosta are white, not yellow, but they're good for adding a bit of variety to the garden in midsummer.

On the foxglove, hosta, lady's mantle, and sedum, clip off the flower stems at the base when the blooms are done. (If you don't want the white flowers of the hosta, feel free to remove the stems before the buds open.) On the foxglove, consider leaving one or two stems in place to produce and drop seeds every few years, so you'll have replacement seedlings available when the original plants die out. Lady's mantle plants can look tired and dull by mid to late summer; if this happens, cut all the leaves back to 2 inches above the ground to get a flush of fresh new foliage for fall. The perennials in this garden can tolerate summer-dry soil to some extent, but it's a good idea to water them during extended dry spells.

Fall and Winter: Lady's mantle and yellow foxgloves occasionally produce some new flowers in fall. Golden Hakone grass flowers then, too, but the airy clusters are golden tan and hardly noticeable against the leaves, which stay bright until cool weather brings out a pinkish blush on them and eventually turns them tan for the winter. 'Frances Williams' hosta sticks around until killed by frost, while 'Angelina' sedum remains through the fall and winter, often taking on orangey hues in ample winter sunlight.

If the hosta, lady's mantle, or sedum is growing out of its allotted space, divide the plants in early to mid fall. For even more yellow next spring, tuck in some golden crocus, daffodils, or other early-flowering bulbs around the hosta clump; they'll bloom and be done by the time the hosta leaves fill out. Other than that, your garden doesn't need further attention until spring.

Digging Deeper

THIS RECTANGULAR PLANTING would work well as a foundation planting against a house or outbuilding. Or, consider using it as a border around a deck, patio, or other sitting area; the plants are low enough that you can still see over them if you're seated, so they'll add beauty without blocking your view. A simple border like this, repeated end to end as many times as needed, is an elegant option for edging a driveway or sidewalk as well.

Most folks think of ornamental grasses only for sunny gardens, but there are some well suited for shade, too, including one of the most beautiful choices for a yellow garden: golden Hakone grass (*Hakonechloa macra* 'Aureola'). The gracefully arching blades are actually green with yellow stripes, but the markings are so bold that the clumps appear just bright yellow from more than a few feet away. There's also a selection with completely yellow leaves, known as 'All Gold'. Both of these are rarely bothered by either pests or diseases, and their slowly expanding clumps seldom need to be divided. In fact, the only maintenance they really need is a yearly trim each spring to remove the old foliage.

Blooms for Shade

There's no rule that says that only sunny gardens get all the great color. With some careful plant choices, you can create a shady perennial planting that rivals the most sun-drenched borders for a pure pop of hot hues. It does help to have a site with at least a few hours of direct sun a day — morning sun and afternoon shade is ideal — but even light, all-day shade can support good growth on an abundance of brightly colored flowering and foliage perennials.

▼ 'Burning Hearts' dwarf bleeding heart (*Dicentra*)

▼ 'Fanal' astilbe (*Astilbe*)

▲ 'Citronelle' heuchera (*Heuchera*)

◄ Wild columbine (*Aquilegia canadensis*)

◄ Cardinal flower (*Lobelia cardinalis*)

119

The Garden Plan

Shopping List

❶ 'FANAL' ASTILBE
Astilbe | 5 plants
Zones 4–9
Alternates: 'Red Sentinel' or other red astilbe
or another 2- to 3-foot-tall, shade-tolerant
perennial with brightly colored flowers, such
as 'Songbird Cardinal' or other columbine
(*Aquilegia*) [5 plants] or 'Britt-Marie Crawford'
or 'Othello' ligularia (*Ligularia dentata*)
[3 plants]

❷ 'CITRONELLE' HEUCHERA
Heuchera | 5 plants
Zones 4–8
Alternates: 'Peach Flambe' or other colored-
leaved heuchera or another 9- to 18-inch-tall,
shade-tolerant perennial with brightly colored
leaves or flowers, such as 'Stoplight' heucherella
(× *Heucherella*) [5 plants] or 'Kabitan' or 'Little
Aurora' hosta (*Hosta*) [5 plants]

❸ WILD COLUMBINE
Aquilegia canadensis | 3 plants
Zones 3–9
Alternates: Another 2- to 3-foot-tall, shade-
tolerant perennial with brightly colored
flowers, such as 'Alexander' yellow loosestrife
(*Lysimachia punctata*) [3 plants]

❹ CARDINAL FLOWER
Lobelia cardinalis | 4 plants
Zones 3–9
Alternates: Another 2- to 3-foot-tall, shade-
tolerant perennial with brightly colored flowers,
such as 'Grape Knee-Hi', 'Ruby Slippers',
or other lobelia (*Lobelia*) [4 plants] or a
globeflower (*Trollius*) [3 plants]

**❺ 'BURNING HEARTS' DWARF
BLEEDING HEART**
Dicentra | 5 plants
Zones 3–8
Alternates: Another 6- to 9-inch-tall, shade-
tolerant perennial with brightly colored flowers,
such as yellow corydalis (*Corydalis lutea*)
[5 plants] or green-and-gold (*Chrysogonum
virginianum*) [5 plants]

Planting Plan

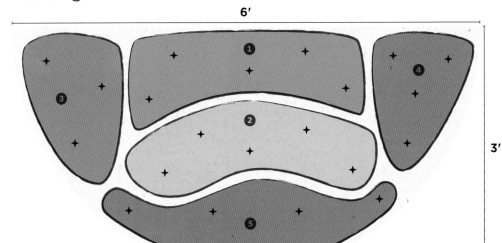

Season by Season

Spring: Start the growing season with a bang of color in mid and late spring: the nodding red-and-yellow blooms of wild columbine, the rosy red hearts of 'Burning Hearts' dwarf bleeding heart, the reddish lacy new shoots of 'Fanal' astilbe, and the broad brilliant yellow leaves of 'Citronelle' heuchera. The cardinal flower is just green leaves now.

Early to mid spring is the ideal time for tackling spring cleanup tasks. Cut down any remaining dead top growth, and clip off any winter-damaged leaves. Every 3 years or so, divide the heuchera clumps to keep them vigorous; also divide the astilbe and cardinal flower now if they were outgrowing their space last year. Top the soil with a fresh layer of organic mulch.

Summer: Wild columbine and 'Burning Hearts' dwarf bleeding hearts keep blooming into early summer, with occasional rebloom later on, too. They're joined by the loose, rosy red plumes of 'Fanal' astilbe, usually at its peak in early summer. Cardinal flower may also begin blooming in early summer, but it's generally at its best in mid to late summer. 'Citronelle' heuchera continues to add a jolt of color all through the summer months, though it may turn more greenish yellow in heavy shade. It also produces loose spikes of tiny, cream-colored flowers, mostly in early to midsummer; they don't add much to the garden, though.

Summer maintenance is mostly a matter of removing flowering parts when the blooms are done. On the columbine, clip off the stalks at the base of the plant; on the cardinal flower, cut them off just above a side shoot or the main leafy part of the stem; and on the astilbe, cut off the browned flower plumes just above the foliage or leave them for fall and winter interest. Clip off the flowering stems of the heuchera as soon as they appear, or wait until the blooms are finished. The dwarf bleeding heart may drop some or all of its lacy, blue-gray leaves if the soil dries out too much but will usually recover if you water thoroughly and regularly during summer dry spells.

Fall and Winter: There's still some lingering color into fall, with some possible rebloom on the cardinal flower and the 'Burning Hearts' dwarf bleeding heart. The yellow leaves of 'Citronelle' heuchera and bronzy astilbe seed heads continue to add interest through fall and into winter — even all winter long in mild-winter areas.

There's not much late-season maintenance to do here. Keep snipping off the finished flower spikes on the cardinal flower, except possibly leaving one or two to drop seeds so you get seedlings to replace the original plants if they die out. (If you go that route, hold off on mulching around the base of your lobelia plants next spring so you don't smother the tiny emerging seedlings.) Leave any remaining top growth on these perennials for the winter.

Digging Deeper

THIS GARDEN IS PLANNED AS A BORDER, with the taller plants at back and short plants at the front, making it well suited to fit against a wall, fence, or other vertical surface. The plants are short enough to see over if you're sitting down, though, so you could just as easily enjoy it as an edging for a deck, porch, or patio. Other options include flipping the plan along its straight side and joining the two parts to create a circular bed or else separating them with a path. Accenting the double-sized planting with a brightly painted bench, arbor, or ornament is a great way to add extra color to the perennial planting all year round.

If you'd like to shift the biggest show of color in this garden from spring to later in the season, consider replacing the wild columbine (*Aquilegia canadensis*) or 'Burning Hearts' dwarf bleeding heart (*Dicentra*) with bright red, orange, or yellow-flowered, shade-tolerant annuals, such as 6- to 10-inch-tall 'Super Elfin Red' or 1- to 2-foot-tall 'Jungle Gold' impatiens (*Impatiens*), 8- to 12-inch-tall 'Prelude Scarlet' wax begonias (*Begonia*), or 6- to 12-inch-tall Non-Stop Series tuberous begonias.

Classic bleeding heart (*Dicentra spectabilis*), with its heart-shaped pink blooms, is a favorite perennial with many gardeners, who just wish it would flower for more than a few weeks each spring. Happily, it's possible to enjoy a somewhat similar, though scaled-down, effect with dwarf bleeding heart species (*D. eximia* and *D. formosa*) and hybrids. These little beauties are typically at their peak in late spring and early summer, often with scattered rebloom through the rest of the growing season.

Pretty Pastels

Pastel-colored flowers — baby blues, pale pinks, lovely lilacs, and mellow yellows — are positively made for the shade. Their light faces stand out well against the gloom, adding welcome bits of brightness all through the growing season. With the addition of some white-marked leaves for extra zip and rich green leaves for contrast, you have all the ingredients for a shade garden that is sure to please.

‹ 'Stairway to Heaven' creeping Jacob's ladder (*Polemonium reptans*)

▲ 'Biokovo' hardy geranium (*Geranium* × *cantabrigiense*)

▾ Dwarf Chinese astilbe (*Astilbe chinensis* var. *pumila*)

▲ 'Etain' viola (*Viola*)

‹ 'Camelot Rose' foxglove (*Digitalis*)

Shopping List

❶ 'CAMELOT ROSE' FOXGLOVE
Digitalis | **3 plants**
Zones 4–8
Alternates: Another foxglove or other 30- to 48-inch-tall, shade-tolerant perennial with pastel-colored flowers, such as common bleeding heart (*Dicentra spectabilis*) [1 plant] or 'Sinonome' toad lily (*Tricyrtis*) [3 plants]

❷ 'STAIRWAY TO HEAVEN' CREEPING JACOB'S LADDER
Polemonium reptans | **3 plants**
Zones 3–8
Alternates: 'Touch of Class' creeping Jacob's ladder or another 1- to 2-foot-tall, shade-tolerant perennial with pastel-colored flowers or leaves, such as 'Blue Mouse Ears' hosta (*Hosta*) [3 plants] or 'Mrs. Moon' lungwort (*Pulmonaria*) [3 plants]

❸ 'BIOKOVO' HARDY GERANIUM
Geranium × cantabrigiense | **1 plant**
Zones 4–8
Alternates: Another 6- to 12-inch-tall, shade-tolerant perennial with pastel-colored flowers, such as a dwarf bleeding heart (*Dicentra*) [1 plant] or 'Sugar and Spice' or other foamflower (*Tiarella*) [1 plant]

❹ DWARF CHINESE ASTILBE
Astilbe chinensis var. *pumila* | **4 plants**
Zones 4–8
Alternates: 'Lilliput', 'Sprite', or other dwarf astilbe or another 6- to 12-inch-tall, shade-tolerant perennial with pastel-colored flowers, such as 'Purple Torch' ajuga (*Ajuga reptans*) [4 plants] or 'Cameo Mix' fan columbine (*Aquilegia flabellata*) [4 plants]

❺ 'ETAIN' VIOLA
Viola | **4 plants**
Zones 4–8
Alternates: Another viola or other 6- to 18-inch-tall, shade-tolerant perennial with pastel-colored flowers, such as woodland phlox (*Phlox divaricata*) [4 plants] or a Lenten rose (*Helleborus × hybridus*) [2 plants]

Planting Plan

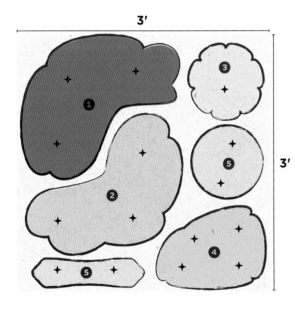

Season by Season

Spring: Pastels are a classic color range for spring, and this garden offers them in abundance. 'Etain' viola is generally the first to bloom, with fragrant, soft yellow flowers that are edged with lavender-purple. 'Stairway to Heaven' creeping Jacob's ladder joins in soon after, with clusters of lightly scented, light blue flowers over white-and-green leaves that are heavily blushed with pink. And by late spring — if not earlier — the pale pink blossoms of 'Biokovo' hardy geranium open, too. 'Camelot Rose' foxglove is usually in bud by late spring, and the dwarf Chinese astilbe has ferny green leaves that may be tinged with bronze.

Early spring is a good time to tackle the simple cleanup chores: cut down any remaining dead top growth, and clip off any winter-damaged leaves on the perennials that held their foliage through the winter. (If the entire clumps of 'Biokovo' geranium look tattered, shear off all the leaves about 2 inches above the ground.) Divide the geranium and the astilbe, too, if they were starting to outgrow their space last year. Both the foxglove and the viola may be short-lived, so if you don't see new growth on them in early spring, set out new plants in their place. Finish up by spreading a fresh layer of organic mulch over the soil.

Summer: The pageant of pastels peaks in early summer. 'Etain' viola, 'Stairway to Heaven' creeping Jacob's ladder, and 'Biokovo' hardy geranium are still going from spring, with the addition of 'Camelot Rose' foxglove, with its showy spikes of spotted, rich pink flowers. These may all continue into midsummer but are usually finishing up about the time that the dwarf Chinese astilbe sends up its perky lavender-pink plumes.

Regularly removing the flowers when they are finished helps to encourage this extended bloom period. Cut off the bloom spikes of the foxglove and creeping Jacob's ladder at the base of the plants, and pinch or clip off the individual flowers of the viola. If the viola plants stop blooming in midsummer, cut them back to 3 to 4 inches. Water the garden during summer dry spells.

Fall and Winter: Other than another round of flowers on the 'Etain' viola, foliage is the main feature of this garden in fall. 'Biokovo' geranium is especially colorful, with its green leaves taking on shades of red, orange, and yellow. The white-and-green leaves of 'Stairway to Heaven' creeping Jacob's ladder often become blushed with pink again now, as well. Most of the perennials in this garden hold their leaves through much or all of the winter. The dwarf Chinese astilbe's leaves turn brown with frost, but if you left the seed heads in place, they too will add winter interest.

Divide the astilbe and geranium in early fall if they are outgrowing their places, and keep pinching off the dead flowers of the viola. Other than that, your pastel garden doesn't need any more care until spring.

Digging Deeper

A SIMPLE SQUARE GARDEN like this one is a great choice for a starter garden. By itself, it would fit easily into a corner, and you could dig and plant it in just a few hours. If you have more time and more space to fill, you could flip the plan and use two squares to flank a bench, arbor, doorway, or set of steps.

Deep green leaves make a great backdrop for pastel-colored flowers, but if you want even more contrast, consider adding some extra-dark foliage, such as deep purple 'Obsidian' heuchera or even ebony black mondo grass (*Ophiopogon planiscapus* 'Nigrescens'). Or, if you love the look of light colors in your shade garden, pair pastel flowers with shade-tolerant perennials that have equally pale blue, gray, or silvery leaves, such as lamb's ears (*Stachys byzantina*), lungworts (*Pulmonaria*), spotted deadnettle (*Lamium maculatum*), and many hostas (*Hosta*).

Hardy geraniums (*Geranium*) have long been favorites for sunny perennial gardens, and some of them can adapt quite well to life in partially shady sites, too. Pale pink 'Biokovo' and darker pink 'Biokovo Karmina', both selections of *G. × cantabrigiense,* are excellent choices for multiseason interest. They typically bloom for a month in late spring to early summer, but in some areas, they may be in bloom pretty much any time from spring to fall. Their foliage usually takes on shades of yellow, orange, and red in fall and sticks around through most or all of the winter.

Spring into Action

Partial to full shade

◆ Average soil

It's hard to think of a better way to celebrate surviving a long, dreary winter than a garden filled with an abundance of cheery flowers and lush leaves. Fortunately, spring happens to be peak bloom time for many shade-tolerant perennials, because the ample sunlight gives them the energy they need to produce flowers — at least until the leaves of nearby deciduous trees expand fully and block much of the light.

➤ Forget-me-not (*Myosotis sylvatica*)

❯ 'White Nancy' spotted deadnettle (*Lamium maculatum*)

▲ Foamflower (*Tiarella cordifolia*)

➤ 'McKana Hybrids' columbine (*Aquilegia*)

➤ Lenten rose (*Helleborus* × *hybridus*)

125

The Garden Plan

Shopping List

❶ 'MCKANA HYBRIDS' COLUMBINE
Aquilegia | **3 plants**
Zones 3–8
Alternates: Another 2- to 3-foot-tall
columbine or other shade-tolerant perennial
that flowers in spring, such as Jacob's
ladder (*Polemonium caeruleum*) [3 plants]
or variegated Solomon's seal (*Polygonatum
odoratum* 'Variegatum') [3 plants]

❷ LENTEN ROSE
Helleborus × hybridus | **4 plants**
Zones 4–9
Alternates: Another 9- to 18-inch-tall, shade-
tolerant perennial that flowers in spring, such as
a lungwort (*Pulmonaria*) [4 plants] or Siberian
bugloss (*Brunnera macrophylla*) [4 plants]

**❸ 'WHITE NANCY' SPOTTED
DEADNETTLE**
Lamium maculatum | **4 plants**
Zones 3–8
Alternates: Another 6- to 9-inch-tall, shade-
tolerant perennial that flowers in spring, such
as 'Burgundy Glow' ajuga (*Ajuga reptans*)
[4 plants] or 'Home Fires' creeping phlox
(*Phlox stolonifera*) [4 plants]

❹ FORGET-ME-NOT
Myosotis sylvatica | **4 plants**
Zones 3–8
Alternates: Another 9- to 12-inch-tall, shade-
tolerant perennial that flowers in spring, such as
a dwarf bleeding heart (*Dicentra*) [4 plants] or
sweet violet (*Viola odorata*) [4 plants]

❺ FOAMFLOWER
Tiarella cordifolia | **3 plants**
Zones 4–9
Alternates: Another 6- to 9-inch-tall, shade-
tolerant perennial that flowers in spring, such
as red barrenwort (*Epimedium × rubrum*)
[3 plants] or heart-leaved bergenia (*Bergenia
cordifolia*) [3 plants]

Planting Plan

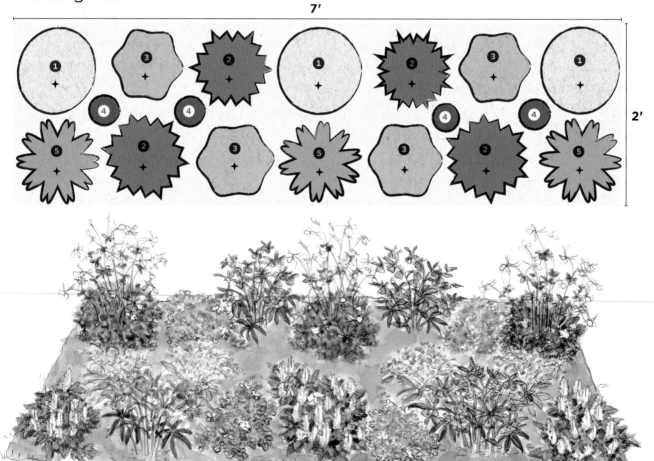

Season by Season

Spring: Lenten roses are among the earliest perennials to bloom in spring. In fact, they may even begin flowering in late winter in mild areas, gracing the garden with nodding, bowl-shaped blooms, usually in solid or spotted white or shades of pink to reddish purple. The dainty, sky-blue blossoms of the forget-me-nots and clustered, bright white flowers of 'White Nancy' spotted deadnettle come along soon after, usually in mid spring but possibly earlier or later, depending on your climate. Foamflowers send up their fuzzy spikes of white to pinkish flowers in mid to late spring. And to round out the season, the graceful, long-spurred blooms of 'McKana Hybrids' columbine flower in a wide range of colors in late spring.

The action starts early in this garden, so you want to do the spring cleanup as soon as possible — even in late winter, if the weather allows. Cut down any remaining tops on the columbines, trim any winter-damaged parts off the foamflowers and spotted deadnettles, and clip off the remaining Lenten rose leaves right at the base,

being careful not to cut into the emerging flower stalks. Then, treat the whole garden to a fresh layer of organic mulch to provide a tidy setting for the spring bloom extravaganza.

Summer: Forget-me-nots and Lenten roses are generally finished flowering by the end of spring, but columbines often continue flowering through early summer, and so may the foamflower and 'White Nancy' spotted deadnettle.

On the columbines, foamflowers, and Lenten roses, clip off the flower stems at their base when the blooms finish to tidy the plants, if you wish. You may want to leave a few finished stalks on the columbines to produce and drop seeds, so you'll have replacement plants coming along when the originals die out after a few years. Cut off the top one-half to two-thirds of the forget-me-not plants to prevent them from self-sowing and possibly extend their life for another year, or let the plants turn brown, pull them out, and shake them over the bare spot that's left to scatter the seeds. Look for

seedlings to appear in mid to late summer. Water the garden during extended summer dry spells.

Fall and Winter: Apart from possible scattered rebloom on the foamflower and 'White Nancy' spotted deadnettle, the main fall and winter interest in this perennial garden comes from the various greens and silvers of the leaves. The foamflower leaves may also blush with deep red to bronzy shades in cold temperatures.

There's not much end-of-the-season maintenance to do in this garden, other than shifting or dividing plants. Early to mid fall is the season to move or divide foamflowers and spotted deadnettles, if they're getting too big for their space. Lenten roses tend to fill out slowly and seldom require division, but if you do want to divide them, early fall — or even late summer — is a good time. Transplant the fuzzy-leaved forget-me-not seedlings to any bare spots then, too.

Digging Deeper

THIS RECTANGULAR PLANTING would fit easily into a narrow foundation bed against a home or outbuilding. Or, use it to line one or both sides of a garden path, sidewalk, or driveway; simply repeat the plan as often as needed to fill any length. Even though it's planned primarily for spring flowers, this garden includes many perennials that also have attractive, long-lasting leaves, so it remains attractive through the rest of the year, too.

It's possible to pack even more excitement into this spring garden by adding a variety of early-blooming bulbs, such as crocuses (*Crocus*), daffodils (*Narcissus*), Dutch hyacinths (*Hyacinthus*), grape hyacinths (*Muscari*), and snowdrops (*Galanthus*). These early risers pop up early, contribute their flowers to the spring extravaganza, and then disappear back underground by early to midsummer. Tuck them among the clumps of forget-me-nots, into the carpets of spotted deadnettle, and around the outer edges of the columbine, foamflower, and Lenten rose clumps.

Spotted deadnettle (*Lamium maculatum*) is a go-to perennial for many shade gardeners, both for its pretty pink or white blooms and its bright silver-and-green leaves. It starts as a distinct clump; then produces long, trailing stems through its main spring bloom season. In a large space, this habit lets it fill in quite quickly, and it can make a great groundcover. In a small garden, gather up the trailing stems and cut them back by one-third to one-half to reduce the size of the plants.

Summer Sanctuary

When summer heat sends you scurrying for shade,
a comfortable bench set in a lush and leafy perennial garden offers the perfect
place to lounge and linger. Plants with purple, yellow, or showily striped foliage
offer high-impact color but need minimal maintenance, so you can enjoy
having a great-looking garden without making yourself a lot of extra work.

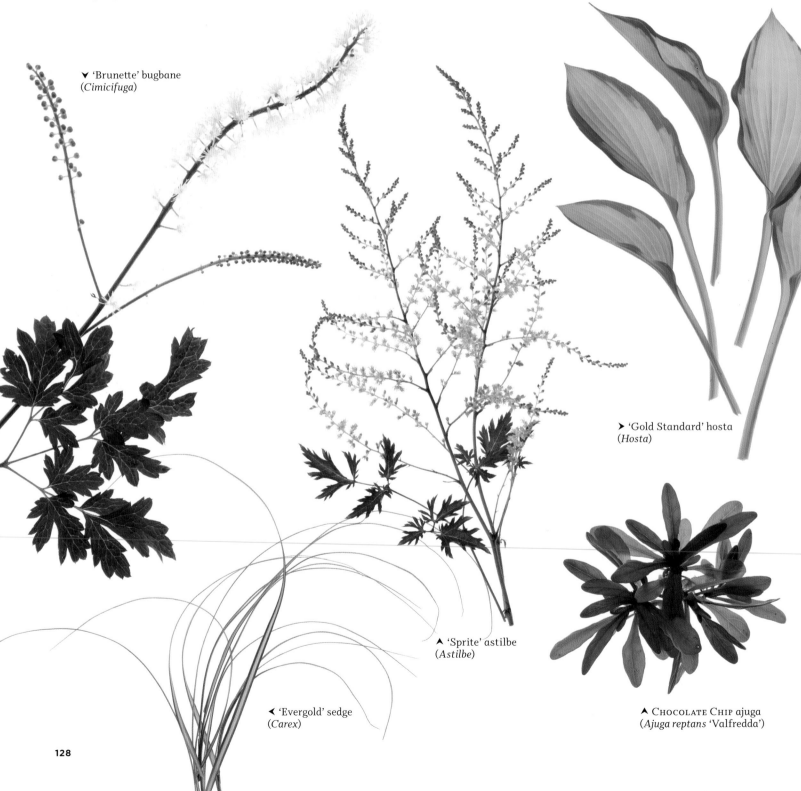

▾ 'Brunette' bugbane
(*Cimicifuga*)

▸ 'Gold Standard' hosta
(*Hosta*)

▴ 'Sprite' astilbe
(*Astilbe*)

◂ 'Evergold' sedge
(*Carex*)

▴ Chocolate Chip ajuga
(*Ajuga reptans* 'Valfredda')

The Garden Plan

Shopping List

❶ 'BRUNETTE' BUGBANE
Cimicifuga | **2 plants**
Zones 4–8
Alternates: 'James Compton' or other dark-leaved bugbane, or another 2- to 4-foot-tall, shade-tolerant perennial with showy summer flowers and/or leaves, such as 'Bridal Veil' astilbe (*Astilbe*) [2 plants] or 'Zweiweltenkind' goat's beard (*Aruncus dioicus*) [2 plants]

❷ 'GOLD STANDARD' HOSTA
Hosta | **2 plants**
Zones 3–8
Alternates: 'Golden Tiara' or another hosta with green-and-yellow or green-and-white leaves, or another 1- to 2-foot-tall, shade-tolerant perennial with showy summer flowers and/or leaves, such as 'Stoplight' heucherella (× *Heucherella*) [2 plants] or blue lobelia (*Lobelia siphilitica*) [2 plants]

❸ 'SPRITE' ASTILBE
Astilbe | **6 plants**
Zones 4–8
Alternates: Another dwarf astilbe or other 6- to 18-inch-tall, shade-tolerant perennial with showy summer flowers and/or leaves, such as Japanese painted fern (*Athyrium niponicum* var. *pictum*) [6 plants] or a dwarf bleeding heart (*Dicentra*) [6 plants]

❹ 'EVERGOLD' SEDGE
Carex | **2 plants**
Zones 5–9
Alternates: 'Ice Dance' or other sedge with green-and-white or green-and-yellow leaves, or another 6- to 18-inch-tall, shade-tolerant perennial with showy summer flowers and/or leaves, such as golden Hakone grass (*Hakonechloa macra* 'Aureola') [2 plants] or variegated blue lilyturf (*Liriope muscari* 'Variegata') [2 plants]

❺ Chocolate Chip AJUGA
Ajuga reptans 'Valfredda' | **6 plants**
Zones 3–9
Alternates: 'Black Scallop' or other dark-leaved ajuga, or another 4- to 9-inch-tall, shade-tolerant perennial with showy summer flowers, fruits, and/or leaves, such as green-and-gold (*Chrysogonum virginianum*) [4 plants] or dwarf mondo grass (*Ophiopogon japonicus* 'Nanus') [6 plants]

Planting Plan

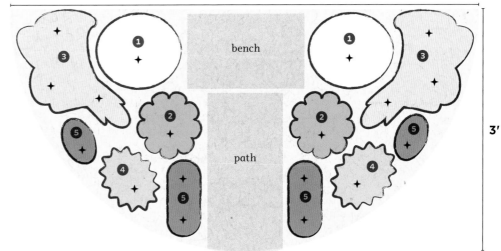

Season by Season

Spring: Even though this collection of perennials is planned for summer interest, its season starts much earlier, with the purple-blue spikes of CHOCOLATE CHIP ajuga beginning in mid to late spring. There's also plenty of early foliage color: chocolate brown from 'Brunette' bugbane and the ajuga, yellow from 'Gold Standard' hosta and 'Evergold' sedge, and bronzy green from 'Sprite' astilbe.

A thorough spring cleanup gets this garden off to a great start for the growing season. Cut down any remaining stems of the astilbe, bugbanes, and hostas, and rake out any dead leaves and other debris. If the sedge has some dead leaves, rake through the clumps to pull them out. Or, if the plants look very tattered, cut off all the leaves about 3 inches above the ground. Apply a fresh layer of organic mulch, too.

Summer: By early summer, your perennials should be filling out quickly. In midsummer, 'Gold Standard' hosta sends up very pale purple, trumpet-shaped blooms; enjoy the flowers or cut off the bloom stalks if you think they detract from the leaves. 'Sprite' astilbe blooms in mid to late summer, with light pink plumes that add another touch of color to the show of lovely summer leaves. You might also see flowers on 'Brunette' bugbane clumps in late summer, but they usually wait until autumn. 'Evergold' sedge' and CHOCOLATE CHIP ajuga continue to add foliage color throughout the summer.

Summer maintenance is minimal: just trim off the bloom spikes of the ajuga once the flowers are done, if you wish, and water during extended dry spells.

Fall and Winter: The colorful foliage you enjoyed all summer continues well into autumn, with the bonus of spiky, scented white blooms on 'Brunette' bugbane in early fall.

Do a quick cleanup pass in mid to late fall to remove the frost-killed tops of the astilbe, bugbane, and hosta, if desired, or leave everything in place to provide some winter interest and protect the dormant plants over winter.

Digging Deeper

THIS HALF-CIRCLE SHAPE is perfectly suited for a site against a wall, fence, or hedge. If you'd prefer to use it in an open site, flip the plan along the straight side to create a circle-shaped garden with room for a larger seat in the middle.

When you set any border against a vertical surface, leave some space between it and the plants at the back. That way, you'll be able to get behind the garden to maintain the wall, fence, or hedge without trampling the plants. It also allows room for perennials at the back to expand and makes it easier for you to maintain the garden without having to step *into* the planting. A strip that's 18 to 24 inches wide is adequate for most sites.

Keep in mind that any time you add furniture or an ornament, such as a bench or birdbath, to a garden, you also need a way to reach it without trampling your perennials. You could add a formal brick or stone path (in a small garden, that could be a fun do-it-yourself project); make it a simple strip of gravel or bark mulch; or just lay out some stepping stones.

Hostas (*Hosta*) are one of the last perennials to sprout in spring, but that doesn't mean you have to be stuck with a large mostly empty circle until they fill out. Fill that space with crocuses (*Crocus*), hyacinths (*Hyacinthus*), mini daffodils (*Narcissus*), or other spring-blooming bulbs for early color. By the time their leaves are ready to die back to the ground in early summer, the hosta leaves will be growing vigorously and cover them up in no time.

Fall Flowers & Foliage

It's easy to plan a flower-filled shade garden for spring, but the show doesn't have to stop when spring does. A combination of late-blooming flowers and perennials with colorful fall leaves celebrates the end of the growing season in style. Autumn colors in shady gardens tend to be more muted than those in sun — mostly deep reds, buttery yellows, soft pinks, and cool blues — but they're no less lovely in the landscape.

❯ 'Running Tapestry' foamflower (*Tiarella cordifolia*)

⌄ Autumn fern (*Dryopteris erythrosora*)

⌄ Variegated Solomon's seal (*Polygonatum odoratum* 'Variegatum')

⌄ Blue lobelia (*Lobelia siphilitica*)

❯ 'Miss Manners' obedient plant (*Physostegia virginiana*)

131

The Garden Plan

Shopping List

❶ 'MISS MANNERS' OBEDIENT PLANT
Physostegia virginiana | 3 plants
Zones 3–9
Alternates: Another 2- to 4-foot-tall, shade-tolerant perennial with colorful flowers or leaves in fall, such as yellow waxbells (*Kirengeshoma palmata*) [3 plants] or a bugbane (*Cimicifuga*) [3 plants]

❷ VARIEGATED SOLOMON'S SEAL
Polygonatum odoratum 'Variegatum' | 5 plants
Zones 4–8
Alternates: Another 18- to 24-inch-tall, shade-tolerant perennial with colorful flowers or leaves in fall, such as 'Francee' or 'Patriot' hosta (*Hosta*) [5 plants] or white turtlehead (*Chelone glabra*) [5 plants]

❸ BLUE LOBELIA
Lobelia siphilitica | 3 plants
Zones 3–8
Alternates: Another 18- to 30-inch-tall, shade-tolerant perennial with colorful flowers or leaves in fall, such as a toad lily (*Tricyrtis*) [3 plants] or hardy begonia (*Begonia grandis*) [3 plants]

❹ AUTUMN FERN
Dryopteris erythrosora | 2 plants
Zones 5–9
Alternates: Another 18- to 24-inch-tall, shade-tolerant perennial with colorful flowers or leaves in fall, such as golden Hakone grass (*Hakonechloa macra* 'Aureola') [2 plants] or 'Wayside' hardy ageratum (*Eupatorium coelestinum*) [2 plants]

❺ 'RUNNING TAPESTRY' FOAMFLOWER
Tiarella cordifolia | 2 plants
Zones 4–9
Alternates: Any other foamflower or another 4- to 9-inch-tall, shade-tolerant perennial with colorful flowers or leaves in fall, such as 'White Nancy' spotted deadnettle (*Lamium maculatum*) [2 plants] or green-and-gold (*Chrysogonum virginianum*) [2 plants]

Planting Plan

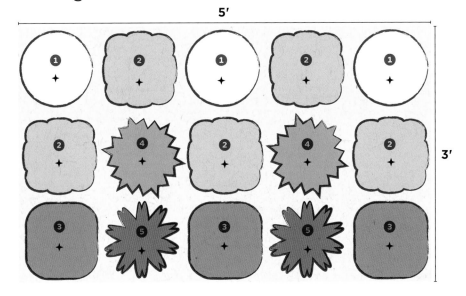

Season by Season

Spring: A perennial garden planned for fall interest can still look good during the rest of the growing season. This one offers loads of spring excitement from the emerging leaves — especially the stout pink sprouts of variegated Solomon's seal, which quickly shoot up into arching stems with green-and-white leaves and dangling white bells by mid to late spring. The bottlebrush spikes of white blossoms on 'Running Tapestry' foamflower open around the same time. The coppery, curled fiddleheads of autumn fern may not appear until late spring, but they're worth waiting for.

A few simple cleanup steps will get your fall garden off to a good start in spring. First, cut off any remaining dead or damaged leaves in early to mid spring. (Wait until new growth appears on the autumn fern before cutting off the previous year's fronds.) If any of the perennials were outgrowing their space last year, divide them now. Rake out any debris, and add a fresh layer of organic mulch.

Summer: Variegated Solomon's seal and 'Running Tapestry' foamflower typically continue flowering into early summer, though you may not notice the flowers on the Solomon's seal now because they're hidden by the showy foliage. 'Miss Manners' obedient plant is just green leaves through the summer, and so is the blue lobelia — at least until they begin blooming in mid to late summer. Though you might guess from its name that autumn fern isn't very interesting until fall, its best time is really any time it's sending up new fronds, because they're a very showy pinkish orange color. They eventually age to deep green, but flushes of new growth may continue through the summer if you're lucky.

Pinching or snipping off the foamflower bloom stems once the blossoms drop may encourage some new flowers to appear through the summer. Also, consider cutting back your lobelia plants to about half their height in early summer, to delay their main bloom display until later in the season. Water the garden during extended dry spells.

Fall and Winter: The pure white blooms of 'Miss Manners' obedient plant are the stars of this garden in early to mid fall, but they're not the only source of interest. Cooler weather often encourages some rebloom on the 'Running Tapestry' foamflower and can bring out another flush of colorful new growth on the autumn fern. The blue lobelia also adds its flowers to the mix in early fall. As the season progresses, the foamflower leaves often take on touches of maroon, and variegated Solomon's seal turns yellow. That's a whole lot of color from one small garden!

The fern and foamflower leaves often stay attractive into winter and may even stay evergreen all winter in mild areas, so they don't need any attention now. Simply snip off the finished flower stems of the lobelia, clip off the dead stalks of the Solomon's seal, and you're done until spring.

Digging Deeper

PERENNIALS THAT ARE PRIZED FOR THEIR FLOWERS generally need more light than those loved mostly for their leaves. Sun is usually abundant in spring, but once nearby trees and shrubs leaf out, there may be too much shade for flowering perennials to make the energy they need for great late-season bloom. So, save this garden for the brightest shade you have: a site with morning sun and afternoon is ideal, but light all-day shade can be fine, too.

This simple rectangular garden is planned to be seen mainly from one side, with tall plants at the back and lower growers toward the front. It's perfectly suited to show off against a vertical surface, such as a wall, fence, hedge, or deck. You can easily extend it to fit a longer space by repeating the plan as many times as needed, linking the sections end to end.

Besides its copper-colored new foliage, autumn fern offers another subtle but special feature: bright red, dotlike "sori" (spore cases) on the back of each frond in fall. They don't show up from a distance, but they're very interesting up close. So, don't mistake them for some unusual pest or disease problem: enjoy their pretty patterns.

Winter Delights

If your idea of gardening is all about the flowers, it's easy to overlook the possibility of having a garden that looks nice in winter, too. True, you don't get an abundance of eye-catching blooms, but you can still enjoy a tapestry of attractive evergreen leaves and interesting seed heads through the colder months. It's a great idea for a spot you frequently see from inside, such as just outside a kitchen or home-office window.

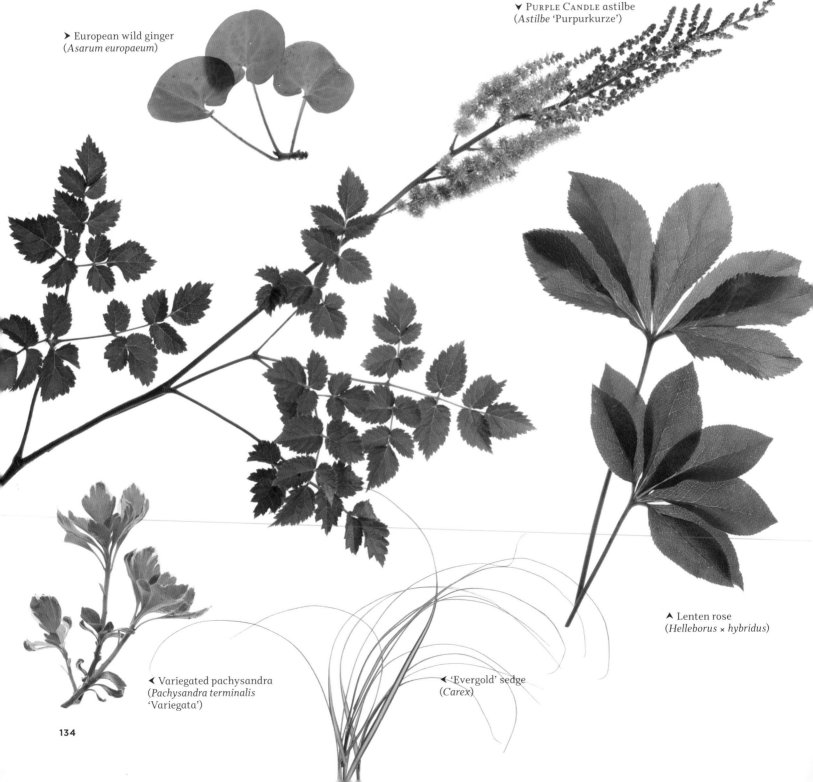

➤ European wild ginger
(*Asarum europaeum*)

❯ PURPLE CANDLE astilbe
(*Astilbe* 'Purpurkurze')

▲ Lenten rose
(*Helleborus* × *hybridus*)

◀ Variegated pachysandra
(*Pachysandra terminalis*
'Variegata')

◀ 'Evergold' sedge
(*Carex*)

The Garden Plan

Shopping List

❶ PURPLE CANDLE ASTILBE
Astilbe 'Purpurkurze' | **3 plants**
Zones 4–9
Alternates: Another astilbe or other 18- to 36-inch-tall, shade-tolerant perennial with attractive winter leaves or seed heads, such as bearsfoot hellebore (*Helleborus foetidus*) [3 plants] or autumn fern (*Dryopteris erythrosora*) [3 plants]

❷ VARIEGATED PACHYSANDRA
Pachysandra terminalis 'Variegata' | **4 plants**
Zones 4–9
Alternates: Another 6- to 18-inch-tall, shade-tolerant perennial with attractive winter leaves or seed heads, such as golden Hakone grass (*Hakonechloa macra* 'Aureola') [4 plants] or 'Silver Dragon' mondo grass (*Ophiopogon japonicus*) [4 plants]

❸ LENTEN ROSE
Helleborus × hybridus | **3 plants**
Zones 4–9
Alternates: Another 6- to 18-inch-tall, shade-tolerant perennial with attractive winter leaves or seed heads, such as bigroot geranium (*Geranium macrorrhizum*) [3 plants] or Christmas fern (*Polystichum acrostichoides*) [3 plants]

❹ 'EVERGOLD' SEDGE
Carex | **2 plants**
Zones 5–9
Alternates: GOLD FOUNTAINS ('Kaga-nishiki') sedge or another 6- to 12-inch-tall, shade-tolerant perennial with attractive winter leaves or seed heads, such as 'Silvery Sunproof' blue lilyturf (*Liriope muscari*) [2 plants]

❺ EUROPEAN WILD GINGER
Asarum europaeum | **3 plants**
Zones 4–8
Alternates: Mottled wild ginger (*A. shuttleworthii*) or another 3- to 9-inch-tall, shade-tolerant perennial with attractive winter leaves or seed heads, such as hardy cyclamen (*Cyclamen coum* or *C. hederifolium*) [3 plants] or heart-leaved bergenia (*Bergenia cordifolia*) [3 plants]

Planting Plan

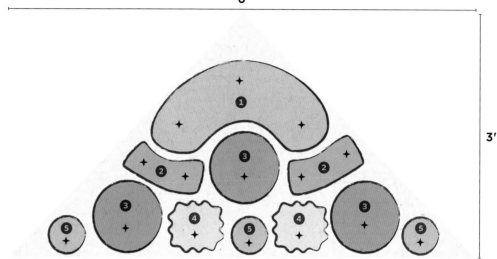

Season by Season

Spring: This garden may be planned for winter features, but it's not attractive *only* in winter. Lenten roses welcome the return of milder weather with nodding, bowl-shaped blooms, mostly in white or shades of pink to deep red, starting in early to mid spring. Variegated pachysandra usually starts blooming around the same time, but you may not notice the short, brushy spikes of white flowers against the green-and-white leaves. There's additional foliage interest from the fresh yellow-and-green-striped leaves of 'Evergold' sedge, the emerging spouts of Purple Candle astilbe, and the glossy green leaves of the European wild ginger. The ginger also produces reddish-brown flowers in mid to late spring, but they're hidden by the leaves.

In early to mid spring, cut off the dried seed heads of the astilbes close to ground level, and trim off any winter-browned leaves on the pachysandra and wild ginger. The hellebore leaves may still look good now, or they may look tattered; either way, trimming them all off right at the base makes the garden look tidier. Rake or pluck out any damaged leaves on the sedge, or cut off all of the foliage about 3 inches above the ground. Apply a fresh layer of organic mulch, and your garden is ready for the growing season.

Summer: The variety of leaf colors and textures provides most of the summer interest in this garden, with the bonus of purplish pink, plumy blooms on Purple Candle astilbe, usually in early to midsummer.

Summer maintenance is minimal: just watering during summer dry spells. Remember to leave the astilbe seed heads in place after the flowers are done so you'll have them for winter interest.

Fall and Winter: The lovely summer leaves continue to look good in fall and through most, if not all, of the winter, too. The one exception is the Purple Candle astilbe: frosts will kill the leaves, but the plumy seed heads turn golden brown and stick around all through the off season.

Digging Deeper

A TRIANGULAR GARDEN LIKE THIS ONE fits easily into a corner where two walls or fences meet. That kind of site is ideal, because it provides some shelter from drying winter winds, which can dry out exposed evergreen leaves and make them turn brown. Another option is to flip the plan along one of the short sides and repeat it, and then flip and repeat it again, to create a planting that could wrap around the outside corner of a deck or patio.

Perennial gardens that depend on evergreen leaves for winter interest are generally most satisfying in areas that get minimal winter snowfall. Evergreen perennials tend to be low growing, so where snow falls early and sticks around for weeks or months, the leaves will be covered up anyway. Light snowfalls, on the other hand, provide a crisp, clean background for the evergreen foliage. And when they melt, they provide moisture, which helps to keep the leaves plump and fresh looking.

Lenten roses (*Helleborus* × *hybridus*) may take a year or two to settle in and begin blooming, but once they start, they get better each year, with more and more flowers each spring and an abundance of lush leaves for the rest of the year. The plants are seldom bothered by pests, diseases, or deer, and they rarely need division, making them among the most low-maintenance perennials around. Clipping off the remaining leaves in spring is a good idea but not absolutely necessary. The same goes for the flower stems once the blooms are finished: cut them off, if you wish, or simply let the new leaves cover them up. If you let the flower stems stay, you may eventually find seedlings, which you can transplant to other parts of your garden.

A Year-Round Garden

◑   Partial shade

◆   Average soil

Creating a perennial garden that looks great all year long is a tall order, and it's even more challenging when you're working in a small space. It important to choose the plants very carefully, making sure each one offers interesting features in at least three seasons, and ideally all year long. An extended bloom season is one key trait; evergreen foliage is another. Other multiseason features to look for include colorful leaves, fall color changes, and interesting seed heads.

➤ Lenten rose
(*Helleborus* × *hybridus*)

➤ Chocolate Chip ajuga
(*Ajuga reptans* 'Valfredda')

❮ 'All Gold' Hakone grass
(*Hakonechloa macra*)

❯ 'Hillside Black Beauty'
bugbane (*Cimicifuga*)

➤ Allegheny pachysandra
(*Pachysandra procumbens*)

The Garden Plan

Shopping List

❶ 'HILLSIDE BLACK BEAUTY' BUGBANE
Cimicifuga | **1 plant**
Zones 4–8
Alternates: 'Brunette' or other dark-leaved bugbane (*Cimicifuga*) or another 3- to 5-foot-tall, shade-tolerant perennial with multiseason interest, such as 'Chocolate Wings' Rodger's flower (*Rodgersia pinnata*) [1 plant] or a tall astilbe (*Astilbe*) [1 plant]

❷ LENTEN ROSE
Helleborus × hybridus | **4 plants**
Zones 4–9
Alternates: Another 9- to 18-inch-tall, shade-tolerant perennial with multiseason interest, such as bearsfoot hellebore (*Helleborus foetidus*) [4 plants] or 'Southern Comfort' or other colored-leaved heuchera (*Heuchera*) [4 plants]

❸ 'ALL GOLD' HAKONE GRASS
Hakonechloa macra | **4 plants**
Zones 5–9
Alternates: Golden Hakone grass (*H. macra* 'Aureola') or another 1- to 2-foot-tall, shade-tolerant perennial with multiseason interest, such as variegated blue lilyturf (*Liriope muscari* 'Variegata') [4 plants] or variegated Solomon's seal (*Polygonatum odoratum* 'Variegatum') [4 plants]

❹ Chocolate Chip AJUGA
Ajuga reptans 'Valfredda' | **6 plants**
Zones 3–9
Alternates: 'Black Scallop' or other ajuga or another 4- to 8-inch-tall, shade-tolerant perennial with multiseason interest, such as black mondo grass (*Ophiopogon planiscapus* 'Nigrescens') [6 plants] or green-and-gold (*Chrysogonum virginianum*) [6 plants]

❺ ALLEGHENY PACHYSANDRA
Pachysandra procumbens | **6 plants**
Zones 5–9
Alternates: Another 6- to 18-inch-tall, shade-tolerant perennial with multiseason interest, such as 'Stairway to Heaven' creeping Jacob's ladder (*Polemonium reptans*) [2 plants] or 'Majeste', 'Milky Way', or other lungwort (*Pulmonaria*) [2 plants]

Planting Plan

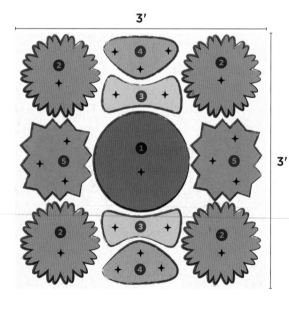

Season by Season

Spring: Lenten roses rise early, with bowl-shaped blooms mostly in white or shades of pink to reddish purple, and flower through much of the spring. Allegheny pachysandra blooms now, too, with brushy clusters of white flowers mostly in early to mid spring. And then there's CHOCOLATE CHIP ajuga, with spikes of small but densely packed purple-blue blossoms in mid to late spring. The dark shoots of 'Hillside Black Beauty' bugbane and bright yellow sprouts of 'All Gold' Hakone grass add extra color to the show.

Tidy the garden for spring by clipping off any dead stems, cut off the evergreen leaves of the Allegheny pachysandra and Lenten rose close to ground level, and rake out any remaining debris. Early to mid spring is also a good time to divide the bugbane and Hakone grass if the clumps are getting too big for their space. When your spring cleanup is done, spread a layer of fresh mulch over the soil.

Summer: Interesting foliage is the key feature of this multiseason garden through the summer months. The Allegheny pachysandra and Lenten roses are done flowering by early summer, but they send up bright green new leaves that darken to deep green. 'Hillside Black Beauty' bugbane forms large clumps of lacy, deep brown leaves, close in color but different in scale to the very small, slender leaves of CHOCOLATE CHIP ajuga. And for a jolt of color, 'All Gold' Hakone grass lives up to its name, with gracefully arching, bright yellow blades that contrast beautifully with darker-leaved companions.

Other than clipping off the finished flower stems of the ajuga and the Lenten rose, and watering during summer dry spells, there's little maintenance to do now.

Fall and Winter: This is often a quiet time in most shady gardens, but there are a lot of changes going on in this one. 'Hillside Black Beauty' bugbane sometimes starts flowering in late summer, but it's usually in peak bloom in early fall, with fuzzy spikes of scented, pinkish white blossoms that turn into dark seed heads and hang around through the winter, even though the leaves disappear. The dainty brown flower heads of 'All Gold' Hakone grass are hardly noticeable in autumn, but its yellow leaves often develop a pinkish blush in cool weather, and eventually dry to a golden tan and remain for winter interest. Allegheny pachysandra leaves develop silvery gray mottling in fall; they remain well into winter in most areas and may even be evergreen in mild climates. CHOCOLATE CHIP ajuga, too, often stays attractive through the entire winter in mild climates, and the leathery foliage of the Lenten roses looks great all through the cooler months.

The only maintenance to do now is dividing the Lenten rose (in early fall, or even late summer) and ajuga (in early fall) if the plants are outgrowing their allotted spaces.

Digging Deeper

THIS SMALL, SQUARE GARDEN is perfect for a corner space: the shape fits easily, and the plan is meant to be seen mostly from just two sides. You can easily use it as the basis for a larger planting, as well. Use two squares to flank an arbor, a bench, or a set of steps, or join two or more repetitions end to end to form a longer multiseason border for a shady foundation planting.

Some of the most outstanding shade perennials — including bugbanes (*Cimicifuga*), hostas (*Hosta*), and Lenten roses (*Helleborus* × *hybridus*) — are also some of the longest-lived plants you can add to your garden. They're also some of the easiest to care for, living happily for 5 years or even much longer without your having to dig up and divide them. Their durability comes at a price, though. Because they grow slowly, they can be more expensive to buy, and they can take several years to settle in and start looking lush. Think of them as an investment, though, and in the meantime, fill in around them with forget-me-nots (*Myosotis sylvatica*), begonias (*Begonia*), or other fast-growing perennials or annuals for the first few years.

Allegheny pachysandra (*P. procumbens*) is a great alternative to the well-known Japanese pachysandra (*P. terminalis*), because it's equally as tough but its creeping habit is much more restrained, so you can enjoy it as a ground cover in a small yard or even mix it with other shade-loving perennials in a woodland-type planting.

Color for Dry Shade

◐ ○ Partial to full shade

◇ ◇ Average to dry soil

A site that's both shady and dry is one of the toughest landscaping challenges. Before you set your heart on planting a garden there, grab a trowel and try digging a few small holes. If hard-packed soil or a dense mat of roots makes digging difficult, your best option might be to simply cover the area with mulch and add a bench and some pots of shade-tolerant annuals and perennials. But if it turns out that you can dig a few holes without too much trouble, then there's a good chance that you'll have luck with a garden of perennials that are adapted to both shade and drought.

➤ Yellow barrenwort
(*Epimedium* × *versicolor*)

➤ White wood aster
(*Aster divaricatus*)

˅ Christmas fern (*Polystichum acrostichoides*)

˅ Allegheny pachysandra
(*Pachysandra procumbens*)

˄ Variegated Solomon's
seal (*Polygonatum odoratum*
'Variegatum')

140

The Garden Plan

Shopping List

❶ VARIEGATED SOLOMON'S SEAL
Polygonatum odoratum 'Variegatum' |
3 plants
Zones 4–8
Alternates: Another 1- to 3-foot-tall perennial
that can tolerate shade and dry soil, such as
gooseneck loosestrife (*Lysimachia clethroides*)
[3 plants] or 'Samobor' or 'Margaret Wilson'
mourning widow (*Geranium phaeum*) [3 plants]

❷ CHRISTMAS FERN
Polystichum acrostichoides | 5 plants
Zones 3–9
Alternates: Another 1- to 2-foot-tall perennial
that can tolerate shade and dry soil, such as
Japanese painted fern (*Athyrium niponicum*
var. *pictum*) [5 plants] or bigroot geranium
(*Geranium macrorrhizum*) [5 plants]

❸ WHITE WOOD ASTER
Aster divaricatus | 6 plants
Zones 4–8
Alternates: Another 12- to 30-inch-tall
perennial that can tolerate shade and dry soil,
such as heart-leaved aster (*Aster cordifolius*)
[2 plants] or a hosta (*Hosta*) [2 plants]

❹ YELLOW BARRENWORT
Epimedium × *versicolor* | 5 plants
Zones 5–8
Alternates: Another barrenwort or other 6-
to 12-inch-tall perennial that can tolerate shade
and dry soil, such as sweet woodruff (*Galium
odoratum*) [5 plants] or lily-of-the-valley
(*Convallaria majalis*) [5 plants]

❺ ALLEGHENY PACHYSANDRA
Pachysandra procumbens | 7 plants
Zones 5–9
Alternates: Another 6- to 12-inch-tall
perennial that can tolerate shade and dry
soil, such as Canada wild ginger (*Asarum
canadense*) [7 plants] or 'Evergold' sedge
(*Carex*) [5 plants]

Planting Plan

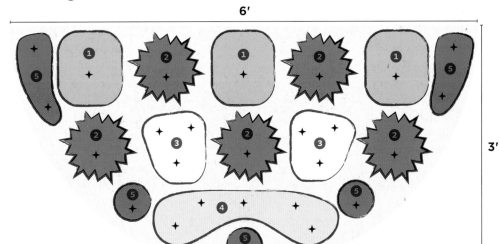

Season by Season

Spring: Like many other shady gardens, this collection of perennials for dry shade offers up an abundance of color for the spring season. The plump pink shoots of variegated Solomon's seal are one of the first features to appear, quickly shooting up into arching stems clad in cream-edged leaves, with small white bells dangling below in mid to late spring. Early to mid spring also brings out the pink-stemmed clusters of fragrant white flowers on the Allegheny pachysandra. And then there are the sprays of dainty blooms on yellow barrenwort, which appear by mid spring, joined quickly by the heart-shaped leaves, which may be green heavily blushed with deep red or even a solid chocolate brown. The unfurling "fiddleheads" of the Christmas fern and emerging dark stems of white wood aster are attractive, too, though not nearly as showy as their flowering companions.

An early spring cleanup session will set up your dry shade garden for a successful growing season. Cut down any remaining dead top growth, and clip off any winter-damaged leaves on the barrenwort, fern, and pachysandra. (Unless the barrenwort stays completely evergreen in your climate, it's often easiest to just shear off all the leaves at ground level; that will make the flowers show up better, too.) Divide the aster, fern, or Solomon's seal clumps if they were starting to crowd out their companions last year and you didn't get around to dividing them in fall. As a finishing touch, spread a fresh layer of organic mulch over the soil.

Summer: Fabulous foliage is the key feature of this garden in summer. Though variegated Solomon's seal finishes flowering by early summer, the green-and-cream or -white leaves look lovely for most, if not all, of the summer. The yellow barrenwort and Allegheny pachysandra also finished in late spring, but their new leaves add a fresh look now, as do the fully expanded fronds of the Christmas fern. White wood aster may begin blooming as early as late summer, but it's mostly just a subtle player in summer, with medium to deep green leaves on its near black stems.

There's nothing to do now, maintenance-wise, except to water occasionally during summer dry spells, especially for the first few years.

Fall and Winter: White wood aster is in peak form in early fall, with clouds of small, starry white flowers, and may keep blooming into mid fall. Its tops dry to brown after frosts, but the fluffy seeds stick around to provide interest for a while longer. The leaves of yellow barrenwort take on a reddish blush in fall, and the green leaves of Allegheny pachysandra develop a silvery gray mottling; both usually look good well into winter, or even through the entire off-season in mild-winter areas. Variegated Solomon's seal turns butter yellow as fall progresses and then drops its leaves for the winter. And then there's the Christmas fern, which holds its good looks from summer through to the following spring.

If the barrenwort, fern, pachysandra, or Solomon's seal clumps are crowding out their companions, early fall is a fine time to divide them. Otherwise, this garden doesn't need much attention in fall or winter, either; just cut down the dead Solomon's seal stems, if you wish, or leave them for spring cleanup.

Digging Deeper

THIS LOW, WOODLAND-STYLE PLANTING offers lots of placement options. Set the flat side against a wall or fence, or against the edge of a deck, patio, or walkway. Or, flip the plan along the flat side, and join the two parts to create a circular bed, or separate the parts with a through-path or a short path ending in a bench.

When you're planting under trees, it's tempting to simply dump a layer of loose topsoil over the area so you don't have to struggle with digging through roots. If you do that, though, you run the risk of smothering the roots of your trees, stressing or even killing them. A much better option is to dig individual planting pockets (roughly 6 inches deep and wide), avoiding cutting through the tree roots as much as possible. Once your perennials are in place, give them a generous layer of organic mulch, and water them regularly for the first year or two, at least, to help them settle in. Once their roots are well established, they'll be able to tolerate drier conditions.

Wet-Site Wonders

There are all kinds of reasons that soil can stay soggy. It might be high in clay, holding tightly to whatever water comes by and slowing the process of its draining away. It might be saturated by water coming up from below, or from a nearby creek, stream, or pond, or it might be a low spot that collects runoff water from surrounding areas. Whatever the reason, lawn grass probably won't thrive there, and ordinary garden plants may suffer, too. There's no need to invest in an expensive drainage system, though: choosing perennials that are adapted to conditions like these can turn that problem site into a gorgeous garden.

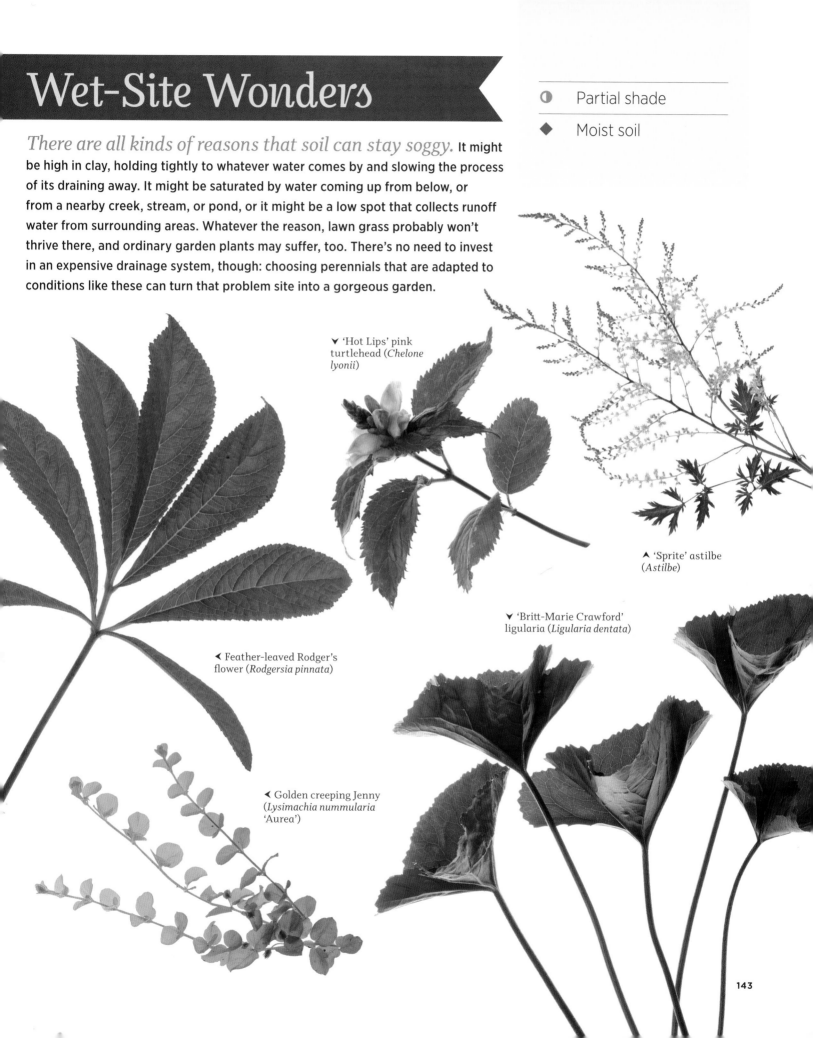

∨ 'Hot Lips' pink turtlehead (*Chelone lyonii*)

∧ 'Sprite' astilbe (*Astilbe*)

∨ 'Britt-Marie Crawford' ligularia (*Ligularia dentata*)

◀ Feather-leaved Rodger's flower (*Rodgersia pinnata*)

◀ Golden creeping Jenny (*Lysimachia nummularia* 'Aurea')

143

The Garden Plan

Shopping List

① FEATHER-LEAVED RODGER'S FLOWER
Rodgersia pinnata | 2 plants
Zones 4–7
Alternates: Another Rodger's flower (*Rodgersia*) or other 3- to 5-foot-tall perennial that can tolerate shade and moist to wet soil, such as cinnamon fern (*Osmunda cinnamomea*) [2 plants] or royal fern (*Osmunda regalis*) [2 plants]

② 'BRITT-MARIE CRAWFORD' LIGULARIA
Ligularia dentata | 1 plant
Zones 4–8
Alternates: 'Desdemona' or 'Othello' ligularia or another 18- to 30-inch-tall perennial that can tolerate shade and moist to wet soil, such as variegated Japanese iris (*Iris ensata* 'Variegata') [1 plant] or variegated sweet flag (*Acorus calamus* 'Variegatus') [1 plant]

③ 'HOT LIPS' PINK TURTLEHEAD
Chelone lyonii | 6 plants
Zones 3–9
Alternates: Another turtlehead (*Chelone*) or other 18- to 36-inch-tall perennial that can tolerate shade and moist to wet soil, such as Japanese primrose (*Primula japonica*) [6 plants] or a toad lily (*Tricyrtis*) [6 plants]

④ 'SPRITE' ASTILBE
Astilbe | 3 plants
Zones 4–8
Alternates: 'Visions', 'White Wings', or another 1- to 2-foot-tall astilbe or other perennial that can tolerate shade and moist to wet soil, such as dwarf goat's beard (*Aruncus aethusifolius*) [3 plants] or 'Ice Dance' sedge (*Carex*) [3 plants]

⑤ GOLDEN CREEPING JENNY
Lysimachia nummularia 'Aurea' | 5 plants
Zones 3–8
Alternates: Another 3- to 12-inch-tall perennial that can tolerate shade and moist to wet soil, such as dwarf golden sweet flag (*Acorus gramineus* 'Minimus Aureus') [5 plants]

Planting Plan

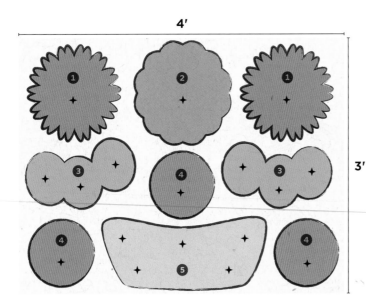

Season by Season

Spring: Early-season excitement in this garden comes mainly from the emerging leaves, especially the red to bronzy, multiparted foliage of the feather-leaved Rodger's flower, the rounded near-black leaves of 'Britt-Marie Crawford' ligularia, the bronzy green shoots of 'Sprite' astilbe, and the rounded bright yellow leaves of golden creeping Jenny. Feather-leaved Rodger's flower and 'Sprite' astilbe may begin to bloom by the end of spring in southern gardens.

Early to mid spring is a good time to divide any of the perennials that have started outgrowing their space. Golden creeping Jenny may need dividing every year or two to keep it in check; slow-growing Rodger's flower can last many, many years without ever needing to be disturbed. Dividing every 3 to 5 years generally works well for the other perennials.

Summer: Early summer is typically peak bloom time for both the large, pink to reddish plumes of the feather-leaved Rodger's flower and the much daintier, pale pink blooms of 'Sprite' astilbe. The astilbe may continue flowering into midsummer. After bloom, the leaves of both are mostly green for the rest of the summer, but there's still plenty of color from the deep purple leaves and the mid- to late summer golden orange daisies of 'Britt-Marie Crawford' ligularia, as well as the rosy pink flowers of 'Hot Lips' turtlehead in late summer. Golden creeping Jenny stays eye-catching through the summer, as well: it produces cupped yellow flowers in summer, but you'll hardly notice them against the ground-hugging yellow foliage.

Clip off the finished flower plumes of the Rodger's flower and astilbe just above the foliage, or leave them for later-season interest. Other than that, there's nothing much to do maintenance-wise, except for watering during extended dry spells if the soil starts to dry out.

Fall and Winter: Flowering interest from 'Britt-Marie Crawford' ligularia and 'Hot Lips' pink turtlehead continues into early fall, with both of them then producing interesting seed heads. There are also the seed heads of the feather-leaved Rodger's flower and 'Sprite' astilbe, if you didn't clip them off earlier. Rodger's flower leaves typically turn reddish to bronzy again when cooler weather returns. The dark ligularia and bright creeping Jenny leaves keep their summer color well into fall; golden creeping Jenny may stick around through most or all of the winter, as well, in mild climates.

Doing a thorough cleanup in mid to late fall removes all of the frost-killed stems and leaves, reducing the chance of rotting problems over the winter.

Digging Deeper

A SIMPLE RECTANGULAR BORDER like this is perfectly suited for a site backed by a vertical surface, such as a wall, fence, or hedge, or as an edging for a stream or lined pond. If you'd like to fill a larger space, repeat the plan as many times as you have room for. Keeping the repetitions identical creates a very formal look; for a border with more variety, replace some of the main plants with the suggested alternates to mix things up a bit.

Instead of tackling soil preparation for your new garden in spring, you might want to wait until a rain-free spell in summer, because it will be easier to dig when the soil isn't mucky mud. And when you plant out the perennials, set the crowns (the point where the stems meet the roots) an inch or so above the soil level, instead of even with it as you normally would, to reduce the chance of rotting.

Once the garden is established, consider holding off on mulching until late spring or even early summer, to give the wet soil a chance to warm up more quickly. (Mulch-covered soil tends to stay cool in spring and can slow the sprouting of your perennials.)

Rain Garden for Shade

Just as they do in sunny sites, rain gardens in shady yards offer an attractive solution for areas that are exposed to stormwater runoff, such as the outlets of gutter downspouts. This keeps rainwater from flowing off your yard and into a sewer; instead, the water has a chance to soak into the soil and return to the natural groundwater system. And while it's soaking in, it's also supporting the growth of a beautiful bunch of perennials!

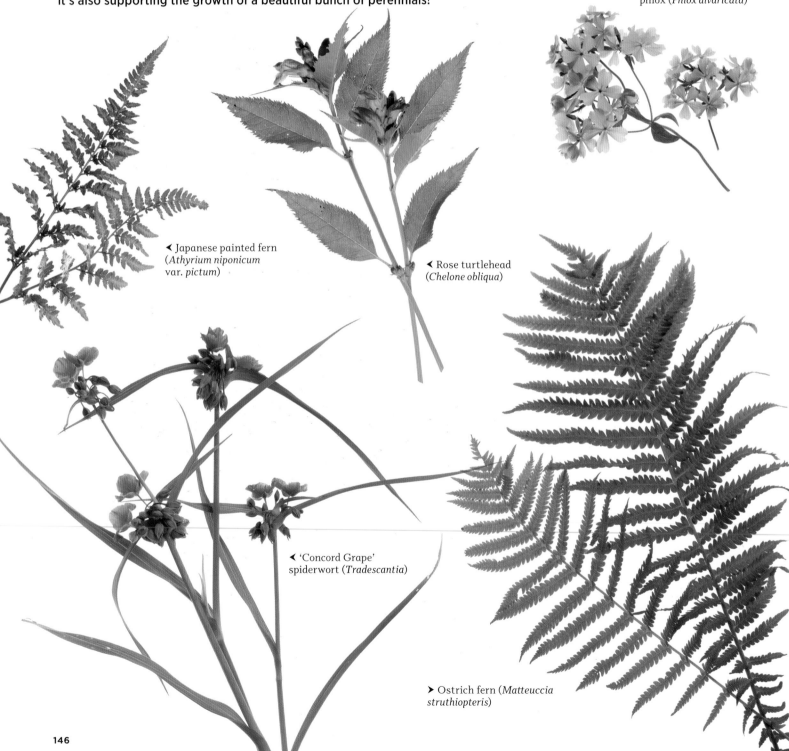

▼ 'London Grove' woodland phlox (*Phlox divaricata*)

◄ Japanese painted fern (*Athyrium niponicum* var. *pictum*)

◄ Rose turtlehead (*Chelone obliqua*)

◄ 'Concord Grape' spiderwort (*Tradescantia*)

➤ Ostrich fern (*Matteuccia struthiopteris*)

The Garden Plan

Shopping List

❶ OSTRICH FERN
Matteuccia struthiopteris | 3 plants
Zones 3–8
Alternates: Another 2- to 3-foot-tall, shade-tolerant perennial that can adapt to occasionally wet soil, such as interrupted fern (*Osmunda claytoniana*) [3 plants] or cinnamon fern (*Osmunda cinnamomea*) [3 plants]

❷ ROSE TURTLEHEAD
Chelone obliqua | 6 plants
Zones 5–9
Alternates: Another turtlehead (*Chelone*) or other 2- to 4-foot-tall, shade-tolerant perennial that can adapt to occasionally wet soil, such as wild bergamot (*Monarda fistulosa*) [6 plants] or obedient plant (*Physostegia virginiana*) [6 plants]

❸ 'CONCORD GRAPE' SPIDERWORT
Tradescantia | 4 plants
Zones 4–8
Alternates: Another spiderwort or other 1- to 2-foot-tall, shade-tolerant perennial that can adapt to occasionally wet soil, such as blue lobelia (*Lobelia siphilitica*) [4 plants] or Bᴜɴɴʏ Bʟᴜᴇ sedge (*Carex laxiculmis* 'Hobb') [4 plants]

❹ JAPANESE PAINTED FERN
Athyrium niponicum var. *pictum* | 4 plants
Zones 4–9
Alternates: Another 9- to 18-inch-tall, shade-tolerant perennial that can adapt to occasionally wet soil, such as 'Stairway to Heaven' creeping Jacob's ladder (*Polemonium reptans*) [4 plants] or wild columbine (*Aquilegia canadensis*) [4 plants]

❺ 'LONDON GROVE' WOODLAND PHLOX
Phlox divaricata | 6 plants
Zones 3–8
Alternates: Another woodland phlox or other 6- to 12-inch-tall, shade-tolerant perennial that can adapt to occasionally wet soil, such as dwarf goat's beard (*Aruncus aethusifolius*) [6 plants] or Canada wild ginger (*Asarum canadense*) [6 plants]

Planting Plan

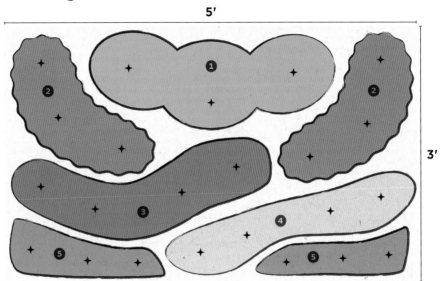

Season by Season

Spring: This rain garden jumps into growth early, starting with the 'London Grove' woodland phlox, with its clouds of fragrant, light lavender-blue blooms in mid and late spring. The 'Concord Grape' spiderwort's grassy leaves rise quickly through the spring, joined by the unfurling fronds of the Japanese painted fern and ostrich fern and the rich green shoots of rose turtlehead.

A bit of attention in early spring will get your rain garden off to a rousing start. Cut down any remaining dead top growth, and trim away any winter-damaged bits on the woodland phlox. If any of the perennials were outgrowing their space last year, this is a fine time to divide them, too. Finish up by applying a fresh layer of organic mulch over the soil.

Summer: In summer, ostrich fern sends up spiky spore-bearing fronds in the center of their vaselike green clumps, echoed through the summer by the much shorter, silvery gray fronds of Japanese painted fern. 'London Grove' woodland phlox usually finishes in early summer, if not sooner, but the rich purple-blue blooms of 'Concord Grape' spiderwort jump in by the start of the summer and keep going into midsummer, at least. Rose turtlehead's rosy pink flowers start appearing in late summer.

Clip or shear off the flower stems of the woodland phlox when the blooms are finished. And if the spiderwort plants sprawl or stop blooming in midsummer, cut them back by half, or even all the way down to the ground, to get fresh new growth. The garden will need watering only during extended summer dry spells.

Fall and Winter: Rose turtlehead is at peak bloom in early to mid fall, and then forms interesting seed heads that last through the winter. 'Concord Grape' spiderwort often produces some scattered rebloom in fall, but it usually dies back once freezing weather returns. Japanese painted fern also dies back after frost. Ostrich fern's green plumes tend to look tattered by early fall, but the center fronds age to a rich, deep brown and last into winter. 'London Grove' woodland phlox also sticks around to contribute a bit of color through the colder months, as the foliage takes on reddish purple shades in fall and winter.

Early fall is an acceptable time to divide the ferns, spiderwort, or woodland phlox if they're crowding out their companions. Other than that, there's not much to do in this garden until spring.

Digging Deeper

THIS RECTANGULAR PLAN is on the small side for a rain garden, especially if you have a lot of runoff water from a large roof area, but it's a great place to start. If you find that runoff water frequently overflows the basin after a normal rain, expand it out from your house, repeating the plan exactly or flipping it along the side with the phlox. For variety, replace some of the plants with the suggested alternates.

Avoid placing your rain garden in a site that's already wet or that tends to collect and hold water during rainy spells. The idea is to choose a spot where the runoff water will soak in relatively quickly, not just sit there and become stagnant, allowing mosquitoes to breed.

Want to add more height and color to your rain garden while you're waiting for the perennials to fill out? Consider adding some camassias (*Camassia*). These bulbs are well adapted to sites that are moist in spring to early summer, when they produce showy spikes of starry flowers, and then drier later on, once the bulbs have died back to the ground for the season. Large camas (*C. leichtlinii*) reaches 24 to 30 inches tall with blue or creamy white flowers; small camas or quamash (*C. quamash*) usually reaches 1 to 2 feet tall.

Shady Slope Planting

◐ ○ Partial to full shade

◆ ◇ Average to dry soil

Sloping sites can be problems or opportunities, depending on your perspective. They can be very dry, if rainfall runs off before it soaks in, and that runoff water can carry topsoil with it, carving gouges out of the slope and depositing the soil on the lawn or walkway at the base of the slope. On the plus side, slopes offer great drainage for perennials that don't like wet soil. They also create a great display area for delicate flowers.

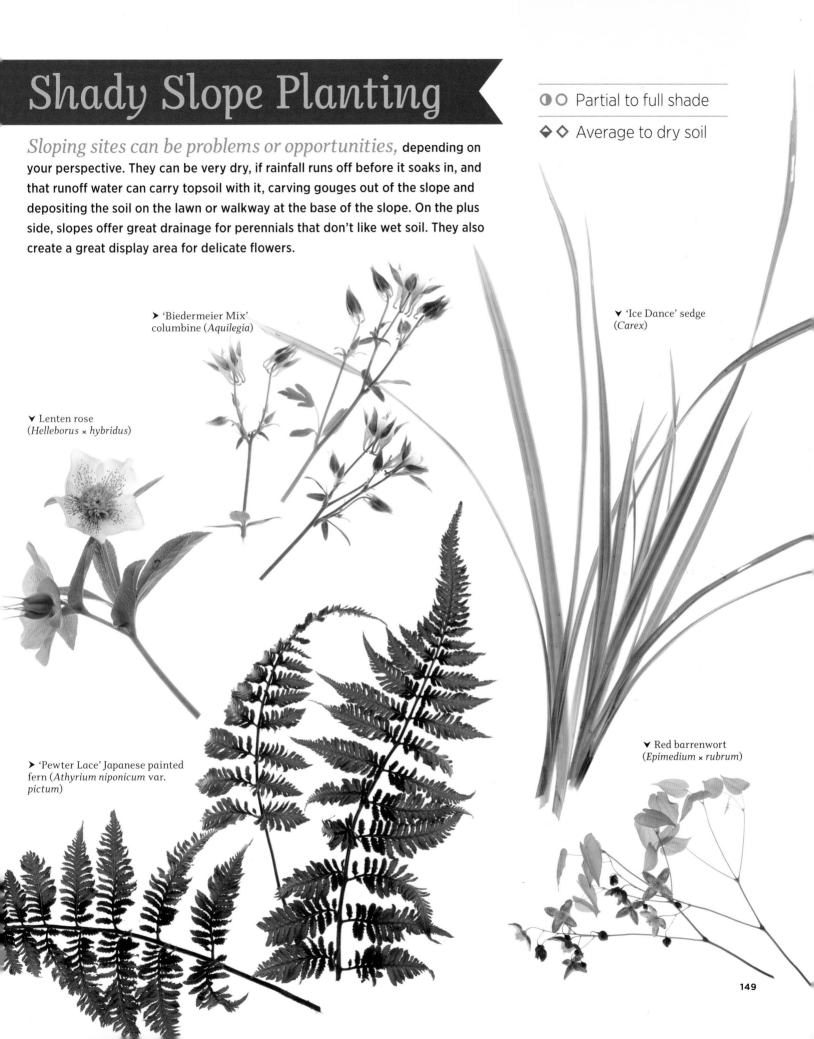

➤ 'Biedermeier Mix'
columbine (*Aquilegia*)

➤ 'Ice Dance' sedge
(*Carex*)

➤ Lenten rose
(*Helleborus × hybridus*)

➤ 'Pewter Lace' Japanese painted
fern (*Athyrium niponicum* var.
pictum)

➤ Red barrenwort
(*Epimedium × rubrum*)

The Garden Plan

Shopping List

❶ 'ICE DANCE' SEDGE
Carex | 5 plants
Zones 5–9
Alternates: Another 6- to 18-inch-tall, shade-tolerant perennial with evergreen leaves, such as 'Big Blue' blue lilyturf (*Liriope muscari*) [5 plants] or variegated Japanese pachysandra (*Pachysandra terminalis* 'Variegata') [5 plants]

❷ LENTEN ROSE
Helleborus × *hybridus* | 4 plants
Zones 4–9
Alternates: Another 6- to 18-inch-tall, shade-tolerant perennial with evergreen leaves, such as a heart-leaved bergenia (*Bergenia cordifolia*) [4 plants], 'Autumn Bride' heuchera (*Heuchera villosa*) [4 plants], or 'Dale's Strain' heuchera (*Heuchera americana*) [4 plants]

❸ 'PEWTER LACE' JAPANESE PAINTED FERN
Athyrium niponicum var. *pictum* | 3 plants
Zones 4–9
Alternates: Another Japanese painted fern or other 1- to 2-foot-tall, shade-tolerant perennial, such as Christmas fern (*Polystichum acrostichoides*) [3 plants] or autumn fern (*Dryopteris erythrosora*) [3 plants]

❹ 'BIEDERMEIER MIX' COLUMBINE
Aquilegia | 9 plants
Zones 3–8
Alternates: Another columbine or other 6- to 18-inch-tall, shade-tolerant perennial, such as white wood aster (*Aster divaricatus*) [9 plants] or 'Espresso' wild geranium (*Geranium maculatum*) [9 plants]

❺ RED BARRENWORT
Epimedium × *rubrum* | 9 plants
Zones 4–8
Alternates: Another barrenwort or other 6- to 12-inch-tall, shade-tolerant perennial, such as a foamflower (*Tiarella cordifolia*) [9 plants], creeping phlox (*Phlox stolonifera*) [9 plants], or green-and-gold (*Chrysogonum virginianum*) [9 plants]

Planting Plan

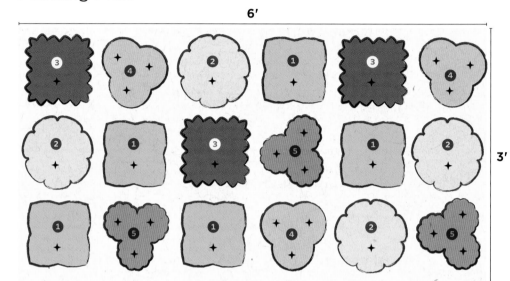

Season by Season

Spring: The garden is filled with flowers in spring, taking advantage of the available sunlight before the expanding leaves of deciduous shrubs and trees cast summer shade. The nodding, bowl-shaped blooms of Lenten roses show up especially well on sloping sites and bloom through much of the spring, pairing prettily with the delicate sprays of starry red barrenwort blooms. The 'Biedermeier Mix' columbine, too, may join the show in late spring with flowers in a range of colors, along with the emerging fresh foliage of 'Ice Dance' sedge and Japanese painted fern.

Get a jump-start on the season by cleaning up the garden as early as you can in spring. First, clip off any remaining dead leaves and stems. Gardeners usually clip the leaves off Lenten roses now, too, even if the foliage is still green, to make a tidy background for the emerging flowers. On a slope, though, you may want to skip that step, so the leaves help protect the soil from erosion by spring rains. New leaves will come up after flowering to cover them up anyway. The sedge usually still looks good after winter, but if the clumps turn brown, it's fine to cut off all the leaves 3 to 4 inches above the ground. After cleanup, add a fresh layer of organic mulch.

Summer: Enjoy the 'Biedermeier Mix' columbine blooms in early summer, along with the fresh, lush leaves of the other perennials, which continue to add interest through the rest of the summer.

Clip off the flower stalks of the columbines as soon as the petals drop. Or, leave them in place until they turn brown so the seeds can ripen; then, cut off the stalks and crumble the seed capsules over the garden or over other parts of your yard to get new plants. Water this slope planting during summer dry spells, especially during the first few years.

Fall and Winter: The interplay of leaf colors and textures makes this garden look good well into fall, and even into winter.

Frosty weather will eventually brown the columbines and fern, but leave the tops in place to protect the soil over the winter. In early fall, you could divide any of the perennials that are outgrowing their space, but that shouldn't happen often. For extra color next spring, tuck some crocus (*Crocus*), snowdrops (*Galanthus*), or other early bulbs into the border in early to mid fall.

Digging Deeper

IT'S EASY TO EXPAND THIS RECTANGULAR PLANTING to fit a larger slope by repeating it end to end as many times as needed, or by doubling it along the long side. If your slope is steep, or if it's much higher than 6 feet, consider breaking it up with one or more low retaining walls; that will reduce the angle of the slope and make planting and maintenance much easier.

The key to successful slope plantings is keeping the soil covered as much as possible. One way to do that is to put the perennials close together at planting time, so they fill in quickly. If that's too expensive to do all at once, install one section at a time over a period of years, or use impatiens or other shade-tolerant annuals in place of some of the perennials for a year or two.

Covering the soil between the plants with mulch is an important part of maintaining a garden on a slope, because it protects the soil from being washed away by pounding rain and provides ideal conditions for the perennial roots to settle in and spread out. Avoid lightweight mulches such as cocoa shells, loose compost, grass clippings, or small wood chips, however, because they can be carried away easily by rain runoff. Shredded mulches usually work well, because they knit together to form a mat that stays in place but remains loose enough for rainfall to soak through it.

Around the House

Clipped evergreen shrubs are a traditional choice for planting along the front wall of a house, but they're not your only option. Instead of looking exactly the same all year round, a planting of mixed perennials offers changing features from season to season. Plus, you won't be stuck with the boring pruning chores necessary to keep foundation shrubs in shape, or have to worry about the plants covering up your house if you *don't* prune. Flowering and foliage perennials also supply more color, interesting textures, and a much more welcoming appearance overall.

➤ 'Bressingham Beauty' astilbe (*Astilbe*)

▲ 'Langtrees' Siberian bugloss (*Brunnera macrophylla*)

◀ Variegated Solomon's seal (*Polygonatum odoratum* 'Variegatum')

▼ Lenten rose (*Helleborus × hybridus*)

▲ 'Pink Pewter' spotted deadnettle (*Lamium maculatum*)

Shopping List

❶ VARIEGATED SOLOMON'S SEAL

Polygonatum odoratum 'Variegatum' |
3 plants
Zones 4–8
Alternates: Another 18- to 36-inch-tall, shade-tolerant perennial with green-and-white or green-and-yellow leaves, such as variegated obedient plant (*Physostegia virginiana* 'Variegata') [3 plants] or 'Snow and Sapphires' Jacob's ladder (*Polemonium caeruleum*) [3 plants]

❷ 'BRESSINGHAM BEAUTY' ASTILBE

Astilbe | **4 plants**
Zones 4–9
Alternates: Another 18- to 36-inch-tall astilbe or other shade-tolerant perennial, such as heart-leaved aster (*Aster cordifolius*) [4 plants] or autumn fern (*Dryopteris erythrosora*) [4 plants]

❸ LENTEN ROSE

Helleborus × hybridus | **4 plants**
Zones 4–9
Alternates: Another 6- to 12-inch-tall, shade-tolerant perennial with evergreen leaves, such as heart-leaved bergenia (*Bergenia cordifolia*) [4 plants] or blue lilyturf (*Liriope muscari*) [4 plants]

❹ 'LANGTREES' SIBERIAN BUGLOSS

Brunnera macrophylla | **1 plant**
Zones 3–8
Alternates: Another Siberian bugloss or other 6- to 18-inch-tall, shade-tolerant perennial with green-and-silver leaves, such as a lungwort (*Pulmonaria*) [1 plant] or 'Pewter Lace' Japanese painted fern (*Athyrium niponicum* var. *pictum*) [1 plant]

❺ 'PINK PEWTER' SPOTTED DEADNETTLE

Lamium maculatum | **3 plants**
Zones 3–8
Alternates: Another spotted deadnettle or other 6- to 12-inch-tall, shade-tolerant perennial with green-and-silver or blue leaves, such as 'Callaway' mottled wild ginger (*Asarum shuttleworthii*) [3 plants] or dwarf bleeding heart (*Dicentra eximia*) [3 plants]

Planting Plan

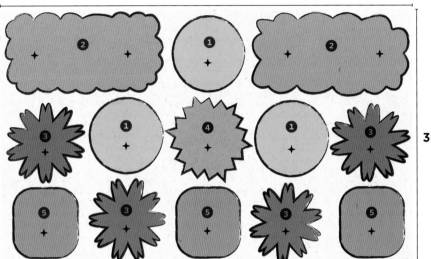

Season by Season

Spring: This garden jumps into the growing season as soon as the weather warms up a bit, with the bowl-shaped blooms of Lenten roses in white or shades of pink to reddish purple starting in early to mid spring. Variegated Solomon's seal is another early riser, with plump, pink shoots that rise quickly into arching stems carrying cream-striped green leaves and dangling white, bell-shaped blooms by mid spring. The dainty, sky-blue blossoms of 'Langtrees' Siberian bugloss, too, start in early to mid spring, joined by the clustered pink flowers of 'Pink Pewter' spotted deadnettle by mid spring. 'Bressingham Beauty' astilbe is the only one not flowering yet, but its bronze-tinted leaves do add some spring interest.

Get an extra-early start on cleanup for this garden — in very early spring or even late winter — so things will be tidy for the extravaganza of spring bloom. Cut down any remaining dead growth, and clip off the Lenten rose leaves close to ground level. If the spotted deadnettle plants look browned or tattered, gather up the trailing stems and cut them back by one-third to one-half of their length. Divide the Solomon's seal, astilbe, and spotted deadnettle clumps if you noticed that they were crowding their companions last year. Finish up by spreading a fresh layer of organic mulch over the soil.

Summer: Most of the early flowers are done by the end of spring, but there's plenty of interesting foliage for summer. Variegated Solomon's seal remains showy through this season, with its cream- to white-striped foliage. New, bright green leaves rise on the Lenten rose soon after bloom, aging to deep green. 'Langtrees' Siberian bugloss, too, produces new leaves after flowering, and the broad, deep green leaves are lightly spotted with silver, complementing the silver-and-green leaves of 'Pink Pewter' spotted deadnettle. The spotted deadnettle may also produce a few flowers in summer, but the main bloom show comes from the rich pink plumes of 'Bressingham Beauty' astilbe, which usually appear in midsummer but may bloom a few weeks earlier or later, depending on your climate.

Just a little attention will keep your foundation planting looking fresh and neat all through the summer. Clip off the flowering stems of the Lenten rose and Siberian bugloss plants right at the base as soon as the blooms are done. If the spotted deadnettle looks a little tired by midsummer, you could cut it back again by one-third to one-half to get a flush of lush new leaves. Water the garden during summer dry spells, too.

Fall and Winter: Other than some scattered flowers on 'Pink Pewter' spotted deadnettle, leaves continue to be the stars of this perennial foundation garden well into fall, at least. The variegated Solomon's seal plants turn a beautiful buttery yellow color in cooler weather, and then drop their leaves for winter. Frosts eventually kill the leaves of 'Bressingham Beauty' astilbe and 'Langtrees' Siberian bugloss, as well. Spotted deadnettle generally holds its foliage into early winter and may even stay around all winter in mild climates. The Lenten roses, too, hold their leathery, deep green leaves all through the winter.

If the Solomon's seal, Lenten rose, Siberian bugloss, or spotted deadnettle clumps are outgrowing their places, divide them in early fall (or even late summer for the Lenten rose). Clip off the seed heads of the astilbe just above the leaves, or let them stay for fall and winter interest, and cut down the Solomon's seal stems when they drop their leaves.

Digging Deeper

THIS RECTANGULAR BORDER is perfectly suited to fit against the wall of a house or a garage, shed, or other outbuilding; repeat the plan as many times as needed to fill the available space. It could also work well as a welcoming entry planting on either side of a door, or as an edging for a driveway or sidewalk.

The soil close to a house foundation can be very dry, because the overhanging roof edge blocks rain from reaching it. One way to deal with this challenge is to leave an unplanted strip at least 18 inches wide between the wall and the back of the border. This moves the border out of the bone-dry zones, with the added benefit of giving you easy access to your house for painting, window cleaning, and other home-maintenance tasks.

Elegant Edging

What could be more welcoming than a walkway lined with flowers and foliage chosen for color, texture, and fragrance? Edging paths and sidewalks with perennials encourages passersby to stop and admire delicate blossoms and intricately patterned leaves up close. A planted strip also keeps lawn grass from growing right up to paved surfaces, so it eliminates the need for frequent trimming to keep those edges looking tidy.

◄ 'Cameo Mix' fan columbine (*Aquilegia flabellata*)

▲ 'Blue Cadet' hosta (*Hosta*)

➤ 'Blue Ridge' creeping phlox (*Phlox stolonifera*)

◄ 'Burgundy Glow' ajuga (*Ajuga reptans*)

➤ 'Evergold' sedge (*Carex*)

The Garden Plan

Shopping List

① 'BLUE CADET' HOSTA
Hosta | **3 plants**
Zones 3–8
Alternates: 'Blue Mouse Ears', 'June', or other compact hosta or another 9- to 18-inch-tall, shade-tolerant perennial, such as lady's mantle (*Alchemilla mollis*) [3 plants] or 'Obsidian' or other heuchera (*Heuchera*) [3 plants]

② 'EVERGOLD' SEDGE
Carex | **3 plants**
Zones 5–9
Alternates: Bunny Blue (*C. laxiculmis* 'Hobb'), Gold Fountains ('Kaga-nishiki'), or other sedge or another 6- to 12-inch-tall, shade-tolerant perennial, such as golden Hakone grass (*Hakonechloa macra* 'Aureola') [3 plants] or Christmas fern (*Polystichum acrostichoides*) [3 plants]

③ 'BURGUNDY GLOW' AJUGA
Ajuga reptans | **12 plants**
Zones 3–9
Alternates: Another ajuga or other 4- to 8-inch-tall, shade-tolerant perennial, such as 'Sugar and Spice' or other foamflower (*Tiarella cordifolia*) [12 plants] or 'White Nancy' spotted deadnettle (*Lamium maculatum*) [4 plants]

④ 'BLUE RIDGE' CREEPING PHLOX
Phlox stolonifera | **6 plants**
Zones 4–8
Alternates: Another creeping phlox or other 6- to 12-inch-tall, shade-tolerant perennial, such as woodland phlox (*Phlox divaricata*) [6 plants] or yellow barrenwort (*Epimedium × versicolor*) [6 plants]

⑤ 'CAMEO MIX' FAN COLUMBINE
Aquilegia flabellata | **6 plants**
Zones 3–8
Alternates: Another 6- to 12-inch-tall columbine or other shade-tolerant perennial, such as 'Lilliput' or another dwarf astilbe (*Astilbe*) [6 plants] or a dwarf bleeding heart (*Dicentra*) [6 plants]

Planting Plan

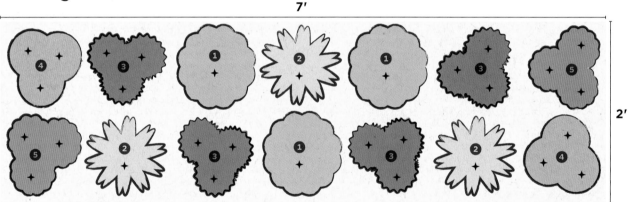

Season by Season

Spring: This simple edging strip begins the growing season with a cheerful abundance of bloom. It starts early with the soft purple-blue clusters of 'Blue Ridge' creeping phlox, quickly joined by the more intense purple-blue spikes of 'Burgundy Glow' ajuga, and then, toward the end of the spring, the spurred flowers of 'Cameo Mix' fan columbine in white and shades of blue or pink. 'Blue Cadet' hosta usually emerges late in the spring, and the new leaves of 'Evergold' sedge are showily striped with bright yellow.

An early spring cleanup lets all of this perennial beauty show off to best advantage. First, clip off any remains of the hosta and columbine. The phlox and ajuga may be evergreen but often brown, at least partly, by spring; snip off the damaged parts, if desired, or just let the new leaves cover them up. 'Evergold' sedge is even more likely to be evergreen; rake the clumps to pull out any damaged blades, or cut off all of the foliage about 3 inches above the ground. If you noticed last year that the hostas or sedges are getting too big for their places, early spring is a good time to divide them. When you're done with spring maintenance, cover the soil with a fresh layer of organic mulch.

Summer: 'Blue Ridge' creeping phlox and 'Burgundy Glow' ajuga usually finish flowering by the end of spring but may continue into early summer in cool areas, along with main bloom of the 'Cameo Mix' fan columbines. The yellow stripes of 'Evergold' sedge eventually age to a cream color, but the clumps still look colorful for the summer, along with the pink-, white-, and green leaves of the ajuga. 'Blue Cadet' hostas' blue-green leaves expand fully in early summer and are topped by stalks of light purple, trumpet-shaped flowers in midsummer.

Once their flowers drop, trim off the flower stalks of the columbines and hostas near the base of the plant, and cut off those of the ajugas and creeping phlox just above the leaves. Water the garden during extended summer dry spells.

Fall and Winter: The mix of leaf colors and textures keeps your edging garden looking attractive well into fall. 'Burgundy Glow' ajuga leaves are mostly bronzy green with a pink blush on the newest foliage by late fall; they stay that way for the winter in mild areas but often turn brown by later winter in colder climates. 'Evergold' sedge and 'Blue Ridge' creeping phlox leaves usually look pretty much the same through winter.

Early to mid fall is a good time to divide the ajuga, hosta, or phlox plants if they are outgrowing their spaces. Once cold weather turns the hosta and columbine tops yellow or brown, cut them off, if desired, or leave the garden cleanup until spring.

Digging Deeper

THIS LONG, NARROW PLANTING is designed for a straight path, but it's easy enough to adapt it to a curving one. Shift the plants around a bit to fill the space, or add a few plants to outside curves and remove a few along inside curves so the planting looks equally full but not crowded. If you have the space, repeat the planting on both sides of the path.

A narrow border of perennials up to about 18 inches tall is a good choice for a new pathway planting, because it's not a huge project to tackle. Plus, it's easy enough to step over the plants if you need to get off the path for some reason. If you find that you really like having a perennial-lined path, you could expand the effect by adding another strip of taller plants behind the existing edging.

If you're planning to plant a strip of perennials along a shady paved area where you use deicing salts in winter, it's smart to consider plants that are also salt-tolerant. For suggestions, check out Salt in the Earth on page 158.

Salt in the Earth

If you live along a coastline, you probably aren't surprised to find out that you need to consider salt tolerance when you choose perennials for your garden. But even gardens far inland can have a problem with salty soil: specifically, plantings sited along streets, sidewalks, and other surfaces where deicing salts are used in winter. You can still have a pretty garden in these tough spots, though, if you choose perennials that can tolerate some salt.

▾ Blue lilyturf (*Liriope muscari*)

➤ Wild columbine (*Aquilegia canadensis*)

▾ Lady's mantle (*Alchemilla mollis*)

▾ 'Angelina' sedum (*Sedum rupestre*)

➤ Japanese painted fern (*Athyrium niponicum* var. *pictum*)

Shopping List

1 WILD COLUMBINE
Aquilegia canadensis | 3 plants
Zones 3-9
Alternates: Another 1- to 3-foot-tall perennial
that can tolerate shade and salt, such as
'Brunette' bugbane (*Cimicifuga*) [1 plant] or
a tall astilbe (*Astilbe*) [3 plants]

2 LADY'S MANTLE
Alchemilla mollis | 4 plants
Zones 3-9
Alternates: Another 8- to 30-inch-tall
perennial that can tolerate shade and moist
soil, such as 'Citronelle' or 'Obsidian' heuchera
(*Heuchera*) [4 plants] or yellow foxglove
(*Digitalis grandiflora*) [4 plants]

3 JAPANESE PAINTED FERN
Athyrium niponicum var. *pictum* | 5 plants
Zones 4-9
Alternates: Another 8- to 18-inch-tall
perennial that can tolerate shade and salt,
such as 'Hermann's Pride' yellow archangel
(*Lamiastrum galeobdolon*) [5 plants] or Lenten
rose (*Helleborus* × *hybridus*) [5 plants]

4 BLUE LILYTURF
Liriope muscari | 3 plants
Zones 5-9
Alternates: Another 6- to 12-inch-tall
perennial that can tolerate shade and salt, such
as lamb's ears (*Stachys byzantina*) [3 plants]
or dwarf Chinese astilbe (*Astilbe chinensis* var.
pumila) [3 plants]

5 'ANGELINA' SEDUM
Sedum rupestre | 6 plants
Zones 3-8
Alternates: Another 4- to 8-inch-tall perennial
that can tolerate shade and salt, such as barren
strawberry (*Waldsteinia ternata*) [6 plants] or
'Illumination' periwinkle (*Vinca minor*) [6 plants]

Planting Plan

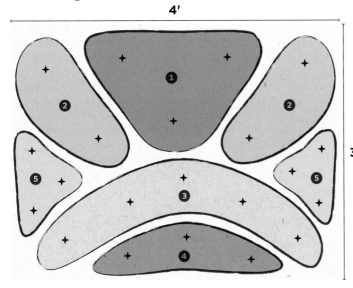

Season by Season

Spring: The growing season kicks off early with a flush of fresh new leaves on most of the perennials — the bright yellow foliage of 'Angelina' sedum is especially showy — with the purplish fronds of Japanese fern coming up a few weeks later. It doesn't take long for flowers to join in: first the nodding, red-and-yellow blossoms of wild columbine, usually starting in mid spring, and soon followed by the frothy greenish yellow clouds of lady's mantle.

Spring cleanup is minimal: simply snip off any remaining leaves on the blue lilyturf, rake out any debris, and add a fresh layer of organic mulch.

Summer: Wild columbine finishes flowering in early summer, if it hasn't already, and so does the lady's mantle — just about the time that 'Angelina' sedum sends up its clustered yellow blooms. (You may not notice the sedum flowers, though, against the bright yellow foliage.) The gray fronds of Japanese painted fern and rich green lilyturf leaves look good all through the summer. Blue lilyturf is also accented with spikes of small purple-blue blooms in late summer.

Trimming off the columbine and lady's mantle flower stalks when the blooms are done will make the plants look tidier for the summer and may even promote some late summer rebloom on the lady's mantle. Or, leave them in place until they turn completely brown, if you'd like to give them a chance to drop their seeds and produce seedlings. Most of these perennials can tolerate dryish soil, but it's a good idea to water this garden during extended dry spells, especially for the first few years after planting.

Fall and Winter: Fall interest in this salt-tolerant garden mostly comes from the variety of leaf shapes and colors. Freezing weather will nip the wild columbine and Japanese painted fern first, and eventually the lady's mantle; cut off the dead tops in mid to late fall. 'Angelina' sedum and blue lilyturf can remain attractive through the winter months.

Early to mid fall is a fine time to divide any of the perennials that are outgrowing their space. (The sedum, in particular, can spread somewhat quickly once it settles in.)

Digging Deeper

USE THIS RECTANGULAR PLANTING to fill a corner between your driveway and sidewalk, or as a mini-border in any site where salty soil is a problem. If you need to fill a larger space, or if you want to use this simple plan as the basis for a longer border to edge a driveway or sidewalk, simply repeat it end to end as many times as needed.

Gardens right next to streets and roadways are subject to salt-laden spray from passing cars, and even salt-tolerant perennials can benefit from extra protection in these tough sites. Try applying a protective mulch, such as cut evergreen branches or straw, to catch some of the salt; remove it at the end of the snow season.

Wild columbine (*Aquilegia canadensis*) is less likely than most other columbines to be damaged by leaf miners (tiny pests that chew pale, winding tunnels in the leaves), but if you do notice a lot of leaf damage, it's fine to cut off all of the top growth in midsummer; new leaves will appear in a few weeks. A similar midsummer shearing also works well on lady's mantle if the leaves look dull and tattered.

Hummingbird Magnet

Many perennials that are best-known as hummingbird favorites thrive in full sun, but there are some equally lovely options for shadier yards — especially sites with half-day sun and half-day shade or light all-day shade. Including a few perennials that produce nectar-rich flowers in spring attracts the attention of early-arriving hummingbirds; pairing them with later-bloomers keeps the hummers coming back for more through the rest of the growing season.

‹ 'Hot Lips' pink turtlehead (*Chelone lyonii*)

➤ Blue lobelia (*Lobelia siphilitica*)

‹ Wild columbine (*Aquilegia canadensis*)

‹ August lily (*Hosta plantaginea*)

▲ 'Dixie Chip' ajuga (*Ajuga reptans*)

161

The Garden Plan

Shopping List

❶ 'HOT LIPS' PINK TURTLEHEAD
Chelone lyonii | **3 plants**
Zones 3–9
Alternates: Another turtlehead or other 2- to 3-foot-tall, shade-tolerant perennial with red and/or nectar-rich flowers, such as an obedient plant (*Physostegia virginiana*) [3 plants] or wild bergamot (*Monarda fistulosa*) [3 plants]

❷ BLUE LOBELIA
Lobelia siphilitica | **7 plants**
Zones 3–8
Alternates: 'Ruby Slippers', cardinal flower (*Lobelia cardinalis*), or other lobelia or another 18- to 36-inch-tall, shade-tolerant perennial with red and/or nectar-rich flowers, such as a toad lily (*Tricyrtis*) [7 plants] or hardy begonia (*Begonia grandis*) [7 plants]

❸ WILD COLUMBINE
Aquilegia canadensis | **3 plants**
Zones 3–9
Alternates: Another columbine or other 12- to 30-inch-tall, shade-tolerant perennial with red and/or nectar-rich flowers, such as a dwarf bleeding heart (*Dicentra*) [3 plants] or Indian pink (*Spigelia marilandica*) [3 plants]

❹ AUGUST LILY
Hosta plantaginea | **2 plants**
Zones 3–9
Alternates: Another hosta or other 1- to 2-foot-tall, shade-tolerant perennial with red and/or nectar-rich flowers, such as a heuchera (*Heuchera*) [6 plants] or an astilbe (*Astilbe*) [6 plants]

❺ 'DIXIE CHIP' AJUGA
Ajuga reptans | **5 plants**
Zones 3–9
Alternates: Another 4- to 12-inch-tall, shade-tolerant perennial with red and/or nectar-rich flowers, such as woodland phlox (*Phlox divaricata*) [5 plants] or creeping phlox (*Phlox stolonifera*) [5 plants]

Planting Plan

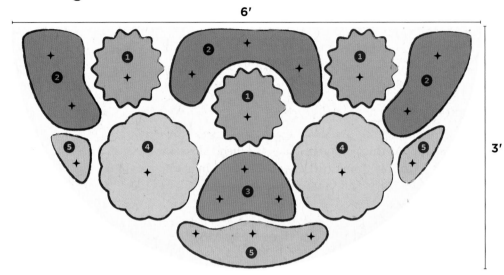

Season by Season

Spring: It's hard to predict when hummingbirds will start checking out your garden, because the migration patterns of the different species vary. But with the small but abundant, purple-blue 'Dixie Chip' ajuga flowers and the nodding red-and-yellow blossoms of wild columbine in mid- to late spring, you'll have a supply of nectar-filled flowers ready for them whenever they show up. At this point, the blue lobelia and 'Hot Lips' pink turtlehead plants are only leafy, and the August lily is just beginning to sprout.

Get your hummingbird garden ready for the season in early to mid spring. Cleanup is mostly a matter of cutting down any dead stems and leaves. If the lobelias and turtleheads were getting too big for their spot last year, divide them now, too. Then, spread a fresh layer of organic mulch over the soil. If the turtlehead stems were floppy last year, try pinching off the top few inches of each stem tip in late spring to encourage bushier growth.

Summer: 'Dixie Chip' ajuga generally finishes flowering by early summer, but the wild columbine continues for a few more weeks. The spikes of blue lobelia come along in midsummer, joined by the fragrant white trumpets of August lily and bright 'Hot Lips' pink turtlehead blossoms in late summer to provide an abundance of nectar for hungry hummers all summer.

Keep the garden tidy by clipping off the bloom stalks of the ajugas and columbines at their base once the flowers are finished. On the lobelias, cutting off the top part of each stem (just above the main leafy part) when the blooms drop can encourage the plants to produce more flowers later in the season. Water the garden during extended dry spells.

Fall and Winter: 'Hot Lips' pink turtlehead plants are filled with plenty of flowers in early fall, providing an ample supply of nectar for hummingbirds to feed on. August lily blooms, too, may linger into early fall, and blue lobelias may continue even into mid fall, especially if you kept the finished flower spikes clipped off.

Once freezing weather returns, your hummingbirds are likely long gone. It's fine to let the garden go into winter without any special attention, except for dividing the ajugas, hosta, lobelias, and turtleheads in early to mid fall if they've outgrown their allotted space. The leaves of 'Dixie Chip' ajuga stay attractive into winter, eventually turning droopy or dying back completely in cold-winter areas. The seed heads of the turtleheads also add some winter interest.

Digging Deeper

A HALF-CIRCLE PLAN like this fits easily against a vertical feature, such as a wall, fence, or deck. Just remember to leave 12 to 18 inches between the back of the garden and the vertical surface, so the plants have room to expand without crowding. This mini-path also makes it easier for you to reach both the back of the garden and the vertical surface for later maintenance without stepping on your perennials.

Male hummingbirds can be rather territorial, but if your yard has ample areas for them to feed, you'll likely see several hummers hanging around, including females and their offspring. Flipping this planting plan along the straight side to form a larger circular garden offers an even greater abundance of feeding opportunities for them. If you have a large enough property, consider planting two or more hummingbird gardens in different parts of your yard to give more visiting hummers a chance to feed without being chased away by a resident male.

Perennial lobelias — both blue lobelia (*Lobelia siphilitica*) and the red-blossomed kind known as cardinal flower (*L. cardinalis*) — are top-notch choices for attracting hummingbirds to your yard. In full-sun sites, they like lots of moisture, but they can also adapt to drier conditions in gardens with morning sun and afternoon shade or light all-day shade. Both kinds produce lots of seed, so you may end up with many seedlings if you don't regularly clip off the finished flower spikes. Consider letting one or two spikes stay, though, so you'll have a few replacement seedlings in case the original plants die. (If you try this trick, wait until early summer to apply mulch around the patches of lobelia, so the tiny seeds can sprout more easily in spring.)

Deter the Deer

◑ Partial shade

◆ Average soil

Nibbled blooms, chomped leaves, and trampled stems:
dealing with deer damage can take all the fun out of gardening. While no perennials are completely deer-proof — these critters will try pretty much anything if they're hungry enough — choosing plants that are less appealing to them may encourage the deer to pass by your garden in search of a more enticing meal.

➤ Golden Hakone grass
(*Hakonechloa macra* 'Aureola')

◀ 'Brunette' bugbane
(*Cimicifuga*)

◡ 'Looking Glass' Siberian
bugloss (*Brunnera macrophylla*)

➤ Foamflower (*Tiarella wherryi*)

➤ Lenten rose
(*Helleborus* × *hybridus*)

The Garden Plan

Shopping List

❶ 'BRUNETTE' BUGBANE
Cimicifuga | **1 plant**
Zones 4–8
Alternates: Another bugbane or other 3- to 4-foot-tall, shade-tolerant, deer-resistant perennial, such as a ligularia (*Ligularia*) [1 plant] or a monkshood (*Aconitum*) [1 plant]

❷ LENTEN ROSE
Helleborus × hybridus | **3 plants**
Zones 4–9
Alternates: Another 1- to 3-foot-tall, shade-tolerant, deer-resistant perennial, such as bearsfoot hellebore (*Helleborus foetidus*) [3 plants] or strawberry foxglove (*Digitalis × mertonensis*) [3 plants]

❸ GOLDEN HAKONE GRASS
Hakonechloa macra 'Aureola' | **7 plants**
Zones 5–9
Alternates: 'All Gold' or other Hakone grass or another 12- to 18-inch-tall, shade-tolerant, deer-resistant perennial, such as variegated blue lilyturf (*Liriope muscari* 'Variegata') [7 plants] or 'Luxuriant' or other dwarf bleeding heart (*Dicentra*) [7 plants]

❹ 'LOOKING GLASS' SIBERIAN BUGLOSS
Brunnera macrophylla | **2 plants**
Zones 3–8
Alternates: Another Siberian bugloss or other 6- to 18-inch-tall, shade-tolerant, deer-resistant perennial, such as a lungwort (*Pulmonaria*) [2 plants] or 'White Nancy' spotted deadnettle (*Lamium maculatum*) [2 plants]

❺ FOAMFLOWER
Tiarella wherryi | **4 plants**
Zones 4–9
Alternates: Another foamflower or other 6- to 12-inch-tall, shade-tolerant, deer-resistant perennial, such as dwarf goat's beard (*Aruncus aethusifolius*) [4 plants] or lady's mantle (*Alchemilla mollis*) [4 plants]

Planting Plan

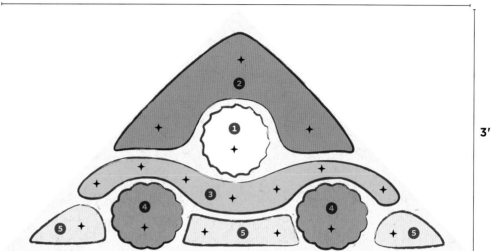

165

Season by Season

Spring: Spring is prime bloom time for this deer-resistant garden, starting in early to mid spring with the white, pink, or reddish purple Lenten rose and sky-blue 'Looking Glass' Siberian bugloss. The white foamflower joins in a few weeks later, with an added dash of color from the bright yellow shoots of the golden Hakone grass. The ferny, deep brown leaves of the emerging 'Brunette' bugbane add additional interest.

Early spring is a good time to tackle any needed cleanup and apply a fresh layer of organic mulch. (Though it's not absolutely necessary, cutting off the remaining leaves of the Lenten rose makes the plants look much tidier for the spring bloom season.) If the bugbane or Hakone grass is outgrowing its space, lift and divide the clumps in early to mid spring.

Summer: Lenten roses and 'Looking Glass' Siberian bugloss usually finish flowering in late spring or early summer, and then send up fresh-looking new leaves. Foamflowers wind up their main flush of bloom a few weeks later but may produce additional blooms here and there through the summer. 'Brunette' bugbane might start flowering in late summer but usually waits until autumn, so the primary summer interest here is from the foliage of the golden Hakone grass and the other perennials.

Cut off the bloom stalks of the Lenten rose and Siberian bugloss to reduce the chance of getting unwanted seedlings, or just let the flush of new leaves cover them up. Foamflowers seldom produce many seedlings, but you may want to clip off their dead flower spikes just to tidy the plants. It's also a good idea to water during extended summer dry spells.

Fall and Winter: In most areas, 'Brunette' bugbane starts flowering in early fall, with dense spikes of white flowers; you may get some additional blooms on the foamflowers then, too. As temperatures cool, the foamflower leaves take on red tones, and the yellow-striped blades of golden Hakone grass develop a pinkish blush.

Eventually, frosts and freezes will brown the golden Hakone leaves and kill the top growth of the bugbane, but the dried leaves and seed heads can still look interesting in winter. The Lenten rose leaves hold their good looks through most or all of the winter, and the foamflowers and 'Looking Glass' Siberian bugloss usually last into early winter, at least. So, you may want to do a light cleanup in late fall, but consider waiting until late winter or early spring to remove the bulk of the dead or damaged bits. If you notice that the foamflowers, Lenten roses, or Siberian bugloss are outgrowing their places, early to mid fall is an ideal time to dig up and divide them.

Digging Deeper

THIS TRIANGULAR GARDEN is well suited for an inner corner site, but you could expand it for a larger site. Flip it on one of the short sides and join the two parts to create a larger triangular border; flip it one more time to create a plan perfect for wrapping around an outer corner. Or flip it along the long side to create a square and add a 2- to 3-foot-wide path between the two parts for a walk-through planting.

If deer are already a serious problem in your yard, adding one deer-resistant planting isn't likely to help the situation much. But if you make note of which plants are frequently fed on and replace them with less-palatable plants, you'll be more likely to have a good-looking garden. For extra protection, apply Plantskydd or some other kind of commercial repellent spray, starting early in the growing season, to encourage deer to go elsewhere before they make a habit of snacking on your plants.

Foamflowers (*Tiarella*) are a great choice for shady sites, but you need to pay attention to which kind you buy. Plants sold as *Tiarella wherryi* or *T. cordifolia* var. *collina* stay in distinct clumps, while those labeled simply as *T. cordifolia* usually produce new plants on slender "runners," creating a carpetlike effect. The spreading kinds tend to fill in more quickly, which can be a plus if you have a lot of space to fill, but you may need to dig out or trim off some of the runners now and then to keep them from creeping beyond the bounds of the garden.

Perfumed Perennials

◑ Partial shade

◆ Average soil

A garden that smells as good as it looks is a scent-sational addition to a shady yard. Put it near a deck or patio where you like to relax or entertain guests, or next to a window so you can enjoy the fragrance indoors. The secret to a successful scented garden is to include scented flowers that bloom at different times; that way, their perfumes won't clash or be overwhelming, and you'll have something pleasing to sniff over the longest possible season.

❮ 'Stargazer' lily
(*Lilium*)

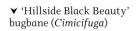
❮ 'Hillside Black Beauty'
bugbane (*Cimicifuga*)

▲ 'Clouds of Perfume' woodland
phlox (*Phlox divaricata*)

❯ Lily-of-the-valley
(*Convallaria majalis*)

❯ August lily (*Hosta
plantaginea*)

167

The Garden Plan

Shopping List

❶ 'HILLSIDE BLACK BEAUTY' BUGBANE
Cimicifuga | 1 plant
Zones 4–8
Alternates: Another bugbane or other 1- to 4-foot-tall, shade-tolerant perennial with scented flowers and/or leaves, such as white baneberry (*Actaea pachypoda*) [1 plant] or 'Golden Jubilee' hyssop (*Agastache*) [1 plant]

❷ AUGUST LILY
Hosta plantaginea | 1 plant
Zones 3–9
Alternates: 'Fragrant Bouquet', 'Royal Standard', or other fragrant hosta, or another 18- to 40-inch-tall, shade-tolerant perennial with scented flowers and/or leaves, such as variegated meadowsweet (*Filipendula ulmaria* 'Variegata') [3 plants]

❸ 'STARGAZER' LILY
Lilium | 7 plants
Zones 3–8
Alternates: 'Casa Blanca' or other fragrant lily or another 2- to 5-foot-tall, shade-tolerant perennial with scented flowers and/or leaves, such as variegated Solomon's seal (*Polygonatum odoratum* 'Variegatum') [5 plants] or 'Stairway to Heaven' creeping Jacob's ladder (*Polemonium reptans*) [5 plants]

❹ 'CLOUDS OF PERFUME' WOODLAND PHLOX
Phlox divaricata | 7 plants
Zones 3–8
Alternates: Another woodland phlox or other 6- to 18-inch-tall, shade-tolerant perennial with scented flowers and/or leaves, such as a foamflower (*Tiarella*) [7 plants] or variegated lemon balm (*Melissa officinalis* 'Variegata') [5 plants]

❺ LILY-OF-THE-VALLEY
Convallaria majalis | 9 plants
Zones 2-7
Alternates: Another 6- to 9-inch-tall, shade-tolerant perennial with scented flowers or leaves, such as a sweet violet (*Viola odorata*) [7 plants] or cowslip primrose (*Primula veris*) [9 plants]

Planting Plan

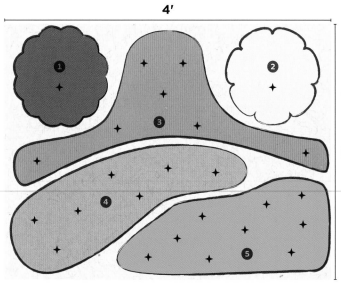

Season by Season

Spring: With so many lovely fragrant perennials flowering in spring, it's hard to avoid having their bloom times overlap at least a bit. Color and scent are so welcome this time of year, though, that it's not a big deal to have two perfumed perennials blooming now. The lily-of-the valley usually starts first — often as soon as early spring, or mid spring in northern gardens — quickly followed by the 'Clouds of Perfume' woodland phlox. The other perennials are also gradually emerging now, but their leafy sprouts aren't nearly as interesting as the early bloomers.

The growing season starts with a bang in this garden, so get an early start on cleanup. Snip off any remaining dead top growth, and rake out any debris. If you noticed that the bugbane or hosta was getting too big last year, divide the clumps now, too. Then, add a fresh layer of organic mulch.

Summer: There's a bit of a break in early summer, when the lily-of-the-valley and 'Clouds of Perfume' woodland phlox have finished and the other flowers haven't started yet. Still, you can admire the lush leaves now — especially those of the lacy, brown 'Hillside Black Beauty' bugbane and the bold, light green August lily. In between the two, the shoots of pink-and-white 'Stargazer' lily will rise, produce buds, and finally flower for several weeks in midsummer. Not surprisingly, late summer is peak time for the large, bright white, trumpet-shaped blooms of August lily. The bugbane, too, may flower in late summer, but it usually waits until fall.

No need to stress out about summer garden maintenance: simply snip off dead flowers, if you wish, and water thoroughly during dry spells. Most importantly, take time to enjoy the delightful summer sights and scents. (Evening is an especially good time to experience the amazing fragrance of the August lily.)

Fall and Winter: August lily may continue to bloom into early fall, overlapping with the beginning of 'Hillside Black Beauty' bugbane's bloom season, which usually continues through September. The bugbane's seed heads are interesting, too, and its leaves, along with those of the August lily and 'Clouds of Perfume' woodland phlox, normally look good until frost.

Early to mid fall is the ideal season to divide the lily-of-the-valley and woodland phlox if they're starting to outgrow their places. Clean up the dead top growth in the garden in mid to late fall, or leave that job until early spring.

Digging Deeper

SCENTED GARDENS ARE GREAT FOR SHELTERED SITES, where a wall, fence, or hedge blocks the breeze and allows the perennial perfumes to collect. This mini-border would be perfect for planting next to a patio, porch, deck, or your favorite garden bench, where you and your guests will be tempted to linger and appreciate the fragrant flowers.

Lining a walkway with a fragrant border allows you to get up close and personal with your plants, a plus when you'd like to slow down and enjoy the sights and scents. Expand this simple planting into an edging by repeating it as many times as space allows, keeping the shorter plants next to the walkway and the tall plants at the back. Or, for a truly scent-sual experience, repeat the linked planting on the other side of the path to create an elegant double border.

If you replace the woodland phlox with a perennial that has aromatic leaves, such as variegated lemon balm (*Melissa officinalis* 'Variegata') or bigroot geranium (*Geranium macrorrhizum*), you'll release the scent every time you pass the garden and brush by the leaves.

Lily-of-the-valley (*Convallaria majalis*) can spread quickly in good soil, so you may need to divide it every 2 or 3 years to keep it in check. Replant what you need in the garden, and tuck the extra divisions into the soil around trees and shrubs in your yard, where they can creep freely and create a great groundcover.

Backyard Flower Shop

If you enjoy having fresh flowers in your home or office, if you like to share the bounty of your flower garden with friends and family, adding a cutting garden to your yard could be a great project. Sure, you can snip blooms from any flower-full planting if you collect them only occasionally, but you don't want to strip your pretty perennial gardens of all of their color at once. With a garden planned specifically for harvesting, you can feel free to cut flowers and foliage as much as you wish, whenever you wish.

◄ 'Fragrant Bouquet' hosta (*Hosta*)

➤ 'Bridal Veil' astilbe (*Astilbe*)

▼ 'Luxuriant' dwarf bleeding heart (*Dicentra*)

▲ Common columbine (*Aquilegia vulgaris*)

➤ Japanese painted fern (*Athyrium niponicum* var. *pictum*)

Shopping List

❶ 'FRAGRANT BOUQUET' HOSTA
Hosta | 1 plant
Zones 3–8
Alternates: Another hosta or other 1- to 3-foot-tall, shade-tolerant perennial, such as a turtlehead (*Chelone*) [1 plant] or obedient plant (*Physostegia virginiana*) [1 plant]

❷ 'BRIDAL VEIL' ASTILBE
Astilbe | 4 plants
Zones 4–9
Alternates: Other astilbes or another 18- to 36-inch-tall, shade-tolerant perennial, such as blue lobelia (*Lobelia siphilitica*) [4 plants], cardinal flower (*Lobelia cardinalis*) [4 plants], or Asiatic lilies (*Lilium*) [12 bulbs]

❸ JAPANESE PAINTED FERN
Athyrium niponicum var. *pictum* | 1 plant
Zones 4–9
Alternates: Other ferns or another 1- to 2-foot-tall, shade-tolerant perennial, such as a heuchera (*Heuchera*) [1 plant] or heucherella (× *Heucherella*) [1 plant]

❹ COMMON COLUMBINE
Aquilegia vulgaris | 2 plants
Zones 3–8
Alternates: Other columbines or another 12- to 30-inch-tall, shade-tolerant perennial, such as Japanese anemone (*Anemone* × *hybrida*) [2 plants] or masterwort (*Astrantia major*) [2 plants]

❺ 'LUXURIANT' DWARF BLEEDING HEART
Dicentra | 1 plant
Zones 3–8
Alternates: Another dwarf bleeding heart or other 1- to 2-foot-tall, shade-tolerant perennial, such as a foamflower (*Tiarella*) [1 plant] or lady's mantle (*Alchemilla mollis*) [1 plant]

Planting Plan

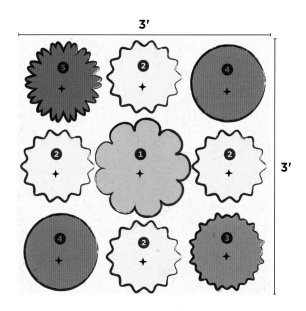

Season by Season

Spring: Blooms begin in mid to late spring, with the dangling, rosy red blooms of 'Luxuriant' dwarf bleeding heart. The columbines join them soon after, with long-spurred blooms in a wide range of colors. Treat yourself to a spring bouquet of either (or both) by clipping the flower stems right at the base when the first flower or two is open on each. Take a few of the blue-green leaves, too.

Get your cutting garden ready for the season with a quick cleanup in early to mid spring. Cut down any remaining top growth, divide the astilbes or hosta if they were getting too large for their space last year, and apply a fresh layer of organic mulch.

Summer: The spring bloomers usually continue into early summer, at least. 'Luxuriant' dwarf bleeding heart may even flower into midsummer, if it's not too hot and the soil doesn't dry out. The white plumes of 'Bridal Veil' appear in early to midsummer; cut them for bouquets when about half of the flowers in each plume are open. And in mid to late summer, enjoy the long-stalked clusters of scented, white trumpets of 'Fragrant Bouquet' hosta indoors by cutting when the first flowers open on each stalk. Remember to include some lovely leaves in your bouquet, including the deeply cut, rich green 'Bridal Veil' astilbe foliage; the lacy, silvery gray fronds of Japanese painted fern; and the broad, cream-edged green leaves of the hosta. (Don't take more than about a third of the leaves from any one plant, though, or you may weaken it.)

If you make the most of your cutting garden, summer maintenance will be minimal, because you'll be clipping off the bloom stalks well before they have a chance to produce seed. And if you do miss a few, there's no need to worry about snipping them off for tidiness unless you want to. In fact, it's a good idea to let the columbines produce some seeds, so you'll have seedlings coming along to replace the original plants when they die out after a few years. Watering your perennial cutting garden during dry spells will keep the flowers coming along and the leaves fresh looking.

Fall and Winter: Foliage is the main source of cutting material in fall, though the 'Luxuriant' dwarf bleeding heart may also produce some flowers when cool weather returns.

In early to mid fall, divide the astilbe, fern, or hosta if the plants are outgrowing their spaces. When frost calls an end to the growing season, leave the remaining top growth in place to provide some winter protection for the plants.

Digging Deeper

A SIMPLE SQUARE GARDEN like this is a snap to prepare and plant, and it's a simple matter to create a cutting garden as large as you want by adding additional squares, with 12- to 18-inch-wide cross-paths between them. Keeping the beds small makes it easy for you to gather flowers and foliage without having to step into the garden or stretch far to reach. Instead of making each square the same, include different colors of the main perennials, or mix in some of the alternate suggestions.

The point of a cutting garden is to produce blooms to harvest, not to look pretty, so you'll probably want to put it in an out-of-the-way spot, such as a side yard. A site with morning sun and afternoon shade, or with light, all-day shade, is ideal. In deep shade, you're not likely to get many flowers, though you can still make interesting arrangements with leaves alone.

For extra-early arrangements, add some spring-blooming bulbs to your cutting garden in early to mid fall. Dutch hyacinths (*Hyacinthus*) are outstanding for fragrance, and grape hyacinths (*Muscari*) and snowdrops (*Galanthus*) are charming in mini-bouquets.

Country Cottage Style

◑   Partial shade

◆   Average soil

Foxgloves, columbines, and many other classic cottage-garden plants can work surprisingly well in a somewhat shady garden. They start growing early, when sunshine is abundant, and are in peak bloom by late spring to early summer, just as deciduous trees are expanding their leaves and providing some shade. A site that's sunny in the morning and shaded in the afternoon is ideal, because protection from strong midday and afternoon sun can help prolong the life of delicate blossoms.

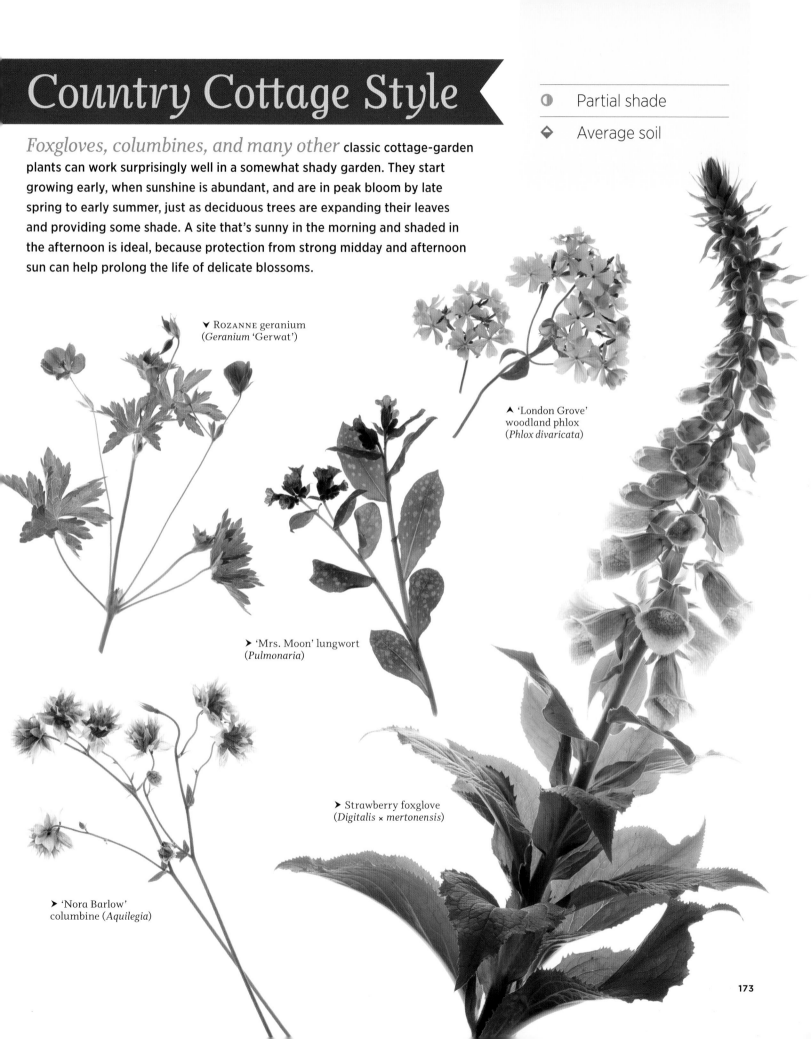

▼ Rozanne geranium
(*Geranium* 'Gerwat')

▲ 'London Grove' woodland phlox
(*Phlox divaricata*)

➤ 'Mrs. Moon' lungwort
(*Pulmonaria*)

➤ 'Nora Barlow' columbine (*Aquilegia*)

➤ Strawberry foxglove
(*Digitalis × mertonensis*)

The Garden Plan

Shopping List

❶ STRAWBERRY FOXGLOVE
Digitalis × mertonensis | **4 plants**
Zones 4–9
Alternates: Yellow foxglove (*Digitalis grandiflora*) or other foxglove, or another 2- to 3-foot-tall, shade-tolerant perennial, such as Japanese anemone (*Anemone × hybrida*) [4 plants] or 'Bressingham Spire' monkshood (*Aconitum*) [4 plants]

❷ 'NORA BARLOW' COLUMBINE
Aquilegia | **6 plants**
Zones 3–8
Alternates: Another columbine or other 12- to 30-inch-tall, shade-tolerant perennial, such as Jacob's ladder (*Polemonium caeruleum*) [6 plants] or 'Langtrees' Siberian bugloss (*Brunnera macrophylla*) [2 plants]

❸ 'MRS. MOON' LUNGWORT
Pulmonaria | **2 plants**
Zones 3–8
Alternates: Another lungwort or other 6- to 12-inch-tall, shade-tolerant perennial, such as lady's mantle (*Alchemilla mollis*) [2 plants] or lamb's ears (*Stachys byzantina*) [2 plants]

❹ 'LONDON GROVE' WOODLAND PHLOX
Phlox divaricata | **6 plants**
Zones 3–8
Alternates: Another woodland phlox or other 6- to 12-inch-tall, shade-tolerant perennial, such as a viola or violet (*Viola*) [6 plants] or a primrose (*Primula*) [6 plants]

❺ ROZANNE HARDY GERANIUM
Geranium 'Gerwat' | **2 plants**
Zones 5–8
Alternates: Another 6- to 12-inch-tall, shade-tolerant perennial such as a dwarf bleeding heart (*Dicentra*) [2 plants], a foamflower (*Tiarella*) [2 plants], or a heucherella (× *Heucherella*) [2 plants]

Planting Plan

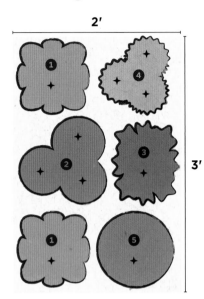

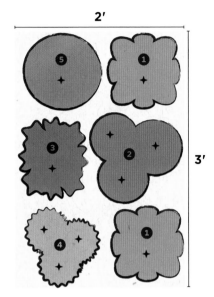

Season by Season

Spring: Start the season with a flurry of flowers in early to mid spring: the scented, flat-faced, light blue blooms of 'London Grove' woodland phlox paired with the nodding, pink buds and blue bells of 'Mrs. Moon' lungwort. As they're finishing up in late spring, the frilly pink-and-white flowers of 'Nora Barlow' columbine join the show, and by this time, the leafy clumps of strawberry foxglove are lush and green. ROZANNE geranium can be slow to sprout but is usually sprouting up by mid to late spring, and it may even be in bloom by the end of the spring.

A thorough cleanup before or just as new growth starts in spring sets the stage for this glorious abundance of flowers and foliage. Cut down any dead bits, and clip off any damaged leaves on the perennials that kept some leaves over the winter. Then, spread a fresh layer of mulch over the soil. If the lungworts are getting too large for their places, divide them as soon as they're finished flowering or wait until fall.

Summer: The earliest bloomers are usually done by early summer, but 'Mrs. Moon' lungwort contributes another round of interest with a flush of fresh leaves after flowering. 'Nora Barlow' columbine peaks in early summer and is soon joined by the rosy pink bells of strawberry foxgloves and simple, purple-blue blooms of ROZANNE geraniums for another bounty of bloom. The geraniums continue flowering into midsummer, at least, and the strawberry foxglove may also bloom in midsummer, especially where summers don't get too hot.

Summer maintenance is mostly a matter of tidying the perennials when they've finished their turn at flowering. On the lungwort and woodland phlox, clip off the remaining bloom stalks, if desired. (On the lungwort, the new leaves will eventually cover them up if you don't remove them.) Cut off the bloom stalks of the columbine and foxglove at the base once all the blossoms are gone. By late summer, ROZANNE geranium's trailing stems can look rather untidy, but you can easily neaten it up by cutting them all off at the base of the plant; new leaves will soon appear, if they haven't already.

Fall and Winter: The main display of this cottage garden is well over by autumn, but it still looks good now. The return of cooler weather often brings out fresh leaves on 'Mrs. Moon' lungwort, and both the lungworts and ROZANNE geranium may rebloom lightly in fall. The geraniums' leaves often take on some reddish tints, too. The leaves of all of these perennials usually stick around for at least part of the winter.

There's not much maintenance to do in this cottage garden in autumn, other than dividing any of the foxglove, geranium, lungwort, or phlox clumps that have outgrown their space.

Digging Deeper

THIS TWO-PART PLANTING is perfectly suited for flanking a charming garden bench, gate, or arbor. Or you could repeat the sections end to end to create an extended pathway planting. Mix in some of the suggested alternate plants, if you wish, to enjoy a wider variety of cottage-garden favorites.

Some of these classic cottage-garden perennials can be prone to pest or disease problems, but there's no need to resort to toxic sprays to treat them. If the leaves of your lungworts develop a gray or white coating in summer — not the normal silvery spots, but larger dusty-looking patches, which are a sign of a fungal disease called powdery mildew — the solution is simple: cut off and destroy the leaves, and water thoroughly to encourage the plants to produce fresh new leaves. This same simple trick works if your columbines develop signs of leaf miners: tiny pests that feed between the top and bottom leaf surfaces, creating pale, winding tunnels.

The tall spires of foxgloves have long been favorites for cottage gardens, but they can be a little tricky to succeed with. Most need a year to settle in and bloom, so don't be disappointed if they don't flower the first summer. Once they do start flowering, they may die out after a season or two. To help extend their life, cut off the flower stalks as soon as the blooms fade and, if the clumps are very leafy, divide them right after the flowering is finished. Strawberry foxglove (*Digitalis* × *mertonensis*) tends to be longer-lived than the common foxglove (*D. purpurea*).

USDA Hardiness Zone Map

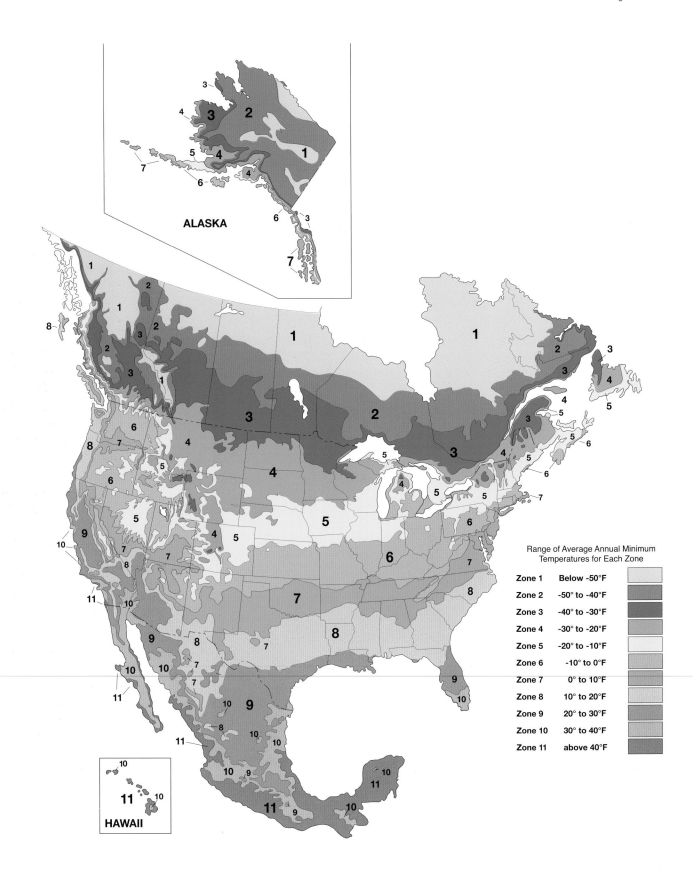

ALASKA

HAWAII

Range of Average Annual Minimum
Temperatures for Each Zone

Zone 1	Below -50°F
Zone 2	-50° to -40°F
Zone 3	-40° to -30°F
Zone 4	-30° to -20°F
Zone 5	-20° to -10°F
Zone 6	-10° to 0°F
Zone 7	0° to 10°F
Zone 8	10° to 20°F
Zone 9	20° to 30°F
Zone 10	30° to 40°F
Zone 11	above 40°F

Page numbers in *italic* indicate photos or illustrations.

Other Storey Titles You Will Enjoy

APR - 2014